Relocating Teams and Expanding Leagues in Professional Sports

Relocating Teams and Expanding Leagues in Professional Sports

How the Major Leagues Respond to Market Conditions

Frank P. Jozsa, Jr.
John J. Guthrie, Jr.

QUORUM BOOKS
Westport, Connecticut • London

Library of Congress Cataloging-in-Publication Data

Jozsa, Frank P., 1941–
    Relocating teams and expanding leagues in professional sports :
how the major leagues respond to market conditions / Frank P. Jozsa,
Jr., John J. Guthrie, Jr.
        p.   cm.
    Includes bibliographical references (p.) and index.
    ISBN 1–56720–193–8 (alk. paper)
    1. Sports franchises—Location—United States.   2. Professional
sports—Marketing—United States.   3. Professional sports—Economic
aspects—United States.   I. Guthrie, John J.   II. Title.
GV716.J69   1999
338.4′7796044′0973—dc21   99–14848

British Library Cataloguing in Publication Data is available.

Library of Congress Catalog Card Number: 99–14848
ISBN: 1–56720–193–8

First published in 1999

Quorum Books, 88 Post Road West, Westport, CT 06881
An imprint of Greenwood Publishing Group, Inc.
www.quorumbooks.com

Printed in the United States of America

The paper used in this book complies with the
Permanent Paper Standard issued by the National
Information Standards Organization (Z39.48–1984).

10 9 8 7 6 5 4 3 2 1

To

Frank P. and Madeline Jozsa

and Helen Guthrie

Contents

Preface

Sports enrich and add diversity to our lives, while professional sports teams and players entertain us. Sports heroes awe our youth. Young fans, for example, swoon over Mark McGwire's towering home runs to left field, Brett Favre's pin-point touchdown passes, or Michael Jordan's slashing drives to the basket for a dunk. Some adults are "sports addicts." They participate in amateur leagues, play scrimmage games in their yard during the half-time of a weekend football game, or compete one-on-one on the basketball court for fun. In the process, sports teaches participants that competition, discipline, sacrifice, and cooperation results in rewards, which prepare them to meet life's challenges.

For half a century we have been dedicated sports fans interested in the accomplishments of professional players, teams, and leagues. During this same period numerous scholars, economists, and historians have studied players, teams, and leagues within professional sports. Their theories and interpretations have established a basis for further research of sports issues from business, economic, historical, political, and legal perspectives. After considering many of the events that have occurred in professional sports since midcentury, specific issues gained our attention. One is the location and success of teams. The other issue concerns the growth of each sport. So, we decided to research these matters further. Our investigation of the movement of professional sports teams from one area to another and the expansion of leagues has resulted in this book.

Written for a wide audience, this book updates and advances much of the scholarship dealing with professional sports. With historical facts to explain when and where professional baseball, football, and basketball teams relocated, and leagues expanded, readers should appreciate and respect the decisions made by owners to earn maximum profits for their teams, which consequently enables sports leagues to survive and prosper.

To measure relocation and expansion between 1950 and 1998, we compiled a variety of demographic, economic, and team-specific data into tables. Besides material furnished by teams and leagues, we gathered statistics and information from books, newspapers, magazines, government publications and from the Internet to analyze team movements and league expansions, as well as to speculate about which, when, and where professional teams will relocate after 2000. But because of unexpected player trades, changes in team ownership, and unanticipated league decisions, our predictions remain uncertain. Undeterred, we studied past events to determine how team owners and leagues responded to market forces then affecting the sports industry. Moreover, by collecting and summarizing over fifty years of published data regarding team movements and league expansions we expose the events and forces that make professional sports a dynamic and integral part of American culture.

This book addresses two important topics. First, it identifies and analyzes the demographic factors of metropolitan areas that influence decisions concerning relocation and expansion. Second, it quantifies and evaluates the success of professional baseball, football, and basketball teams prior to and following relocation, and after expansion. Chapters One and Three detail the relocation of teams. Chapters Two and Four focus on the expansion of leagues. Together these four chapters identify the owners of each relocated and expansion team and highlight significant facts about the owners' investment in the franchise. Chapter Five then ranks the relocated and expansion teams in three sports as either superior, average, or inferior based on a team's success in the 1990s. Chapter Six covers alternative leagues and the status of venues currently planned for construction, including the financial aspects. The Conclusion summarizes our findings and describes why team owners use taxpayer money to subsidize the construction or renovation of a club's ballpark, stadium, or arena.

For their contribution we thank the staff at Pfeiffer University's library and computer center, and at the public libraries in Charlotte and Concord, North Carolina, and Terre Haute, Indiana. Gerald Carpenter of the School of Business and Professional Studies; Mike Riemann, the Executive Vice President for Budget and Finance; and Don Dodson, the former Chancellor of the Charlotte Campus permitted Frank Jozsa to use the facilities at Pfeiffer University as required. Mike Utsman, Assistant Dean of Student Support Services, Duane Dunston, a university technician, and Don Phipps, a computer information services professor assisted Jozsa with his computer files and programs. In addition, Frank Wetta, Dean of Arts and Sciences at Daytona Beach Community College, has encouraged John Guthrie to "do history" and stay active as a scholar. Professor Emeritus James Quirk, retired from California Institute of Technology, and professors Gary Stone, of Winthrop University, and Peg Harman, of Pfeiffer University, read and reviewed the manuscript. As a group, they found and corrected errors of omission or commission and misstatements of facts regarding team- and league-specific information, demographic and economic data, and the chronology of sports events that occurred between 1950 and 1998. Given their contribution, this book more accurately portrays the roles of franchise owners, leagues, and communities in the geographic distribution and development of the professional sports industry as it has evolved in the United States. We greatly appreciate their help. Needless to say, we are responsible for any errors of fact or interpretation that may appear in this book.

Both authors have participated in sports. As an undergraduate John Guthrie ran cross country at Radford College. One year after earning his B.S., he received a graduate assistantship as assistant coach of the school's men's and women's cross-country teams. In 1979, both teams qualified for their respective NAIA championship meet. Guthrie concedes, however, that head coach Tyler Will deserves the most credit for this accomplishment. Guthrie continued running since leaving Radford. He has won two marathons and has run a personal best time of 2:28 for that distance.

Frank Jozsa played twenty years of organized baseball as a pitcher/catcher, from Little League to semi-pro. His all-star team included Tommy John, who went on to pitch for the Cleveland Indians, Chicago White Sox, Los Angeles Dodgers, and New York Yankees. With John pitching and Jozsa catching their team won the Indiana Babe Ruth League title in 1956. Later, Jozsa played on Terre Haute, Indiana's Great Lakes Connie Mack League Championship team. But like many hoosier youths, Jozsa too loved basketball, another sport at which he excelled. Jozsa had the good fortune to play high school hoops for Coaches Bill Welch and Howard Sharpe. Coach Sharpe won 759 basketball games between 1940 and 1987 at six Indiana high schools. Highly respected by his peers, Howard was an inspiration to Jozsa because of his knowledge of sports and for his leadership and concern for his players as student-athletes. While playing for Coach Sharpe at Gerstmeyer High School, Jozsa established an Indiana high school record by sinking forty-one consecutive free throws. His athletic prowess enabled him to play on Indiana State University's varsity basketball and baseball squads.

Besides colleagues, coaches, and teammates we are thankful for the care and affection extended by other people. Family and friends made Frank Jozsa's "Hall of Fame" for providing valuable aid throughout his career. Those inducted on the first ballot include Diana Donnenhoffer, Helen and Jeff Jozsa, Maureen Fogle, and Nancy Altuve. Without the support and love of his parents, the late Frank P. Sr. and Madeline Jozsa, he might not have participated in sports as a youth and maintained an interest in it throughout his career as an educator. They taught Jozsa to respect his opponents, practice hard, and never give up the pursuit to win. Likewise, Guthrie extends his utmost appreciation to his friends and clan—particularly Joe, his favorite Little League coach and Edie, his favorite equestrian—for always being there whenever he requested or needed aid.

Introduction

Since the beginning of the twentieth century, sports have assumed a growing role in American culture.[1] From the comfort of their homes, millions of people watch and listen to daily broadcasts of games and their results, player interviews, as well as various other sports events. Others enjoy weekly games at ballparks, courts, and arenas located in cities, towns, and suburbs across North America. Annual conference, division, and league championships increasingly dominate televised news programs, crowding out political debates, announcements of giant corporate mergers, and international crises. Concurrently, sports controversies have captured the headlines in our major newspapers and magazines. In a more recent trend, fans have fervently discussed an array of sports topics on talk radio and prime-time television programs. Besides addressing disputes between players and management over salaries and other matters, this discourse frequently focuses on the use of taxpayer moneys to finance the construction of new, multimillion-dollar sports facilities. Even minute changes in the operation and ownership of teams receive top billing in the press. Small wonder then, that reporters, analysts, and scholars contribute to the popularity of sports and stimulate the public's seemingly insatiable appetite for information concerning the conduct and decisions of athletes, team owners, and league officials.

Mindful of the above, we wrote this book primarily for sports fans and enthusiasts ranging from players and owners, to professors and undergraduates majoring in sports management, to politicians who advocate further regulation of the sports industry. The book provides an historical account of two phenomena. The first is the relocation of professional sports franchises. The second is the expansion of professional leagues in baseball, football, and basketball. While numerous articles and books deal with these topics, no work focuses exclusively on the dynamics of why, where, and to what extent professional teams have moved or how leagues have expanded during the second half of the twentieth century. In tackling these matters, we argue that the market alone should determine the course and development of professional sports leagues. We discourage intrusion from nonmarket sources and oppose government intervention in, or regulation of, the business of sports. The interaction of supply and demand in a market—which includes communities, fans, leagues, team owners, players, and the media—provides the most efficient allocation of limited sports resources. Sports markets, however, are not purely competitive. Given their economic conduct and performance, professional leagues represent cartels with considerable market power. By restricting the number of teams and the quantity of games played, leagues distort the resources allocated in the sports industry. Likewise, we oppose extensive revenue sharing or the reallocation of revenues from profitable to less profitable, or from large to small market, teams. Instead of successful franchises subsidizing their league opponents, we favor free-market incentives. Franchise relocation is a natural adjustment to market conditions, and no person or institution is better equipped than an owner to make such decisions. After all, owners want to maximize their profits. To do this, they must respond to market conditions.[2]

Discouraging a franchise from relocating to a more profitable location and persuading league officials to place an expansion team at a particular site directly concern communities, fans, players, and team owners. Using demographic and economic statistics and sports-related data, we explore the historical background and reasons for relocation and expansion in three major-league sports. To that end, the text first analyzes historical trends concerning franchise moves and locating expansion sites. Next, it identifies economic and demographic facts specific to home sites and markets. Third, it reveals the strategies of team owners and leagues in managing the quality of existing franchises. Fourth, it ranks teams based on performance, home attendance, and estimated market value. Finally, the book measures the success of relocated and expansion teams at the home site.[3]

Much of our data and information have been extracted from a wide variety of published material. Between 1960 and 1975, several economists investigated and analyzed the professional sports industry.[4] Their work, in general, discussed taxation, labor relations, antitrust laws, and public subsidies as applied to teams and leagues. Roger Noll and James Quirk focused on the economics of club movements and on the business rationale for professional sports league expansions. In their models, the sports business consists of privately or corporately owned team franchises that joined together to form leagues. Franchises have certain privileges, including the exclusive right to provide league contests within a specific geographic area. Owners seek to maximize profits at their respective locations, and leagues operate as a cartel to limit competition by setting franchise operating rules and restricting the supply of teams in the sport.[5] Our analysis incorporates these findings and those of other scholars. Recent studies, for instance, on the appreciating value of sports franchises, on the competition between cities to build and finance extravagant sports venues, and on the financial dilemma of small market teams, have addressed decisions regarding team relocation or league expansion.[6]

One of our key objectives is to examine the long-run trends of franchise relocation. To do this, we provide a cross section of demographic data and team performance statistics on clubs that have relocated. But we make no overriding critique of team owners who have moved their franchises. Our aim is to relate how and why owners strategically place their teams to compete in their respective leagues, while acquiring talented players and winning championships. Another purpose is to explain league expansions since 1950 by illuminating both the performances of new teams and the demographic characteristics of the home site. As with relocation, we leave it for readers to evaluate, or second-guess, the owners and leagues regarding these decisions.

In addition, we examine the relocation in and expansion of Major League Baseball (MLB), the National and American Football Leagues (NFL and AFL), and the National and American Basketball Associations (NBA and ABA). The sports organizations investigated here originated in 1876 with the National League, followed by the American League in 1901, the NFL in 1920, the NBA in 1946, the AFL in 1960, and the ABA in 1967. In essence, our work represents a response to Stephen H. Hardy's call for studies that appreciate sport as a special industry, like agriculture, steel, or medicine, and assume an historical perspective.[7]

Our analysis excludes the franchise movements and league expansions that occurred before 1950 for several reasons. First, the boom in the exposure and popularity of these sports began in the 1950s. Second, MLB and the NFL had long periods of franchise stability prior to 1950, while the NBA experienced excessive volatility in franchise locations from 1946 to 1950. Third, government officials have revised much of the pre-1950 census data for metropolitan area per capita income and other demographic characteristics, rendering such data unreliable for our purposes. Fourth, some specific team information for the years prior to 1950, such as home attendance and venue capacity, is either unavailable or inaccurate.[8]

In a free, competitive market, a franchise owner's decision to relocate his or her team is a business strategy. The owner hopes to maximize total profits, or the value of the franchise, by relocating to an available site having a higher drawing potential in terms of several factors. These include an area's population, its population growth and wealth, and the local and regional markets for radio and television. So if an owner fails to maximize profits at a current site, he or she stands to increase the value of the franchise by moving the team to a more lucrative location. The other owners in the league should approve the move if it is in their best interest. That is, if the relocation increases the value of their respective franchises, owners should approve the relocation.

As noted above, in the 1970s economists interested in the sport industry within the United States first analyzed the business, financial, and economic aspects of franchise relocation. In 1973, James Quirk concluded that franchise moves provide no long-term solution for the tendency of big-city teams to dominate a given sport. Moves in organized baseball, for example, merely intensified the extent of imbalances in playing strengths among teams instead of mitigating such imbalances. Furthermore, MLB has itself created the problem of franchise instability by adopting a business rules structure that undermines a club's survival in small cities. As Quirk put it, only the prudent and equitable application of antitrust legislation will end the abuse of franchise moves and interleague imbalances.[9]

Soon thereafter, Quirk collaborated with Mohamed El Hodiri on team movements and league operations. The four key points in this work echoed Quirk's previous study. For one, they claim that franchises located in areas with high drawing potential compete better than franchises situated in regions with low drawing potential. For another, they contend that the higher the share of television and radio revenues accruing to a team, the greater the salaries of its players. Under those circumstances the chance of survival for clubs in smaller markets lessens. Additionally, leagues could achieve parity of playing strengths among teams, Quirk and Hodiri assert, by assigning franchise rights so as to equalize drawing potential instead of balancing geographic areas. Many of the franchise shifts from the 1940s to the 1970s, according to them, represented the expansion of leagues from regional to national organizations made possible by dependable air transportation and by the growth of population centers on the West Coast.[10]

On the heels of this seminal work came *Government and the Sports Business* (1974). This analogy, edited by sports economist Roger Noll, discusses the economics of expansion in terms of game attendance, player costs, and taxation. Noll and the other contributors used economic theories and statistical evidence to analyze the future prospects for major league expansion in the 1970s and the 1980s. From this, the authors recommended that leagues should pursue an open and effective expansion policy, as opposed to the restrictive rules that leagues had voluntarily adopted or that the government had arbitrarily imposed by the mid-1970s. The work endorsed a larger supply and a more efficient allocation of franchises and favored limiting the anti-competitive behavior of sports enterprises and leagues. In fact, at least one of the proposals—the equitable sharing of national broadcasting revenues—was adopted by the NBA in 1976.[11]

Three related articles, published in the mid-1980s, discuss the relationship between franchise relocation and the enforcement of antitrust law. Federal regulatory attorney James Gattuso, for example, says the rules structure governing sports leagues, which constrain member teams, does several things. Furthering the long-run interests of the leagues and their fans, these rules also effectively maintain a regional balance of franchises. In turn, this promotes the intensity of interleague competition and thereby enhances the long-run stability of the leagues. Internal management policy, according to Gattuso, warrants neither meticulous government oversight nor bureaucratic control. Therefore, the antitrust laws should allow franchises to enforce league rules regarding team relocation, merger, or abandonment.[12]

In contrast, political science professor Arthur T. Johnson favors federal legislation and public policies designed to preserve franchise stability and to maximize the public's access to professional sporting events. Wanting to eliminate the scarcity of franchises, Johnson makes two recommendations. First, force all professional leagues to reduce existing barriers for membership and permit cities without teams to bid for franchises. Second, Congress should protect community interests while assuring the owner's property rights and avoiding unnecessary regulatory mechanisms of league operations.[13]

David Meggyesy, however, opposed congressional grants of antitrust immunity to professional sports leagues. In the interest of communities, players, owners, and fans, he contends that Congress should instead undertake a comprehensive study of league operations and focus especially on the issue of allowing sports associations to pool revenues from television, skyboxes, club seats, and luxury suites.[14]

Three notable books published in the 1990s deal with the interplay and enduring relationship between cities, franchises, and fans. Each book features a description or analysis of franchise relocation in the major leagues during various periods of the twentieth century. *The Business of Professional Sports* (1991), by Paul Staudohar and James Mangan, details the dynamics of the sports business and how it influences, and is influenced by, society at large. Their book stimulates intellectual discourse about ways to change and perhaps improve the operation of the sports industry. In addition to examining sport as a product of television, Staudohar and Mangan also provide a concise review of the literature covering various facets of the sports business from labor-management relations, to sports as a social science, to business and public policy on amateur and professional sports.[15]

In *Playing the Field: Why Sports Teams Move and Cities Fight to Keep Them* (1993), Charles C. Euchner examines the intercity competition to attract professional teams. Among other topics, Euchner analyzes team profits and franchise relocation, the moves of the Raiders from Oakland to Los Angeles and the Colts from Baltimore to Indianapolis, and sports leagues and the dependent city. He also discusses franchise mobility from economic, legal, and political perspectives. Euchner declares that professional "sports is not a dominant industry in any city, yet teams receive the kind of attention one might expect to be lavished on major employers and producers located there." According to Euchner, this occurs because "sports franchises have great leverage. Their demands do not directly affect many interest groups and opponents of stadium projects have difficulty developing coalitions to oppose them." As a result, "civic leaders tend to succumb to the blackmail tactics of professional sports owners rather then develop and support sound economic policies."[16]

In *The Sports Franchise Game: Cities in Pursuit of Sports Franchises, Events, Stadiums, and Arenas* (1995), sports industry analyst Kenneth Shropshire refers to quantitative impact studies to evaluate (a) how Philadelphia and Camden, New Jersey competed to attract professional sports teams, (b) franchise shifts in the San Francisco area, (c) relocation of the Baltimore Colts to Indianapolis, and (d) the efforts by fans in Washington D.C. to secure a baseball franchise for the nation's capital. In the process, he attempts to answer some significant questions. For instance, what value does a sports franchise bring to a city? When should a city battle for a franchise? Why is the competition for a team so vigorous? Should a city build a stadium, ballpark, or arena in the hopes of attracting a franchise? Shropshire concludes that a city's decision to pursue a professional sports franchise is largely subjective. Accordingly, local politicians should consider the community's image and civic need to determine the value of a franchise before financing the construction of a sports facility for a team. Shropshire advocates partial public ownership of a franchise if taxpayer funds are invested in a team. Moreover, he states that with public financing of a facility "it may now be appropriate to expect franchise owners to act more socially responsible in the community." In sum, "a review of economic impact studies of new stadium construction costs and franchise bidding [by cities] warrants the conclusion that there is no clear-cut answer and that there are many issues to consider." Thus in the *Sports Franchise Game*, the reader must measure the true economic and social value of professional sports to American cities.[17]

Over the past several years, an increasing number of articles have appeared in newspapers across the nation that discuss and fret about the possibility of a home team relocating. Many of these news items focus on the threat, explicit or implicit, made by owners to move their franchise if taxpayers refuse to subsidize the construction and operation of a new, home site venue. *Texas Monthly* published a report in 1996 examining Houston's three professional sports teams— the Oilers, the Astros, and the Rockets. According to the study, the owners of the franchises exacted subsidies to finance new multimillion-dollar sports facilities featuring amenities like club seats and luxury suites. In addition, owners demanded a larger share of the venue's advertising, parking, concession, and merchandising revenues. The article concludes that losing these franchises should have slight economic impact on Houston since collectively the teams contribute less than 1 percent of the local economy's output of goods and services.[18]

In his article, "Break Up the Sports League Monopolies," historian Stephen Ross argues that sports leagues exercise monopolistic power by restricting the number of available franchises. By holding down the number of teams, established franchises increase their revenues by earning greater profits from television rights and by inducing greater tax subsidies from cities. If rival sports leagues existed, he contends that established leagues would only realize greater profits by expansion. Failure to expand would result in losses. Yet Ross admits that little data exists about the competitive expansion practices in professional team sports.[19]

In March 1991, *The Sporting News* printed a series of reports on the expansion plans of professional sports. These articles highlight the views of the commissioners of MLB, the NFL, and the NBA. For instance, NBA Commissioner David Stern stated: "Expansion on a precise dollar and cents basis may be less profitable than people think. But if you represent yourself as a national league, and see that there are large regions underrepresented, you have to look carefully at the demand and try to fulfill it." Together the reports underscore the expected risks of expansion as espoused by a sample of owners, economists, and sports analysts. Still, if managed correctly, the reports claim, expansion in the economic environment of 1991 would cause limited financial damage to existing teams while helping leagues flourish. The reports conclude that professional sports leagues confronted a daunting challenge in the 1990s—that is, reigning in costs while finding new, abundant sources of revenue.[20] Six years later *The Sporting News* offered three recommendations for building a successful franchise to the owners of two recent MLB additions, the Arizona Diamondbacks and the Tampa Bay Devil Rays—pick the right star, draft prudently, and have a plan.[21]

Other scholars have viewed the topic from a sociological perspective. In "Blackballing the Inner City," Gary Stix cites Alan P. Sager and Arthur J. Culbert who analyzed the exodus of urban baseball teams from inner city neighborhoods like Brooklyn. To be sure, the advent of jet travel in the 1950s and the existence of two or more teams in the same sport at the same site, partially explain why the Dodgers moved from Brooklyn to Los Angeles. But the two academics conclude that race was a more powerful statistical indicator than the age of the stadium, team standing, or average annual attendance in an owner's decision to evacuate an inner city site. Indeed, Sager and Culbert imply that race proved more crucial than personal income, or any other factor, in explaining why fans feared venturing into Brooklyn's poor neighborhoods to attend games. Even so, critics of the study point out that most teams move for greater profits at an alternative site.[22]

Along these lines, Indiana University professor Mark Rosentraub's *Major League Losers* (1997) explodes the myth that professional teams by virtue of their existence generate so much economic growth and civic pride that they constitute a public benefit worthy of taxpayer-funded subsidies. Rosentraub details the patterns of franchise movements in the major leagues and shows that the social and psychological links between the fans, teams, and cities have frayed as demographic and economic trends redefine the hierarchy of municipalities. Small communities hosting professional teams must either subsidize their club or lose it to larger or wealthier communities. Rejecting subsidies, Rosentraub endorses a market-based approach that would end the sports welfare game conclusively. This approach would stop what he calls "the perverse transfer of public money to wealthy players and wealthier owners."[23]

Some commentators take issue with Rosentraub's compelling thesis. In January 1997, *SportsTravel* featured an article about the commitment made by cities to build inner-connecting infrastructures that will link cities and support their new professional teams. In Jacksonville, Baltimore, Hartford, Phoenix, Columbus, and Toronto, boosters planned and sought funding for new municipal investments in entertainment and sports complexes. As the promoters see it, new state-of-the-art hotels, stadiums, ballparks, arenas, and construction projects promise to spur long-term economic development, create jobs, and boost the city's image as a sport and entertainment capital. Event sponsors, furthermore, claim that collegiate and amateur sports events will gradually migrate to these cities to use the existing professional sports facilities.[24]

While some cities hope to attract a sports franchise, some regional organizations have become more outspoken about losing teams to other states. In a February 1997 posting on their Web site, the Franchise of Americans Needing Sports (FANS) listed three resolutions relative to the relocation of major league baseball, football, and basketball franchises from California. They resolved that the state senate should hold a symposium within three months to discuss professional sports infrastructure in California and its economic and social impact on local communities. They also requested that Congress explore the comprehensive issue of antitrust and its involvement in professional sports and to investigate the related issues of special tax breaks and incentive programs that prompt owners to relocate their teams to other cities. Lastly, they lobbied Congress to enact measures to prevent established teams from being lured away by enticing offers from other cities and jurisdictions. Toward that goal, FANS strongly urged Congress to create a federal agency to keep a watchful eye on sports teams that remain obligated under contract to a local municipality.[25]

Any astute reader of American newspapers and magazines realizes the media hype and press that local civic leaders illicit to attract a sports franchise to an area. The *Wall Street Journal, Business Week,* and newspapers in the major cities of North Carolina, for example, ran numerous stories in 1997 on the probability of major league baseball coming to the twelve-county Triad area, which contains the cities of Greensboro, High Point, and Winston-Salem. The region has great demographics—population size, a high-ranked television market, and twelve minor league baseball teams—and twenty investors who could raise the $100 million entry fee. The Triad emerged as the leading contender, distancing rival sites in northern Virginia, Orlando, Indianapolis, and Charlotte in the race to win a baseball franchise. In a May 1998 referendum, however, Triad-area voters in Guilford and Forsyth Counties, North Carolina, overwhelmingly rejected a tax proposal to help build a $210 million, 45,000-seat baseball stadium. The outcome of the referendum suggests that people in these counties oppose taxpayer subsidies for professional sports facilities because schools, roads, and county infrastructure projects have higher priority.[26]

Although not specifically discussed in this book, the National Hockey League (NHL) is an expanding and popular sports organization. Despite a $75 million entry fee and the highest ticket prices for professional games, nine cities in North America competed eagerly for five NHL franchise openings—one began play in 1997 and four more teams will join the league by 2000. Yet to survive in the long run as a major North American sport, most NHL franchises need additional national television revenues and an excess of cash flows from home attendance and arena amenities. Whether the NHL survives will depend on fans allocating their money and leisure time to watch "the Coolest Game on Earth."[27]

Like the NHL, due to limited popularity and exposure, the Arena Football League is also excluded from this analysis. Founded in 1986, the league played in 1998 with fourteen teams including Arizona, Nashville, New Jersey, New York City, and Tampa Bay, all of which hosted NFL clubs. Lamar Hunt, the owner of the Kansas City Chiefs, has bid for an expansion franchise to play in 20,000-seat Kemper Stadium in 1999. By 2000, Buffalo and New Orleans will join the league. Other sites currently under consideration for teams are Boston, Jacksonville, and San Diego.[28]

Meanwhile, in 1997 *The Sporting News* recognized several North American cities as the best sports sites in terms of their (a) sports climate and atmosphere, (b) fervent and knowledgeable fans, (c) potential venue capacity, and (d) accessible location. Having the right mix of these features would make a city a strong candidate for an expansion franchise. Salt Lake City, Charlotte, and Charleston, South Carolina ranked the highest for MLB. On the other hand, Los Angeles/Anaheim, Toronto, and Salt Lake City scored the highest for an NFL franchise. Pittsburgh, St. Louis, and Tampa/St. Petersburg seemed best suited for an NBA franchise. These cities already have a selection of teams in professional and collegiate sports, a nucleus of hard-core fans who read, watch, and discuss sports, and an appealing array of indoor and outdoor nonsport activities for people to choose from. Considering these criteria, *The Sporting News* rated Denver, Dallas-Fort Worth, and Miami as the top three cities for all sports in 1997.[29]

The procedure for purchasing a new or existing franchise is structured and straightforward. In MLB a prospective owner of an expansion franchise must have a management structure intact and submit to league officials a five-year projection of the financial statements of the club's operations. At the new site, the ballpark must have a seating capacity of nearly forty thousand, and the parking facilities must accommodate at least 25 percent of the ballpark's capacity. A receptive local government, eager to get a new home team, is another requisite for successful ownership. Also, local demographic data such as the number of households with televisions must meet a minimum standard established by the league. To gain ownership, 75 percent of the owners in the league in which the team plays, and 50 percent in the other league, must approve the deal.[30]

Prospective owners of an NBA expansion franchise must first file an application with the league office, and then submit a comprehensive business plan for the operation of the franchise. After a background check of the applicant, the NBA's executive committee interviews the would-be owner while other league officials evaluate the business plan. At least 75 percent of the existing owners must approve the purchase of the franchise by the prospective buyer.[31]

In the NFL, a potential owner initially secures approval from the commissioner's office to purchase a team. Unlike the other leagues, the NFL stipulates that one individual or firm must control a majority interest in the team. If a group seeks ownership, one person in the group must own at least 30 percent of the group's share. As in MLB, the NFL wants a managerial structure in place with someone clearly responsible for running the franchise, and 75 percent of the existing owners must approve the sale of any league club.[32]

The expansion of professional sports leagues in the United States began in the early 1900s. Now, as then, established franchise owners and league committees must jointly consent to add new teams, because of the potential impact on profits. In agreeing to allow expansion, each owner evaluates the financial benefits and costs of increasing the league's membership. Depending on the sport or the existing franchises, from the perspective of a current team owner, the expansion might result in less broadcasting revenues, additional transportation costs, greater seasonal home attendance and competitive rivalries, and a loss of veteran players to a new club. Thus, each current owner makes the twin decisions of whether to expand, and where to locate, after evaluating the net economic benefits to his or her team.

Since few comprehensive texts or collections of readings deal with the decisions, methodologies, and tactics of owners and leagues to expand, we draw much of our material from insightful articles and studies published in the past twenty-five years on why, when, and where professional sports leagues expand. Chapter One documents the history of all major professional sports teams in baseball, football, and basketball that relocated between 1950 and 1977. In doing so, it examines various socioeconomic, demographic, and team-performance factors as background information for the relocation of a team from one site to another and in support of the decisions by owners and league. Throughout this and the ensuing chapters, the discussion will adhere to the following sequence of the sports and leagues: MLB, then the NFL and AFL, and the NBA and ABA. Next, we evaluate the impact of the relocation on both sites.

Chapter Two provides the rationale and incentives for major league expansion between 1950 and 1977. This historical and economic analysis of expansions in professional team sports details the factors that motivate leagues to add new clubs and that encourage prospective owners to choose the best site to locate their franchise. We then offer some insight into how the expansion franchise affects the community, fans, other sports teams, and nonsports activities and events at the new site. We conclude Chapter Two by identifying the principal trends and patterns of expansion in the professional sports industry during the quarter century under investigation.

Chapter Three examines the winning record, changes in attendance, and the estimated market value of teams that relocated since 1977. Initially, we identify individuals or groups owning the franchise, then discuss the success of the team after relocation. After compiling data, we calculate the average winning percentage and home attendance over selected seasons for each team that moved in baseball, football, and basketball. Also, we obtained the sales price and estimated market value of a team from *Financial World* and other sources and used this material as indicators of economic success. Consequently, Chapter Three provides facts and evidence whether playing at a new site matters to a team's players, coaches, owners, fans, and the league. It concludes with a discussion of some recent trends and our predictions concerning the relocation of professional teams into the twenty-first century. This discussion raises three questions. Will small-market clubs in areas having weak demographics continue to struggle to compete with big-city teams in the various professional sports leagues? Do untapped sports markets exist in either the United States or foreign countries? If so, can owners exploit these sites for relocation purposes?

Chapter Four explores the ownership history, win-loss percentages, hometown fan support, and the financial value of all expansion teams in professional baseball, football, and basketball since 1977. As in Chapter Three, we organize team-specific information and demographic statistics and insert it into tables to analyze the progress of the expansion teams in the three sports from 1987 to 1997. We mention the key players of the expansion teams and isolate those clubs that have won division and conference titles and league championships. Additionally, we discuss the history of expansion teams such as the Colorado Rockies and Florida Marlins in baseball, the Carolina Panthers and Jacksonville Jaguars in football, and the Toronto Raptors and Vancouver Grizzlies in basketball to indicate how these teams emerged and began competing. Chapter Four also compares the expansion teams in each league to explain why some teams succeed. It concludes by making predictions concerning future expansions in professional team sports. For example, because the North American sports market has an abundance of teams, would the location of an MLB franchise in

Mexico, an NFL club in Europe, or even an NBA division in Europe, make economic sense for professional sports leagues in the long run?

In Chapter Five each relocated and expansion team is ranked as either superior, average, or inferior. As in Chapters Three and Four, we updated and scored criteria to measure and analyze each club's performance since 1990. Tables list the teams and their winning percentage, home game attendance, and estimated market value, and the overall rank of the team.

In Chapter Six we analyze sports venues and discuss at length the two newest professional basketball leagues for women—the American Basketball League (ABL) and the Women's National Basketball Association (WNBA). In 1997 both leagues began play with eight teams located in different cities. With scheduled play in the fall for the ABL and the summer for the WNBA, the survival of the leagues will depend on the income received from corporate sponsorships, gate attendance, and limited television revenues. The first WNBA season home attendance per franchise averaged 9,669—or 6,300 above their target. Average attendance per game ranged from 11,800 for the New York Liberty to 7,500 for the Charlotte Sting. What is more, over three million viewers per week watched WNBA games on NBC, ESPN, and Lifetime. According to the WNBA commissioner, "professional sports leagues are not made overnight; it's a slow building process and we're in the middle of that process right now."[33]

Since 1990, more than two dozen professional sports stadiums and arenas have been built in the United States and Canada. The *Wall Street Journal* reported that baseball stadiums constructed since the 1970s in Pittsburgh, Minneapolis, and Chicago initially generated more revenues, but once the novelty wore thin attendance declined and revenues followed suit (unless of course the home team maintained or increased its win-loss record).[34] With some of the new facilities costing in excess of $300 million, taxpayers often oppose investing public funds for the benefit of wealthy owners and high-salaried players. We comment on this issue throughout the text.[35]

We conclude the book by highlighting the major findings of the research and speculate about the future of professional sports teams and leagues for the twenty-first century. In our view, the demand for quality sports entertainment will continue to surge in America, at least over the next decade. So the direction, trend, and pattern that team relocation and league expansion follow will matter to fans, television and media executives, current and prospective team owners, and the general public. Although this book, in general, documents what has taken place during the past half century, the Conclusion consolidates our findings and lays a foundation for predicting what might happen in the professional sports industry in the near future. At the same time, we expose those factors that lead television viewers to turn off broadcasts of the World Series, Super Bowl, or NBA Playoffs and instead spend their weekend afternoons watching classic movies or other programs, or participating in outdoor activities.

NOTES

1. In a poll of seven hundred athletes who played in the 1997 AAU Junior Olympics in Charlotte, 53 percent of the boys and 34 percent of the girls expect to play profes-

sional sports some day. Seventy percent of the black youths and 33 percent of the white youths believe they will make the roster of a professional team. For complete results of the poll, see Editorial, *Charlotte Observer* (9 August 1997), 1, 14A.

2. After selling out 364 straight games the attendance of the Charlotte Hornets fell in the 1997–98 season. To expand their fan base and boost future revenues in the Charlotte Coliseum, the marketing department of the team tracks ticket stubs and conducts surveys with focus groups and fans. For further information of the club's strategies see Insider, *Charlotte Observer* (1 December 1997), 2D.

3. Sport history has established itself as a legitimate field of inquiry only over the past thirty years. See S. W. Pope ed., *The New American Sport History: Recent Approaches and Perspectives* (Urbana and Chicago: University of Illinois Press, 1997); Steven A. Riess, *Major Problems in American Sport History* (Boston and New York: Houghton Mifflin Company, 1997). For important historical works on the economic aspects of sports, see Stephen H. Hardy, "Entrepreneurs, Organizations, and the Sports Marketplace," *Journal of Sport History* 13 (1986), 14–33; Allen Guttman, *Sports Spectators* (New York: Columbia University Press, 1986); Roger G. Noll, ed., *Government and the Sports Business* (Washington, D.C.: The Brookings Institution, 1974); James Quirk and Rodney D. Fort, *Pay Dirt: The Business of Professional Sports* (Princeton, N.J.: Princeton University Press, 1992); Gerald W. Scully, *The Market Structure of Sports* (Chapel Hill: University of North Carolina Press, 1995). For the best general overview of American sports since midcentury, see Randy Roberts and James Olsen, *Winning Is the Only Thing: Sports in America Since 1945* (Baltimore and London: Johns Hopkins University Press, 1989).

4. See Henry G. Demmert, *The Economics of Professional Team Sports* (Lexington, Mass.: D. C. Heath and Company, 1973); James Quirk and Mohamed El Hodiri, "An Economic Model of a Professional Sports League," *Journal of Political Economy* 79 (March/April 1975), 1302–1319; Walter Neale, "The Peculiar Economics of Professional Sports," *Quarterly Journal of Economics* 78 (February 1964), 1–14.

5. James Quirk and Mohamed El Hodiri, "The Economic Theory of a Professional Sports League," in Roger G. Noll, ed., *Government and the Sports Business* (Washington, D.C.: The Brookings Institution, 1974), 33–80.

6. Since 1991 *Financial World* has published a series of articles estimating the profits, values, and net worth of professional sports franchises in the United States. See Tushar Atre, Kristine Auns, Kurt Badenhausen, Kevin McAuliffe, Christopher Nikolov, and Michael Ozanian, "Sports, Stocks, and Bonds," *Financial World* (20 May 1996), 53–64; Michael Ozanian, Tushar Atre, Ronald Fink, Jennifer Reingold, John Kinelman, Andre Osterland, and Jeff Skar, "Suite Deals," *Financial World* (9 May 1995), 42–56; Michael Ozanian and Brooke Grabarek, "The Untouchables," *Financial World* (10 May 1994), 42–45. See also Michael Ozanian, "Selective Accounting," *Forbes* (14 December 1998), 124–134; Michael N. Danielson, *Home Team: Professional Sports and the American Metropolis* (Princeton, N.J.: Princeton University Press, 1997).

7. See Stephen H. Hardy, "Entrepreneurs, Organizations, and the Sports Marketplace," *Journal of Sport History* 13 (1986), 14–33.

8. See Frank P. Jozsa, Jr., "An Economic Analysis of Franchise Relocation and League Expansion in Professional Team Sports, 1950–1975," (Ph.D. diss., Georgia State University, 1977) for a wealth of demographic data, statistics, and team performance information dating from 1950.

9. For a comprehensive study of the process of franchise moves in baseball from 1946 to 1972, see James Quirk "An Economic Analysis of Team Movements in Professional Sports," *Law and Contemporary Problems* 38 (Winter/Spring 1973), 42–66.

10. In part, these conclusions were derived analytically and empirically by James Quirk and Mohamed El Hodiri in "The Economic Theory of a Professional Sports League," in Roger G. Noll, ed., *Government and the Sports Business*, 33–80.

11. For why sports firms should receive special privileges from government relative to other forms of business enterprise, see Noll's *Government and the Sports Business.*

12. For why leagues should avoid skewing the market to favor relocation of franchises, see James Gattuso, "Congress and Rule-Making," *Society* (May/June 1986), 6–10.

13. For a compelling argument of reducing barriers to league entry as a policy goal and thereby maximizing access to professional sports for fans, see Arthur T. Johnson, "Balancing Interests," *Society* (May/June, 1986), 11–16.

14. For these views see David Meggyesy, "The National Football League Monopoly," *Society* (May/June, 1986), 16–21. See also Meggyesy's *Out of Their League* (Forestville, Calif.: Ramparts Press, 1970).

15. For a multidisciplinary approach analyzing the sports business, see Paul D. Staudohar and James A. Mangan, eds., *The Business of Professional Sports* (Champaign: University of Illinois Press, 1991).

16. See Charles C. Euchner, *Playing the Field: Why Sports Teams Move and Cities Fight to Keep Them* (Baltimore: Johns Hopkins University Press, 1993).

17. Professional sports franchises impact a community in various ways. Cities across America are clamoring for the opportunity to pay for stadiums and arenas with public funds. This topic is detailed in Kenneth L. Shropshire, *The Sports Franchise Game: Cities in Pursuit of Sports Franchises, Events, Stadiums, and Arenas* (Philadelphia: University of Pennsylvania Press, 1995).

18. The story of how Houston's sports owners sought to betray their hometown begins with the Astrodome. See Robert Draper, "Spoils Sports: Houston Professional Sports Teams Threaten to Relocate," *Texas Monthly* (January 1996), 110–116.

19. Stephen F. Ross, "Break Up the Sports League Monopolies," in *The Business of Professional Sports* (1991), 152–173.

20. Some analysts have depicted the best and worst from expansion by the professional sports leagues. Several view the 1990s as a period of momentous decisions by leagues and television networks. For these problems see Paul Attner, "How Professional Sports Governs Expansion Will Mean Success or Failure for the 21st Century," *The Sporting News* (18 March 1991), 13–19.

21. See Jerry Crasnick, "How to Build a Baseball Franchise," *The Sporting News* (30 June 1997), 27.

22. See Gary Stix, "Blackballing the Inner City," *Scientific American* 269 (September 1993), 152.

23. To what percentage of jobs and payroll in a community does a professional sports franchise contribute? How much return do taxpayers receive when they opt to spend money on a professional sports facility? For an examination of these and other public policy issues see Mark S. Rosentraub, *Major League Losers: The Real Costs of Sports and Who's Paying for It* (New York: Basic Books, 1997); John J. McCormick, "Playing Stadium Games: The Urge to Be a Big-League Town Has Turned Civic Pride Into a Costly—and Vain—Obsession," *Newsweek* (30 June 1997), 55.

24. To learn what six cities have done to upgrade their infrastructure and welcome the arrival of their new professional sports team, see Melissa Minker, "Expansion," *SportsTravel* (January 1997), 30–34.

25. The complete mission of FANS and the relocation resolution is available on the Web at <http://www.consumers.com> cited 10 February 1997.

26. For the sport-hungry Triad area and whether it has a real shot at a ball club, see Justin Catanoso, "Loading the Bases in North Carolina?" *Business Week* (7 April 1997), 98–99. Most financial information and data on professional teams, especially for expansion franchises, captivates the public's interest. When uncovered by the press, the data get immediately documented and publicized in the sports pages. Information such as the purchase price of an expansion franchise, team operating costs, league entry fees, annual net earnings, the present value of a franchise, and owner's rates of return are major financial news items that interest sports fans, and analysts who want to learn the economics of the sports business. Publications like *Financial World, USA Today, Information Please Sports Almanac, Fortune,* and the *Wall Street Journal* have produced articles that report on, and occasionally analyze, the financing of franchise operations. The avid business reader wanting more information on the sports industry should consult *Financial World's Annual 1991–1998 Surveys* for the total market value of existing franchises in MLB, the NFL, and the NBA. The data in the *Surveys* reflect the upward trend in the market values of sports franchises and illuminate how expensive and lucrative investments in venues and players are for cities and owners, respectively. Taxpayers from cities that bid for a new MLB, NFL, or NBA franchise may be stunned by *Financial World's Surveys* and have second thoughts about voting for tax increases that finance the expansion team's venue. For the results of the tax proposals in Guilford and Forsyth Counties, North Carolina, see "Voters Reject Triad Referendum for Baseball Stadium," posted to the Web site <http://www.cnnsi.com> cited 6 May 1998.

27. With a goal of all its teams breaking even in 2000, despite relatively low annual television ratings and revenues, the NHL embarked on a major makeover in the mid-1990s. Along with player salaries, licensing revenue and attendance have soared since the early 1990s as the league has expanded into new cities, added sponsors, moved problem teams to profit-maximizing sites, and stabilized other clubs through league-wide revenue sharing. See Stefan Fatsis, "The 'Coolest Game on Earth' Tries to Match the NHL Hype," *Wall Street Journal* (25 April 1997), B9.

28. See "Hunt for More Football in K.C.? Chiefs Owner, GM Visiting Arena Bowl, May Get Next Team," at the Web site <http://www.cnnsi.com> cited 19 November 1998.

29. See Bob Hille, "TSN's Best Sports Cities," *The Sporting News* (30 June 1997), 14–23.

30. Buying a sports franchise is a major task. Political clout, as well as money, are prerequisites for the league to consider. For understanding the process and requirements for ownership, see Alfred Edmond, Jr., "So You Want to Buy a Team?" *Black Enterprise* (September 1988), 79–88.

31. Ibid.

32. Ibid.

33. See Roger Thurow, "Women's Hoops League Out-Glitzes Rivals," *Wall Street Journal* (19 September 1997), B12; Ellen Alperstein, "WNBA's Rookie Season Is the Start of Something Big," *Charlotte Observer* (31 August 1997), 1G.

34. Allen Barra and Allen St. John, "Debunking Baseball's Stadium Myth," *Wall Street Journal* (18 July 1997), B9.

35. In Roger G. Noll and Andrew Zimbalist, eds., *Sports, Jobs, and Taxes: The Economic Impact of Sports Teams and Stadiums* (Washington, D.C.: The Brookings Institution, 1997) the contributors answer two important questions regarding sports venues. First, should stadium projects be subsidized by taxpayers because of the benefits that sports teams and facilities provide to the local economy? Second, if stadiums are unprofitable investments with low or negative economic returns, why are these facilities still being subsidized by taxpayers? Economists Noll and Zimbalist conclude that local politics and the bargaining power of the teams explain why subsidies continue even while

limited government is being touted and public construction projects have dubious or little value.

Chapter 1 _____

Franchise Relocation, 1950 to 1977

In 1958, during the courtship between Los Angeles and the owner of the Brooklyn Dodgers, Walter O'Malley, one city official promised him the moon, but he asked for more. Norris Poulson, a member of a group of Californians who were then trying to lure the Dodgers to Los Angeles, said one could hardly blame O'Malley. "He had a valuable package in the Dodgers and he knows it." O'Malley made no promises and insisted that he would consider moving his team to Southern California only if Los Angeles agreed to build him a ballpark. Although the city did not construct a new stadium for the Dodgers, it acquiesced to give O'Malley 185 acres of land and to purchase the club an additional 115 acres at a price not to exceed $7,000 per acre. Sweetening the deal further, Los Angeles promised to contribute $2 million toward grading and $2.7 million for constructing access roads. The latter sum came from the state gasoline tax fund. And, the Dodgers moved to the West Coast.[1]

To explore team movements further, this chapter analyzes the relocation of professional baseball, football, and basketball franchises from 1950 to 1977. Along the way, we discuss the pertinent economic, demographic, and team performance characteristics that motivated and justified each move that occurred in MLB, the NFL, AFL, NBA, and ABA. After analyzing such data, we address several questions concerning the relocation of major league teams. For instance, which teams moved? What factors influenced the decision of owners to relocate their franchises? Did the relocation result in greater economic returns to proprietors and the leagues? Do similarities exist in the relocation patterns of the teams in the three sports during the period under investigation?

MAJOR LEAGUE BASEBALL

National League

Established in 1876, the National League of Professional Baseball Clubs (NL) was the first permanent major league. The NL "was a league of 'clubs' rather than players." With eight chartered clubs aligned on an east-west basis, the league adopted rules governing the location of teams and sought to operate on sound business principles. Member cities, for example, "were required to have a minimum of seventy-five thousand inhabitants."[2] League rules also prohibited a team from locating in a city claimed by another team as its home territory, unless the aggrieved team and league approved the relocation. Each club, therefore, retains an exclusive right to sell admissions to league games in its home region. In MLB, a team can select a site in another team's territory in the rival league if the stadiums are located at least five miles apart.[3] From 1900 to 1949, eight NL teams played in Boston, Brooklyn, Chicago, Cincinnati, New York, Philadelphia, Pittsburgh, and St. Louis. Owners chose these sites in moderate to large eastern and midwestern cities because they were then experiencing economic growth, an expanding population, and a rising industrial employment base.[4]

In 1952 organized baseball amended its rules governing franchise moves in two ways. First, those owners wishing to relocate a team required no league consent for moving unless the move encroached upon the other league's territory. To approve the move, owners next needed to secure a three-fourths majority vote of league members, in lieu of unanimous consent. These revisions of the rules gave MLB teams more freedom to change residences. Over the next thirteen years several NL owners took advantage of the new regulations.[5]

The Boston Braves became the first team to exploit the new rules governing franchise relocation. In the early 1950s, the Braves played poorly in league competition. After placing seventh in the 1952 season, and given the presence and success of the American League's Boston Red Sox, owner Lou Perini decided to move the Braves to Milwaukee, a city begging for a big-league franchise. In 1953, the Braves moved to Milwaukee and set a new club record for attendance by drawing over 1.8 million fans to their home games.[6]

In the mid-1950s the industrial economy of the eastern United States seemed stagnant. Walter O'Malley, the owner of the Brooklyn Dodgers, and Horace Stoneham, the owner of the New York Giants, viewed MLB as a high profile, lucrative entertainment industry. Despite drawing over a million fans and having the most profitable television contract in baseball, O'Malley was unhappy in Brooklyn. With merely 35,000 seats, Ebbets Field had little potential for future growth. Its parking facilities appeared inadequate and the neighborhood surrounding the ballpark was rapidly deteriorating. This, coupled with the success of the Braves in Milwaukee, prompted O'Malley to act. Initially he tried to negotiate a deal for a new stadium in Brooklyn, but a city commissioner rejected the notion of using public funds to subsidize a privately owned professional baseball team. With an untapped sports market beckoning on the Pacific Coast, and given the convenience of improved air transportation, O'Malley and Stoneham vacated New York and moved their clubs to Los Angeles and San

Francisco, respectively, after the 1957 season. Two years later the Giants lost the NL pennant to the Dodgers who went on to defeat the Chicago White Sox in the 1959 World Series. In winning the championship, the Dodgers set an attendance record of over 420,000 in the six-game series.[7]

During this era, a Dodger and a Giant became baseball heroes. In the late 1940s and the early 1950s, the first African American to play in the big leagues, Dodger superstar Jackie Robinson, played a prominent role as a defensive infielder, base stealer, and clutch hitter. From 1947 to 1956, Robinson hit 137 home runs and batted .311 with a .474 slugging average. Willie Mays played equally effectively for the Giants by contributing to the success of the team in New York and San Francisco. From 1951 to 1973, Mays batted .302, scored 2,062 runs, struck 3,283 base hits, swatted 660 home runs, and maintained a .557 slugging average.[8]

From 1954 to 1965, as Mays inched closer to Babe Ruth's career home-run record, Hank Aaron diligently pursued the same milestone for the Braves. Despite Aaron's success at the plate and notwithstanding the Braves' 86–76 record and mediocre fifth-place finish in the NL, only 555,500 fans attended Milwaukee's home games in 1965. With grim prospects for fan support in Milwaukee, and lured by an emerging sports market in the sunbelt, the Braves moved to Atlanta in 1966. The shift of the club generated much criticism. Responding to complaints that he did nothing to prevent the move, baseball commissioner William Eckert said, "I think that in this great democracy we live in, if a man wants to take his property somewhere else and can do it legally, then I could not stop him."[9] In any case, Aaron played nine seasons in Atlanta breaking Ruth's career home run record in 1974. He ended his playing days with the Milwaukee Brewers in 1975 and 1976. Aaron's career .305 batting average, .555 slugging average, 3,771 base hits, 624 doubles, 2,297 runs-batted-in, and 755 home runs boosted attendance wherever he played.[10]

As Table 1.1 illustrates, only four NL teams relocated from 1950 to 1977. So during this period, a franchise move occurred on average every seven years in the NL. None of these teams made major player trades in the three-year post-move period. The performances of the Milwaukee Braves and San Francisco Giants significantly improved at their new home site. But the performances of the Dodgers declined at Los Angeles, while those of the Braves remained almost constant at Atlanta.

Even teams of average quality, located in big cities, draw enough fans to earn substantial profits. In James Quirk and Mohamed El Hodiri's study of organized ball, the market population, and games won by a team relate positively. Their analysis of franchise shifts showed that big-city MLB teams compete better and win more games than their small-city counterparts.[11] Given team rankings before and after relocation, how did the move affect home site attendance, both total and relative to the other teams in the league? Table 1.2 indicates clearly that average home attendance increased for each NL franchise, especially in the Braves' move from Boston to Milwaukee. The Los Angeles Dodgers' average attendance almost doubled, despite a decline in the team's performance. Also, each club's home attendance improved dramatically relative to the

Table 1.1
NL Franchise Relocation and Team Performance at Three-Year Pre-Move and Post-Move Intervals

Year	Franchise Move	Pre-Move Performance			Post-Move Performance		
1952–53	Boston to Milwaukee	.539	.494	.418	.597	.578	.552
1957–58	Brooklyn to Los Angeles	.641	.604	.545	.461	.564	.532
1957–58	New York to San Francisco	.519	.435	.448	.519	.539	.513
1965–66	Milwaukee to Atlanta	.516	.543	.531	.525	.475	.500

Note: Year reflects the last year at the pre-move site and the first year at the post-move site. For example, the last season for the Braves in Boston was 1952, and the first season in Milwaukee was 1953. Pre-Move and Post-Move Performance are the team's finish in the league's standings based on win-loss percentages in the three seasons prior to and following relocation. The Boston Braves won 53.9 and 49.4 percent of their games in the 1950 and 1951 seasons, and the Milwaukee Braves won 57.8 and 55.2 percent in the 1954 and 1955 seasons.

Source: The World Almanac and Book of Facts (Mahwah, N.J.: World Almanac Books, 1952–1967).

other league franchises. The population and per capita income surrounding a team's home site play important roles in influencing the relocation decision of owners and leagues. Some studies suggest that these factors influence attendance, which in turn affect a team's revenues and profits. Roger Noll determined that attendance and per capita income are inversely related. The relationship between attendance and income is due to the relatively low price of tickets to MLB games and also to the rise in less physically exerting occupations in the blue-collar cities of the Northeast and Midwest where the sedate pace of baseball seems less attractive. Because of this, he concluded that MLB is a working-class sport. Unsurprisingly, Noll proved that the hometown population is crucial to a team's success.[12]

Table 1.3 shows that NL teams tended to move to cities with smaller populations, greater population growth, and similar per capita income levels relative to the pre-move site. Even so, NL owners and leagues shrewdly decided to leave

Table 1.2
NL Franchise Relocation and Average Attendance for Three Years

		Pre-Move Years		Post-Move Years	
Year	Franchise Move	Home	League	Home	League
1952–53	Boston to Milwaukee	571	675	1,988	963
1957–58	Brooklyn to Los Angeles	1,092	1,047	2,057	1,285
1957–58	New York to San Francisco	702	1,047	1,496	1,285
1965–66	Milwaukee to Atlanta	746	1,231	1,489	1,317

Note: Home and League are, respectively, the team's average attendance per season for the final three seasons at the pre-move site and for the first three seasons at the post-move site. Home and League attendance are in hundreds of thousands.

Source: The World Almanac and Book of Facts, 1952–1967; Quirk, "An Economic Analysis of Team Movements In Sports," *Law and Contemporary Problems* 38 (Winter/Spring 1973), 51.

these sites given the economic and population growth in the southern and west-ern United States since the early 1960s. From 1960 to 1990, for example, the population of the metropolitan areas increased by 158 percent in Boston, 202 percent in New York, 125 percent in Milwaukee, 241 percent in Los Angeles, 236 percent in San Francisco, and 253 percent in Atlanta.[13]

Table 1.4 reveals that the NL teams that migrated from 1950 to 1977 left sites having more intersport competition and MLB teams, in particular, such as the Red Sox in Boston and the Yankees in New York. This in part explains why the Braves moved to Wisconsin and the Dodgers and Giants to California in the 1950s.

American League

The American League of Professional Baseball Clubs (AL) was formed in 1901 by chartering teams in Baltimore, Philadelphia, Boston, Chicago, Cleve-land, Detroit, Washington, and Milwaukee. A year after the inaugural season, St. Louis replaced Milwaukee. In 1903 the financially troubled Baltimore fran-chise relocated to New York in accordance with the NL/AL agreement permit-ting invasion into the other league's territory. "Securing a New York franchise," notes historian Steven A. Riess, "was considered crucial for certifying the American League's major-league status and its financial success." Anyway, from 1903 to 1953 no other AL teams shifted location.[14]

Following the 1952 rule changes in MLB, the fifty-year era of franchise stability ended for the AL. In 1953 owner Bill Veeck sold the St. Louis Browns to a syndicate of civic leaders in Baltimore, and in 1954 the Philadelphia Ath-letics relocated to Kansas City, after the Mack family sold the franchise to

Table 1.3
NL Franchise Relocation and Area Demographic Data, by Site

Year	Franchise Move	Pre-Move Site			Post-Move Site		
		Pop	Income	%Growth	Pop	Income	%Growth
1952–53	Boston to Milwaukee	1.2	1,829	7.4	.9	2,202	24.8
1957–58	Brooklyn to LA	3.7	2,823	11.9	6.2	2,803	54.8
1957–58	New York to SF	3.7	2,823	11.9	2.6	2,871	24.2
1965–66	Milwaukee to Atlanta	1.2	3,308	9.8	1.2	3,115	36.5

Note: Pop is the mean population per franchise in the Standard Metropolitan Statistical Area (SMSA), in millions, at the Pre-Move and Post-Move Sites. Income is the per capita personal in-come in the SMSA in thousands of dollars. The %Growth is the percentage growth in the total population in the pre-move and post-move SMSAs during the decade of the team's relocation. For example, population and income are reported for Boston in 1952, and Milwaukee in 1953. Boston's population grew 7.4 percent from 1950 to 1959, and Milwaukee's increased by 24.8 percent.

Source: U.S. Department of Commerce, Economic and Statistics Administration, *County and City Data Book* (Washington, D.C., 1950–1967); U.S. Department of Commerce, Bureau of Economic Analysis, *Survey of Current Business* (Washington, D.C., 1950–1967); U.S. Department of Com-merce, Bureau of the Census, *Statistical Abstract of the United States* (Washington, D.C., 1961, 1978). We used interpolation to calculate Population and Income for years between the census.

Table 1.4
NL Franchise Relocation and Intersport Competitors, by Site, by Year

| | | Pre-Move Site | | | Post-Move Site | | |
Year	Franchise Move	MLB	NFL/AFL	NBA/ABA	MLB	NFL/AFL	NBA/ABA
1952–53	Boston to Milwaukee	1	0	1	0	1	1
1957–58	Brooklyn to LA	2	1	1	0	1	0
1957–58	New York to SF	2	1	1	0	1	0
1965–66	Milwaukee to Atlanta	0	1	0	0	1	0

Note: Table entries are the number of professional teams in each sport at the Pre-Move and Post-Move Sites during the year prior to and following the team's relocation.

Source: The World Almanac and Book of Facts, 1950–1967.

Arnold Johnson. Since the St. Louis Browns and the Philadelphia Athletics usually placed at or near the bottom of the league's rankings, both clubs remained economically weak.

Clark Griffith was hired to manage the Washington Senators in 1912. Seven years later Griffith purchased 50 percent of the team from the other owners. After the death of Griffith in 1955, the performance and attendance of the Washington Senators worsened. From 1950 to 1959, the average attendance of the Senators declined by 14 percent. As attendance declined so did the performance of the club.[15] Between 1955 and 1959, the Senators finished no higher than seventh place in league standings. The quip that Washington was first in war, first in peace, and last in the American League seemed to ring true. Consequently, the Senators' playing days in the nation's capital had become numbered. In 1960, at the request of Clark's nephew Calvin Griffith, the league approved the relocation of the Senators to Bloomington, a suburb of the Twin Cities in Minnesota. Although smaller than Washington, D.C., the Minneapolis–St. Paul area ranked fourteenth in population and grew nearly 30 percent from 1950 to 1960. With a commitment made by the AL to place an expansion team in Washington in 1961, the Senators relocated to Minnesota and became the Twins. One of the team's leaders in Washington and Minnesota was slugger Harmon Killebrew. Over a twenty-two-year career with Washington, Minnesota, and Kansas City, Killebrew batted .256, scored 1,283 runs, clouted 573 home runs, and maintained a slugging average of .509. He also ranks ninth all-time in MLB with 1,699 career strike-outs.[16]

The expansion Senators averaged 664,000 in attendance at home games per season between 1961 and 1971. The ownership of the club fluctuated, changing in 1963, 1965, and in 1969 when Bob Short purchased the team for $9.4 million. After attendance declined from 918,000 in 1969 to 655,000 in 1971, Short moved the team to Arlington, Texas, and renamed it the Texas Rangers. In 1975 the attendance of the Rangers increased to 1.2 million, and the team improved to a seventh-place finish in the AL.

From 1948 to 1954, the attendance of the Philadelphia Athletics fell from 900,000 to 300,000 per season. The club placed eighth in league attendance in 1954. Meanwhile, the Philadelphia Phillies drew over 900,000 per season between 1950 and 1954. After acquiring the Athletics and Connie Mack Stadium for $8 million in 1954 from the Mack family, Arnold Johnson moved the club to Kansas City. In 1960 Johnson died and the executors of his estate sold the Athletics to Charley Finley for $2 million. In Kansas City, the performance and attendance of the team improved. However, with a dismal tenth-place finish in 1967, and a relatively small market to exploit, the club migrated to Oakland, an emerging sports market in northern California. With this move, Finley's television contract increased from $98,000 to $705,000.[17]

In 1969 the Seattle Pilots finished their first season last in the AL's Western Division and placed tenth in league attendance. The next year the club went bankrupt and was sold for $10.8 million to a syndicate headed by Bud Selig. Despite lawsuits filed by various Seattle groups to halt relocation, in 1970 Selig moved the team to Milwaukee and renamed it the Milwaukee Brewers.[18]

Between 1950 and 1977 an AL franchise relocated approximately every five years. To analyze each move we constructed Tables 1.5–1.8 to portray the changes that occurred for the teams at the post-move sites. Table 1.5 shows that Baltimore, Minnesota, and Oakland teams improved in performance at their post-move sites, while the performance of the Rangers declined in Texas. The performance of the Royals in Kansas City and the Brewers in Milwaukee barely changed after their moves from Philadelphia and Seattle, respectively. These changes in performance by AL teams at their post-move sites appear similar to those of the NL teams that relocated from 1950 to 1976. That is, roughly 50 percent of the MLB teams that moved experienced an improved record during the three-year, post-move period.

The appreciation in average home-team attendance during the three-year, post-move period proved less pronounced in the AL, relative to the teams that moved in the NL, as depicted in Table 1.6. Attendance at home games more than doubled in Baltimore, Kansas City, and Minnesota. For the other AL teams, attendance increased 18 percent in Oakland, 11 percent in Milwaukee, and 6 percent in Texas. Among the relocated NL teams, the Dodgers realized the smallest post-move gain in average attendance. Following the move from

Table 1.5
AL Franchise Relocation and Team Performance at Three-Year Pre-Move and Post-Move Intervals

Year	Franchise Move	Pre-Move Performance			Post-Move Performance		
1953–54	St. Louis to Baltimore	.338	.416	.351	.351	.370	.498
1954–55	Philadelphia to KC	.513	.383	.331	.409	.338	.386
1960–61	Washington to Minn.	.396	.409	.474	.438	.562	.565
1967–68	Kansas City to Oakland	.364	.451	.385	.506	.543	.549
1969–70	Seattle to Milwaukee	–	–	.395	.401	.429	.417
1971–72	Washington to Texas	.531	.432	.396	351	.352	.525

Note: Pre-Move and Post-Move Performance are a team's final standings in the AL based on win-loss percentages for three seasons prior to and following relocation. The Seattle Pilots moved to Milwaukee in 1970 after one season in Seattle.

Source: The World Almanac and Book of Facts, 1953–1973.

Brooklyn to Los Angeles the franchise increased its average attendance by 88 percent, or from 1.09 to 2.05 million per season (see Table 1.2).

After the three-year, post-move "honeymoon" period, did home attendance for these AL teams change? If so, how? Did the fans eventually lose interest in their new team? We calculated the percentage change in the average home attendance from the fourth to the sixth years at the post-move site for each team. The average attendance declined 2 percent in Baltimore, 19 percent in Kansas City, and 4 percent in Minnesota. Average attendance increased 18 percent in Oakland, 44 percent in Milwaukee, and 40 percent in Texas. Thus over the six-year, post-move period the rate of increase in home attendance significantly slowed in only the first three AL team relocations.

Table 1.6 further reveals how the relative (home versus league) attendance of the six teams changed in the three-year, post-move period. Only the home attendance of Kansas City and Minnesota exceeded the league average. These results show that the imbalances in market size (area population) among teams persisted in the AL. In contrast, home team attendance in the NL exceeded the league average after each team relocation. The NL teams relocated to larger markets such as Atlanta, Los Angeles, and San Francisco, than did the AL teams.

The population, population growth, and per capita personal income of consumers in a metropolitan area provide useful data when analyzing a particular area's demand for entertainment including professional sports. We applied these "demographics" earlier in Table 1.3. They demonstrate that of the four franchise moves in the NL, three of the teams relocated to less-populated sites (we divided the population of New York into thirds due to the presence of three major-league teams between 1954 and 1957). In addition, the differences in per capita income of consumers at the pre-move and post-move sites remained small in each of the NL moves, while the population growth at the post-move sites exceeded that at the pre-move sites for each relocation. Apparently population varied more than per capita income relative to the shifting of NL franchises.

Table 1.6
AL Franchise Relocation and Average Attendance for Three Years

Year	Franchise Move	Pre-Move Years		Post-Move Years	
		Home	League	Home	League
1953–54	St. Louis to Baltimore	370	989	938	1,019
1954–55	Philadelphia to KC	431	1,019	1,103	1,043
1960–61	Washington to Minn.	611	1,096	1,365	1,010
1967–68	Kansas City to Oakland	674	1,016	798	1,048
1969–70	Seattle to Milwaukee	678	1,011	755	967
1971–72	Washington to Texas	799	989	847	1,053

Note: Table entries are the average home game attendance (in hundreds of thousands) of a team and the AL for the three seasons prior to and following relocation.

Source: The World Almanac and Book of Facts, 1953–1973; Quirk "An Economic Analysis of Team Movements in Professional Sports," 51.

Do population, growth, and per capita income of an area influence either the owner or the league in deciding to relocate, and to which city? Since the mid-1950s the Dodgers, and since the late 1960s the Braves, have remained stable with little threat of relocating. On the other hand, when considering viable candidates for relocation as analyzed earlier in this chapter, the Giants are usually one of the first teams mentioned. Also, unless they remain competitive, small-city teams like San Diego, Pittsburgh, and Cincinnati seem to have tenuous futures at their present sites.

As Table 1.7 reveals, four of the six AL franchises that relocated from 1950 to 1976 migrated to smaller metropolitan areas. Indeed, only Oakland's and Milwaukee's populations exceeded Kansas City's and Seattle's, respectively. Except for the moves to Minnesota and Milwaukee, moreover, the population growth in Baltimore, Kansas City, Oakland, and Arlington, Texas, exceeded the same at the pre-move sites. Perhaps factors other than total population explain why some franchises move. The differences in consumer income across sites proved minor in the AL except in the cases of Kansas City to Oakland, and Washington to Texas. Oaklanders had higher per capita incomes than residents in Kansas City. Of course, per capita income might be highly skewed, as in Washington where no significant middle class exists. In the nation's capital households in general are either wealthy or poor. But in the affluent suburbs surrounding Washington per capita income ranks above national averages.

Given the six franchise moves in the AL since 1950, it seems apparent that population and population growth play a greater role than per capita income in an owner's decision to select a city. It follows then that AL franchises in Kansas City, Minnesota, and Oakland seemed destined for abandonment because of weak demographics and insufficient home attendance at those sites.

After examining the history of relocation in the NL, we identified the six franchise moves in the AL, ranked the performance and attendance for each team at their pre-move and post-move sites, and described three demographic

Table 1.7
AL Franchise Relocation and Area Demographic Data, by Site, by Year

| | | Pre-Move Site | | | Post-Move Site | | |
Year	Franchise Move	Pop	Income	%Growth	Pop	Income	%Growth
1953–54	St. Louis to Baltimore	1.7	2,019	17.4	1.4	1,952	22.9
1954–55	Philadelphia to KC	3.9	2,085	18.3	.9	2,115	28.7
1960–61	Washington to Minn.	2.0	2,953	38.8	1.5	2,825	23.0
1967–68	Kansas City to Oakland	1.1	3,623	14.9	3.0	4,694	17.4
1969–70	Seattle to Milwaukee	1.3	4,339	28.7	1.4	4,232	9.8
1971–72	Washington to Texas	2.9	5,238	6.9	1.4	3,918	24.6

Note: We used statistical interpolation to calculate the population and income per capita between census years. Pop is the SMSA population in millions. Income is the per capita personal income in the SMSA in thousands of dollars. The %Growth was calculated as in Table 1.3.

Source: County and City Data Books, 1953–1973; Survey of Current Business, 1953–1973; Statistical Abstract of the United States, 1961, 1979, 1992.

characteristics (population, population growth, and per capita income) of the areas where the teams played. Furthermore, in the AL the presence of other professional baseball, football, and basketball teams at the pre-move and post-move sites poses some interesting questions. Table 1.4 indicates that NL teams vacated cities where a number of professional teams existed. Did the same number of sports competitors exist at the sites of the six AL franchises that relocated between 1950 and 1976? If not, how can we account for differences in intersport competition at the post-move sites between the NL and AL?

Relative to the NL, more professional sports teams existed at the AL's post-move locations (see Table 1.8). Two reasons may explain the differences in intersport competition. First, 50 percent of the NL franchise moves occurred when cities had more than two MLB teams. Second, the expansion of the NFL, AFL, NBA, and ABA in the 1960s placed other professional teams in MLB cities. By why some franchises move. The differences in consumer income across sites proved minor in the AL except in the cases of Kansas City to Oakland, and Washington to Texas. Oaklanders had higher per capita incomes than residents in Kansas City. Of course, per capita income might be highly skewed, as in Washington where no significant middle class exists. In the nation's capital households in general are either wealthy or poor. But in the affluent suburbs surrounding Washington per capita income ranks above national averages.

Given the six franchise moves in the AL since 1950, it seems apparent that population and population growth play a greater role than per capita income in an owner's decision to select a city. It follows then that AL franchises in Kansas City, Minnesota, and Oakland seemed destined for abandonment because of weak demographics and insufficient home attendance at those sites.

After examining the history of relocation in the NL, we identified the six franchise moves in the AL, ranked the performance and attendance for each team at their pre-move and post-move sites, and described three demographic preceding the franchise moves of AL teams in the 1960s, the three NL franchises earned "first-mover" advantages. Although the relocation of a sports enterprise entails risk and cost, each NL team had fewer competitors at their post-

Table 1.8
AL Franchise Relocation and Intersport Competitors, by Site, by Year

Year	Franchise Move	Pre-Move Site			Post-Move Site		
		MLB	NFL/AFL	NBA/ABA	MLB	NFL/AFL	NBA/ABA
1953–54	St.Louis to Balt.	1	0	0	0	1	1
1954–55	Phil. to KC	1	1	1	0	0	0
1960–61	Wash. to Minn.	0	1	0	0	1	0
1967–68	KC to Oakland	0	1	0	1	2	2
1969–70	Seattle to Milw.	0	0	1	0	1	1
1971–72	Wash. to Texas	1	1	0	0	1	1

Note: Table entries are the number of professional sports teams at the Pre-Move and Post-Move Sites for the franchises in the year prior to and following relocation.

Source: The World Almanac and Book of Facts, 1953–1973.

move site for the reasons stated. This allowed the relocated NL clubs sufficient time to establish brand loyalty, build a fan base, and stake a claim on consumer expenditures for professional sports games. In retrospect, the wisdom and fore-sight of the NL to approve team relocation's in the 1950s rewarded owners with enhanced profits from gate and television revenues. From 1953 to 1965, for example, per team revenues from local and national baseball broadcasts rights increased 270 percent.[19]

PROFESSIONAL FOOTBALL

National Football League

Inspired by a growing grass-roots interest in amateur football, the sport's first professional game was played in 1895 between two towns, Latrobe and Jeanette, Pennsylvania. Twenty-five years later, the American Professional As-sociation organized to form the first professional football league.[20] With each of its five clubs paying a $25 franchise fee, the new league lacked a set schedule. Because of this, teams played one another wherever and whenever conditions seemed profitable. Following the inaugural season, Joseph Carr reorganized the association into the National Football League (NFL). It struggled until 1925, when the Chicago Bears signed University of Illinois All-American halfback Red Grange to a contract. The Bears and Grange toured the nation playing games with rivals. When Grange's contract proposal was rejected by the Bears, in 1926 he and his manager C. C. Pyle formed the American Football League (AFL I). Due to the financial deficiencies of many AFL I teams, the league failed after playing only one season. The NFL admitted the rival league's most successful team, the New York Yankees, because its star player Red Grange was a top draw in professional football.[21] During the 1920s and 1930s, the NFL re-mained in a state of flux. Twenty-two teams played in 1926 but only eight com-peted in 1932. However unsettled, the NFL reached a watershed in 1936. No teams changed owners or cities, while each team played an equal number of games.

A second NFL rival, AFL II, fielded seven teams in 1936 and 1937, while the AFL III played with six teams in 1940 and four teams in 1941. Neither league proved a formidable threat to the NFL. The teams played in marginal markets such as Milwaukee and Columbus, Ohio, and fans viewed both AFL II and III as minor leagues. According to Quirk and Fort, "In hindsight, AFL II and III were mistakes on the part of the owner-investors in these leagues, over-estimating the profit potential of the pro football market."[22] The All-American Conference, a rival league that began play in 1946, consisted of seven teams, while the NFL comprised ten teams split between two divisions. The All-American Football Conference competed with the NFL from 1946 until 1949. In that year, the conference folded and three of its better franchises—Baltimore, Cleveland, and San Francisco—joined the NFL. Then consisting of thirteen teams, the NFL's National and American Conferences began play in 1950.[23]

In the next section, we discuss the movement of teams in the NFL and its upstart rival, the American Football League. The discussion focuses on the demographic, economic, financial, and team-specific data and information pertinent to an owner's decision to relocate, and to which site. Like MLB, each NFL team has exclusive territorial rights to protect it from encroachment on its market by another franchise in the league. The goal of a franchise is to maximize profits at its site. The objective of the NFL is to approve a franchise relocation if the move serves the interest of the league. The NFL mandates that 75 percent of the league owners must approve a relocation.

By 1950 the NFL's total regular season and post-season attendance averaged over twenty-six thousand per game, an increase of eighteen thousand per game since 1934. The 1950 season began with National Conference teams in Baltimore, Chicago, Detroit, Green Bay, Los Angeles, New York, and San Francisco. American Conference teams played in Chicago, Cleveland, New York, Philadelphia, Pittsburgh, and Washington. From 1950 to 1977, three NFL franchises relocated. The following synopsis provides insight and rationale for each relocation.

The Baltimore Colts played poorly in the All-American Football Conference in the late 1940s, winning less than 50 percent of their games. Along with the Cleveland Browns and the San Francisco FortyNiners, the Colts joined the NFL in 1950 after the 1949 AAFC–NFL merger. Disappointed with the team's performance in the 1950 season, the owner of the Colts abandoned Baltimore and withdrew the franchise from the NFL. With a mediocre performance in 1950, and a last place finish in the 1951 season, the owner of the New York Yankees of the American Conference sold the team for $300,000 to a Dallas textile magnate, Giles Miller, who renamed the team the Dallas Texans. The Texans continued to lose over 90 percent of their games and in 1953 returned to Baltimore as the Colts.[24]

By the late 1950s, the Chicago Cardinals of the American Conference faced a desperate financial condition. The team's annual attendance varied between 99,000 and 151,000 from 1950 to 1958. After ending the 1959 season with a 2–10 record, the Cardinals moved to St. Louis in 1960. During the 1960s, the NFL enjoyed a period of franchise stability that continued following its merger with the AFL in 1969. All NFL franchises remained put until 1982. After a federal circuit court ruled that the NFL had violated the 1890 Sherman Antitrust Act by requiring a three-fourths vote (twenty-one teams) to approve a franchise relocation, owner Al Davis moved the Raiders from Oakland to Los Angeles. Following the move, the Raiders continued practicing in Oakland during the season, but played the 1982 season in the Los Angeles Coliseum.[25]

Did the performance (average winning percentage) and attendance of the Texans, Colts, and Cardinals change after relocating from Dallas, Baltimore, and Chicago, respectively? The performance and attendance of the Cardinals rose because of the leadership of head coaches Wally Lemm and Charlie Winner, and the play of quarterback Charley Johnson, wide receiver Sonny Randall, running back John David Crow, and place kicker Jim Bakken. Meanwhile, the Texans played poorly in Dallas and the team's attendance fell. The Colts played better in Baltimore, but also before sparse crowds.[26]

The demographics of the cities affected the relocations. The population and per capita income in New York and Chicago exceeded those in Dallas and St.

Louis. If so, why did the teams depart from the two largest cities in the United States? Because of enthusiastic fan support for the NFL Giants in New York and the Bears in Chicago, the Texans and Colts moved to cities without professional football clubs. The relocation from Dallas, a small city, to Baltimore, a larger city, was expected given the poor performance, weak attendance, and financial difficulties of the franchise in Texas.[27]

The presence of intersport competition in the pre-move and post-move areas also differed. Prior to relocation, three other professional teams existed in New York, two in Chicago and none in Dallas. After relocation, no intersport competitors played in Dallas, one existed in Baltimore, and two competed in St. Louis. Evidently, the moves that occurred in the NFL between 1950 and 1976 happened because either the teams were uncompetitive or other professional football, baseball, and basketball clubs played in the same city and received more attention from the media and greater support from fans.[28]

American Football League

Three American Football Leagues had existed prior to 1960. They included the AFL I, which played in 1926, the AFL II, which competed in 1936 and 1937, and the AFL III, which lasted from 1940 to 1941. AFL II's existence proved short-lived in part because of the depressed U.S. economy of the 1930s. AFL I and III were adversely affected by financial insecurity, the poor quality of play, lack of competitive balance, and the presence of a rival professional football league. In 1958, after quarterback Johnny Unitas and the Baltimore Colts won a dramatic NFL championship game defeating the New York Giants in a sudden-death overtime, a seemingly insatiable, nationwide demand for professional football surfaced. In this environment, a group of prospective owners organized a fourth American Football League (AFL). They intended to pressure the NFL into expanding by admitting the teams of the new league. Initially the NFL stood firm against its newly organized rival. For example, because of financial problems the owners of the Chicago Cardinals opposed NFL expansion or admission of the AFL teams to the established league.[29] In December 1959 eight AFL team owners selected their first-round draft choices, adopted a cooperative television plan, and elected a new commissioner, Joe Foss. In June 1960 the AFL signed a five-year, $11 million television contract with ABC that guaranteed each franchise $185,000 per year.[30]

The AFL, moreover, was the contrivance of Lamar Hunt, a graduate of Southern Methodist University and a major heir to a billion-dollar fortune accumulated by his oil tycoon father, H. L. Hunt. The son was an ardent football fan who schemed to bring a professional team to Dallas. Clint Murchison, Hunt's business rival in Dallas, had the same ambition. During the 1950s both magnates attempted to buy the original Dallas Texans, the Chicago Cardinals, the Washington Redskins, and the San Francisco FortyNiners. Nonetheless, obstacles always seemed to appear. Discouraged but undaunted, Hunt announced the establishment of the AFL in 1959. Its teams played in Houston, Dallas, New York, Boston, Denver, Los Angeles, Oakland, and Buffalo. Consequently, a recruitment war had begun and the new league forced the NFL to expand through merger or confront the loss of lucrative television markets.[31]

Shortly after the AFL granted Hunt a franchise in Dallas, the NFL awarded Clint Murchison the Dallas Cowboys. After 1960 the younger league struggled to stay intact—many AFL clubs stayed one step ahead of bankruptcy. Hunt eventually moved the Texans to Kansas City in 1963 and renamed the team the Chiefs. Wishing to end the salary wars, the AFL and NFL finally merged in 1966. Interestingly, the federal legislation that exempted the merger from anti-trust laws was sponsored by Senator Russell Long and Congressman Hale Boggs, both Democrats from Louisiana. (The following year, the NFL granted a new franchise to New Orleans. But we are getting ahead of the story.) It is suffi-cient to say the merger brought about a common player draft and shared televi-sion revenues and briefly suppressed the salary wars.[32]

The AFL teams located in Boston, Buffalo, Dallas, Denver, Houston, Los Angeles, New York, and Oakland, which began play in September 1960, com-peted in two divisions. Six of these teams remained at their original sites while two teams moved during the decade-long history of the league. Before examin-ing the relocation of AFL teams, some demographic and team-specific informa-tion on the six AFL teams that stayed put provides a backdrop for better under-standing the franchises that moved. This information appears in Table 1.9. As the table indicates, the six "permanent" AFL rivals proved competitive and nearly equal in performance from 1960 to 1969. An average six percentage-point difference in win-loss records existed between first-place Houston and sixth-place Denver. Buffalo, Houston, and Kansas City each won two champi-onships in the league's history. Other teams that won league titles include Dal-las, New York, Oakland, and San Diego. Except for Houston, the AFL fran-chises located in the larger cities performed better than small-city teams.

Only two AFL teams relocated during the course of the league's existence. Despite a 10–4 record and a 24–16 loss to the Houston Oilers in the AFL cham-pionship game in 1961, the Los Angeles Raiders averaged a meager five thou-sand attendance per home game (95,000 below stadium capacity), ending the

Table 1.9
Selected Data for Six Permanent AFL Franchises, 1960 to 1969

Franchise	Population	%Growth	Performance	Attendance	R&T
Boston	2.6	8.6	.304	149	211
Buffalo	1.3	3.2	.299	240	214
Denver	1.0	32.6	.276	184	206
Houston	1.2	39.8	.335	251	227
Oakland	2.6	17.4	.334	181	205
New York	10.7	4.6	.323	276	212

Note: Population is the SMSA's total population in millions in 1960. The %Growth is the percent-age change in the area's population between 1960 and 1969. Performance, Attendance, and R&T are, respectively, the team's mean win-loss percentage, home attendance in hundreds of thousands, and radio and television revenues in hundreds of thousands of dollars during 1960–1969.

Source: James Quirk and Rodney D. Fort, *Pay Dirt: The Business of Professional Team Sports* (Princeton, N.J.: Princeton University Press, 1992), 492–494; Ira Horowitz, "Sports Broadcasting," in Roger G. Noll, ed. *Government and the Sports Business* (Washington, D.C.: The Brookings Institution, 1974), 287–288; *Statistical Abstract of the U.S.*, 1964, 1974.

season with a financial loss of almost $1 million. So after acquiring the club for $25,000 in 1959, Barron and Conrad Hilton moved the Raiders to San Diego in 1961.

The Dallas Texans ranked second in the league in the 1960 and 1961 seasons, and won the AFL championship game in 1963, upsetting the defending champion Houston Oilers 20–17 in overtime. But with its mean home-game attendance under eleven thousand per season and vying with the NFL Cowboys for media attention, the relocation of the Texans proved inevitable. In February 1963, the team announced it would move to Kansas City and become the Chiefs. The advantages of relocating the team to Kansas City included a larger stadium and a $1 per year stadium rental fee for the 1964 and 1965 seasons. Also, by being the first AFL team in the Midwest, the Chiefs managed to sell fifteen thousand season tickets in Kansas City, a 300 percent increase from the previous season in Dallas. The Chiefs won the AFL title in 1966 and went on to play the Green Bay Packers in the 1967 Super Bowl. Although the Chiefs lost that game 35–10, they returned to the Super Bowl in 1970 and upset the heavily favored Minnesota Vikings 23–7. The Chiefs' victory maintained the AFL's domination of the big game that started with the Jets defeating the Colts 16–7 in the 1969 Super Bowl. Indeed, the AFL/AFC domination of the Super Bowl continued throughout the 1970s as the Miami Dolphins, Oakland Raiders, and Pittsburgh Steelers won eight of the next ten Vince Lombardi Trophies.

Table 1.10 shows that the population and per capita income of Los Angeles exceeded San Diego's, while Kansas City's population and per capita income exceeded that of Dallas. Meanwhile, the population in San Diego and Dallas grew faster than in Los Angeles and Kansas City. Other reasons, however, explain the moves by AFL teams. These include intersport competition, attendance levels at the pre-move site, as well as the stadium amenities and demand for professional football at the post-move site. The other team-specific information appears in Table 1.11, which underscores why the AFL abandoned Los Angeles and Dallas in the early 1960s.

Between 1960 and 1969, the average per-game attendance in the AFL increased by 145 percent, while the NFL saw its attendance grow 36 percent.

Table 1.10
AFL Franchise Relocation and Area Demographic Data, by Site, by Year

Year	Franchise Move	Pre-Move Site			Post-Move Site		
		Pop	Income	%Growth	Pop	Income	%Growth
1960–61	LA to SD	3.0	2,918	16.6	1.0	2,392	31.4
1962–63	Dallas to KC	.9	2,588	36.8	1.1	2,805	14.9

Note: Table entries are the SMSA population in millions, per capita personal income in thousands of dollars, and the percentage growth in population in the SMSA between 1960 and 1970.

Source: Statistical Abstract of the U.S., 1979; U.S. Department of Commerce, Bureau of the Census, *Census of Population,* Social and Economic Characteristics, Metropolitan Areas (Washington, D.C.: 1960–1970).

Although the AFL's attendance increased proportionately from 30 percent to 47 percent of the NFL's during those years, the difference in absolute attendance widened from 2.2 million to 3.2 million. This happened because the NFL extended the playing season to fourteen games and thereby added fifty-two games to its season schedule. Meanwhile, the AFL played only fourteen additional games. Furthermore, many of the AFL teams suffered financial losses until the league signed a five-year, $36 million television contract with NBC that began with the 1965 season. As a result, broadcasting revenues per AFL team increased from $364,000 to $934,000 in 1965, or by 156 percent. By 1969 broadcasting revenues declined to $895,000 per team. In comparison, NFL broadcasting revenues per team increased by 3 percent from 1964 to 1965, and by 23 percent from 1964 to 1969. During the 1960s, the gap in total annual broadcasting revenues between the two leagues grew by over $15 million. The escalation in player salaries, coupled with the growing disparities in total attendance and broadcasting revenues throughout the 1960s, compelled the leagues to merge.

The leagues formed an AFL/NFL alliance in 1966. To that end, they agreed to a common draft and a championship game. In 1967 the AFL and NFL played the first preseason interleague games. By June 1969 the twenty-six AFL and NFL teams had aligned into three divisions in each of two conferences. Various circumstances led to the merger. Most important, the rivalry between the two leagues had magnified salary expectations. To illustrate the point, in 1965 the owner of the New York Jets, Sonny Werblin, signed University of Alabama's star quarterback, Joe Namath, for the then unprecedented annual salary of $400,000. This deal prompted NFL stars like John Brodie and Roman Gabriel to undertake serious contract talks with AFL clubs. Rumors circulated about secret negotiations. According to historians Randy Roberts and James Olson, "On the heels of this came the threat of lawsuits and counter suits. The whole thing bordered on chaos, and everyone involved became dissatisfied. Inevitably the rival leagues initiated peace talks and on June 8, 1966, they agreed to merge."[33]

Table 1.11
AFL Franchise Relocation and Selected Data, by Site, by Year

Year	Franchise Move	Pre-Move Site			Post-Move Site		
		Att	Performance	R&T	Att	Performance	R&T
1960–61	LA to SD	69	.714	198	195	.857	225
1962–63	Dallas to KC	155	.786	25	150	.357	264

Note: At the Pre-Move and Post-Move Sites, Att is the team's mean home-game attendance in thousands. Performance is the team's mean win-loss percentage in the AFL. R&T is the team's mean radio and television revenues in thousands of dollars (for Los Angles in 1960, San Diego in 1961, Dallas in 1962, and Kansas City in 1963).

Source: Quirk and Fort, *Pay Dirt: The Business of Professional Sports*, 479–511; *The World Almanac and the Book of Facts*, 1961–1964.

PROFESSIONAL BASKETBALL

National Basketball Association

In 1898, seven years after James Naismith invented the game of basketball in Springfield, Massachusetts, a group of organizers launched two professional associations—the National Basketball League and the New England League. Within two years both leagues had expired. The American Basketball League (ABL) was formed in 1925, but it never attained prominence in the late 1920s and 1930s due to a lack of interest in professional basketball and to the Depression of the 1930s. The first stable league, the National Basketball League (NBL), emerged in 1937. The NBL played in small and medium midwestern cities such as Buffalo, Cincinnati, Columbus, Fort Wayne, Indianapolis, Kankakee, and Pittsburgh.[34]

By 1947 two professional basketball leagues existed in the United States. The Basketball Association of America (BAA) had formed in 1946 and included such prominent teams as the Boston Celtics, the Philadelphia Warriors, and the New York Knickerbockers. Several NBL clubs, including the Minnesota Lakers, jumped to the BAA in 1948. The next season, six strong NBL franchises followed suit. The two leagues then merged to form the National Basketball Association (NBA). The association tipped-off its first season in 1949.[35]

New NBA teams included Syracuse; Denver; Anderson, Indiana; Sheboygan, Wisconsin; Tri-Cities (Moline, Davenport, and Rock Island, Illinois); and Waterloo, Iowa. Only eight teams played in U.S. metropolitan areas ranked in the top twenty in population. This strategy of placing teams in small towns reflected the origin of most players and basketball's base of popularity at amateur levels. But the strategy failed for NBA franchises in Anderson and Sheboygan, and Waterloo canceled operations before the 1950 season.[36]

One of the pioneers in developing the NBA, Ben Kerner, owned the Tri-City Blackhawks. Since the team played in a league that had clubs in New York, Boston, and Philadelphia, Kerner moved his franchise to Milwaukee and prospered for a couple of years. That is, until the Boston Braves relocated to Milwaukee, and the city went baseball crazy. In the 1950s basketball had little prestige compared to baseball's long-standing tradition as the national pastime. No longer the only game in town, Kerner took a risk and moved his Hawks to St. Louis in the summer of 1955. St. Louis then had the baseball Cardinals. The previous year, the AL's Browns had moved to Baltimore. Moreover, no NFL, NBA, or NHL teams played in St. Louis. As it happened, Kerner made a fortune proving that St. Louis could be an excellent sports market.[37]

For a combination of economic, demographic, and team-specific reasons, four NBA teams relocated in the 1950s, five in the 1960s, four in the 1970s, two in the 1980s, and none since 1990.[38] The migration of teams in the 1950s and 1960s to large cities and the growing importance of television as a revenue source in professional basketball justified many of the pre-1970 franchise moves. Also, the birth of the American Basketball Association (ABA) in 1967 and the location of its teams at strategic sites threatened the NBA.

From 1950 to 1976 one NBA team, on average, moved every 2.5 years. Until 1968, 75 percent of NBA relocation's involved teams moving from eastern to midwestern cities. The move by the Lakers and the Warriors to California in the early 1960s followed the migration of baseball's Dodgers and Giants in 1957. From 1968 to 1976, two teams moved to cities in the South and Southwest.

Approximately one-half of the NBA teams that relocated ranked in the upper third of the league in winning percentage. Two of the worst performing teams that moved were the 1967–1971 and 1978–1984 San Diego Clippers. Both Clipper teams competed better at their new home sites, Houston and Los Angeles.

Table 1.12 lists the NBA franchises that relocated and provides the performance (mean winning percentage) of each team for three seasons before and after the move. It denotes that team performances varied little for the majority of NBA franchises that moved between 1951 and 1973. We anticipated finding no significant differences in performance of these teams merely because they migrated to a new site and arena.

Given the team's performance at the pre-move and post-move sites, we wondered why the eleven NBA franchises changed residences as indicated in Table 1.12, and what factors compelled them to select their new locations?

Roger Noll correlated professional basketball attendance with the area's population, black population, and per capita income, and with team-specific factors such as the fraction of games won and the number of star players, home ticket prices, and whether a team belonged to the NBA or ABA.[39] In one equation, Noll estimated that the area's population, black population, and home ticket prices relate inversely to home-game attendance in the ABA. In a second

Table 1.12
NBA Franchise Relocation and Team Performance at Three-Year Pre-Move and Post-Move Intervals

Year	Franchise Move	Pre-Move Performance			Post-Move Performance		
1951–52	Tri-Cities to Milwaukee	–	.453	.368	.258	.380	.292
1955–56	Milwaukee to St. Louis	.380	.292	.361	.458	.472	.569
1957–58	Fort Wayne to Detroit	.597	.514	.472	.458	.389	.400
1957–58	Rochester to Cincinnati	.403	.431	.431	.458	.264	.253
1960–61	Minneapolis to LA	.264	.456	.333	.456	.675	.663
1962–63	Philadelphia to SF	.653	.582	.612	.388	.595	.213
1963–64	Syracuse to Phil.	.481	.512	.600	.431	.500	.688
1963–64	Chicago to Baltimore	–	.225	.313	.387	.462	.475
1968–69	St. Louis to Atlanta	.450	.481	.683	.585	.585	.439
1971–72	San Diego to Houston	.451	.329	.488	.415	.402	.390
1972–73	Cincinnati to KC	.439	.402	.366	.439	.402	.537

Note: Pre-Move and Post-Move Performances are the final win-loss percentages of a team in the league in the three seasons prior to and following relocation.

Source: The World Almanac and Book of Facts 1950–1974.

equation, total population and attendance related slightly positive in the NBA. Furthermore, he estimated that the fraction of games won, number of star players, and membership in the NBA relate positively to home-game attendance. As Noll put it: "The NBA's relocation and expansions between the mid-1950s and the late 1960s rectified this situation [of locating teams in small cities and relying exclusively on gate receipts] by strategically placing the NBA in all of the large media centers, increasing the value of its product both at the gate and over the air."[40]

We collected some vital statistics pertaining to why NBA teams relocate and to which sites (see Table 1.13). Along with a team's performance, the demographics of the area in which the team is located influence home attendance. For the eleven NBA teams that moved between 1950 and 1976, the following statistics illuminate why franchises migrate.

Table 1.13 indicates that in most cases the pre-move sites had greater population growth. In the majority, the population and per capita income at the post-move sites exceeded those at the pre-move sites. Of the nine moves in the 1950s and 1960s, four teams relocated to sites experiencing above-average (14 percent) population growth, six teams relocated to larger cities, and six teams departed for areas with a higher per capita income. On the other hand, in the 1970s differences in population and per capita income between the pre-move and post-move sites seemed more balanced than in the 1950s or 1960s. And, in San Diego and Kansas City the population grew at a greater rate than in Houston and Cincinnati. Apparently, NBA teams in the 1950s and 1960s relocated to

Table 1.13
NBA Franchise Relocation and Area Demographic Data, by Site, by Year

Year	Franchise Move	Pre-Move Site			Post-Move Site		
		%Growth	Pop	Income	%Growth	Pop	Income
1951–52	Tri-Cities to Milwaukee	15.3	.2	1,915	6.0	.9	2,034
1955–56	Milwaukee to St. Louis	24.8	1.0	2,363	13.6	1.9	2,257
1957–58	Fort Wayne to Detroit	6.4	.2	2,179	14.4	3.6	2,408
1957–58	Rochester to Cincinnati	20.3	.5	2,408	10.3	1.0	2,374
1960–61	Minneapolis to LA	25.1	1.4	2,817	7.9	6.7	3,050
1962–63	Philadelphia to S.F.	10.9	4.4	2,702	9.1	2.8	3,457
1963–64	Syracuse to Phil.	12.8	.5	2,521	16.3	4.5	2,943
1963–64	Chicago to Baltimore	12.2	6.4	3,304	22.2	1.8	2,753
1968–69	St. Louis to Atlanta	12.3	2.3	3,903	22.4	1.3	3,995
1971–72	San Diego to Houston	37.1	1.4	4,262	19.2	2.1	4,591
1972–73	Cincinnati to KC	1.0	1.4	4,510	12.5	1.3	5,051

Note: At the Pre-Move and Post-Move Sites, the %Growth is the percentage growth of the total population in the SMSA during the decade of the relocation. Pop is the SMSA's total population per team in millions. Income measures the per capita personal income in the SMSA in thousands of dollars.

Source: The World Almanac and Book of Facts, 1950–1973; County and City Data Books, 1952, 1967, and 1972; Census of Population, 1950; Survey of Current Business, May 1974; Statistical Abstracts of the U.S., 1961, 1971, 1983.

more populated and higher income areas, while one team in the 1970s moved to a site with above-average growth. The eleven moves suggest that NBA franchise proprietors changed strategies in their decision regarding where to relocate given the demographic trends in the United States and the factors listed in Table 1.13.

In baseball and football, teams moved from sites that hosted other professional teams, especially in the same sport. This raises the question whether NBA teams relocated to areas with fewer professional sports teams. Table 1.14 provides information pertinent to that query. To a greater extent than in baseball or football, NBA teams migrated to areas that hosted other professional teams. Indeed, twelve teams played at the pre-move sites and twenty-one teams at the post-move sites. Perhaps NBA owners worried little about the presence of other sports teams in their market, or, given the growing popularity of professional basketball, especially since the 1960s, the threat of financial competition from rival sports leagues seemed unimportant when NBA owners evaluated new sites for their franchises.[41]

American Basketball Association

Many significant changes that occur in society happen as a result of revolutionaries. In professional basketball, journalist Terry Pluto declared, "It was the ABA that threw the firebombs and demanded that attention be paid." In a variety of ways, wrote Pluto, "The ABA turned pro basketball upside down. The ABA never wanted to be its own league. From the beginning, the goal was to force a merger, to convince the NBA that it needed more teams and more markets."[42] The ABA began play in 1967. With only twelve NBA teams competing that year, an ample supply of players was available for ABA teams to recruit.

Table 1.14
NBA Franchise Relocation and Intersport Competitors, by Site, by Year

		Pre-Move Site			Post-Move Site		
Year	Franchise Move	MLB	NFL/AFL	NBA/ABA	MLB	NFL/AFL	NBA/ABA
1951–52	Tri-Cities to Milwaukee	0	0	0	0	1	0
1955–56	Milwaukee to St. Louis	1	1	0	1	0	0
1957–58	Fort Wayne to Detroit	0	0	0	1	1	0
1957–58	Rochester to Cincinnati	0	0	0	1	0	0
1960–61	Minneapolis to LA	0	0	0	2	1	0
1962–63	Philadelphia to SF	1	1	0	1	2	0
1963–64	Syracuse to Phil.	0	0	1	1	0	0
1963–64	Chicago to Baltimore	2	1	0	1	1	0
1968–69	St. Louis to Atlanta	1	1	0	1	1	0
1971–72	San Diego to Houston	0	1	0	1	1	0
1972–73	Cincinnati to KC	1	1	0	1	1	0

Note: The table contains the number of professional baseball, football, and basketball teams at the Pre-Move and Post-Move Sites during the years indicated.

Source: *The World Almanac and Book of Facts*, 1950–1973.

The eleven original ABA sites consisted of small (Denver, Indianapolis, Louisville, and New Orleans), medium (Dallas, Houston, Pittsburgh, and Minneapolis–St. Paul), and large (New York, Los Angeles, and Oakland) cities. That New York, Los Angeles, and the Oakland area also hosted NBA teams suggests the audacity of the ABA.

Although failing at the box office during its nine-year history, the ABA was a creative league in adopting the three-point shot, a red-white-and-blue basketball, and a strategy of fielding several teams with no distinct home site. Unfortunately, the latter strategy failed, resulting in low fan attendance and insufficient media revenues. Over the course of the ABA's history, franchises in Baltimore, Miami, and Pittsburgh went out of business. So by 1976, only six teams remained in the league. During its nine-year existence, twelve ABA teams relocated and two teams changed sites within the same metropolitan area—New Jersey to New York and Anaheim to Los Angeles after the 1968 season.

According to the criteria in Table 1.15, only one ABA team that moved (New Orleans) declined in performance, but drew more fans to its arena at the post-move site (Memphis). Only in Pittsburgh, Washington (where Rick Barry led the league in scoring), and St. Louis did performance and attendance decline. Interestingly, the 1974 Carolina and 1975 Memphis franchises moved to sites that hosted more professional teams than at the pre-move sites. Such cases suggest that having other professional teams, which play in different seasons, helps establish a location as a major-league city.

While Pittsburgh, Washington, and St. Louis experienced a fall in attendance at the post-move site, Virginia and San Antonio became more competitive

Table 1.15
ABA Franchise Relocation and Selected Criteria, by Site, by Year

Year	Franchise Move	Pre-Move Site		Post-Move Site	
		Performance	Attendance	Performance	Attendance
1968–69	Pittsburgh to Minnesota	.692	–	.462	170
1968–69	Minnesota to Miami	.462	–	.551	249
1969–70	Minnesota to Pittsburgh	.461	170	.345	168
1969–70	Oakland to Washington	.784	223	.523	170
1969–70	Houston to Carolina	.294	64	.500	511
1970–71	NO to Memphis	.500	218	.488	268
1970–71	Los Angeles to Utah	.511	122	.678	512
1970–71	Washington to Virginia	523	170	.654	361
1973–74	Dallas to San Antonio	.333	201	.535	513
1974–75	Carolina to St. Louis	.559	494	.381	387
1975–76	Memphis to Baltimore	.321	325	–	–

Note: The criteria was measured as follows. Performance is the team's win-loss percentage in the final season at the Pre-Move Site and in the first season at the Post-Move Site. Attendance is the regular season attendance in thousands for the final season at the Pre-Move Site and the first season at the Post-Move Site. Attendance for the 1967–68 season is not available. The Baltimore Claws went bankrupt before the 1975–76 season began and withdrew from the league.

Source: The World Almanac and Book of Facts, 1969–1977; Quirk and Fort, *Pay Dirt*, 326.

after relocating and saw attendance improve. A major reason for these positive numbers in Virginia stemmed from the deep pool of talented players that wore Squires uniforms. Although Rick Barry refused to play for the Squires and demanded that the erstwhile Caps trade him to another team, Virginia had one of the most exciting teams in professional basketball history. Besides superstar Julius Erving, all-pros Charlie Scott, George Gervin, and Svenn Nater excited Squires fans in the Norfolk area as they put the tri-colored ball through the hoop.

In addition to the criteria in Table 1.15, we analyzed the pre-move and post-move area's per capita income for the eleven ABA franchises. For most franchise moves in the ABA, the areas of the post-move sites had a higher per capita income level than the areas at the pre-move sites. These results contrast sharply with what occurred in MLB, and in the NFL and AFL where lower per capita income levels existed at the post-move sites. Also, similar to NBA franchises, the owners of ABA teams established sites in regions that lacked other professional teams such as Utah and San Antonio. The ABA also chose sites like Indiana, Kentucky, and North Carolina where basketball dominates amateur and collegiate sports, as well as metropolitan areas with large African American populations such as Memphis and Norfolk.

Four ABA franchises—Indiana, Kentucky, New York, and Denver—remained at their original sites for nine seasons. Indiana's per game attendance exceeded the ABA's average during each season. New York and Denver bested the league average in four seasons. With former University of Kentucky All-American Dan Issel on its squad to draw fans, Kentucky exceeded the league average in eight seasons. Roger Noll has estimated that by adding star center Artis Gilmore to the Colonels in 1971, the ABA franchise drew about three thousand more fans to each home game. In monetary terms, Gilmore earned roughly $250,000 (over arena costs) for the club in gate receipts.[43]

Even though the ABA's average per game attendance increased from 45 percent to over 70 percent of the NBA's in the 1968–69 to 1975–76 seasons, the former never consummated a national broadcasting contract, and few ABA teams received any local broadcasting revenues. These conditions contributed to the abandonment of the Pittsburgh and Miami franchises after the 1971–72 season. Eventually only eight ABA teams remained to compete in the 1975–76 season. In June 1976, the NBA and ABA reached an agreement whereby the top four attendance leaders in the last season joined the NBA. Denver, Indiana, New York, and San Antonio each paid an entry fee to the NBA and an additional payment to the Kentucky and Utah franchises for folding the ABA.[44] In 1970, when the NBA agreed to merge with the ABA (to close the bidding war between them for top players), the older league asked Congress for a special exemption from antitrust laws to enable the merger. Sam Ervin, who headed the Senate committee investigating the matter, responded, "If you want to be exempt from the law of the land to carry out a commercial arrangement you say you need, you'd better show me your tax returns and other data to prove you really need it." Instead of opening its books, the NBA declined respectfully and waited another six years before merging with its rival.[45]

SUMMARY

Between 1950 and 1977 thirty-seven professional sports teams moved. Ten of these moves (27 percent) occurred in organized baseball, five (14 percent) in football, and twenty-two (59 percent) in basketball. Seventy percent of the post-move metropolitan areas of the relocated baseball teams had a smaller population, and 60 percent had households with less per capita personal income than in the pre-move areas. After relocating, most MLB teams improved in winning percentage and all experienced increases in home attendance. Moreover, the majority of post-move areas hosted existing professional football or basketball clubs. On average, the post-move areas of the relocated NFL and AFL teams also had smaller populations, with less per capita personal incomes than in the pre-move areas. The NFL teams played better while the performance of the AFL teams fluctuated, despite the fact that Kansas City and San Diego won three AFL championship games between 1963 and 1969. In the NBA, four teams moved between 1951 and 1958, five between 1960 and 1969, and two between 1971 and 1973. After relocating, seven NBA teams improved in winning percentage and attendance. The teams' post-move areas on average had larger populations, with higher per capita incomes, smaller population growth rates, and a larger proportion of minorities, than the pre-move areas. The ABA teams also moved to sites with similar populations, per capita incomes, and percentage of minorities to those hosting relocated NBA teams.

The demographic factors we identified in this chapter varied in the pre- and post-move areas of the relocated teams in the three sports. The mean winning percentage and home attendance of the teams generally improved after relocation. This contributed to higher revenues and profits for the relocated franchises and leagues during the years 1950 to 1977.

NOTES

1. "Norris Poulson Reveals How Los Angeles Got the Brooklyn Dodgers in 1958" in Seven A. Riess ed., *Major Problems in American Sport History* (Boston and New York: Houghton Mifflin Company, 1997), 408–411.

2. Steven A. Riess, *Sport in the Industrial Age 1850–1920* (Wheeling, Ill.: Harlan Davidson, Inc., 1995), 156.

3. See Roger G. Noll, "The U.S. Team Sports Industry: An Introduction," in Roger G. Noll ed., *Government and the Sports Business* (Washington, D.C.: The Brookings Institution, 1974), 8.

4. Riess, *Sport in the Industrial Age, 1850–1920*, 163. For important works on MLB, see Harold Seymour, *Baseball: The Early Years* (New York: Oxford University Press, 1960); idem., *Baseball: The Golden Age*, 2nd ed. (New York: Oxford University Press, 1989); Benjamin G. Radar, *Baseball: A History of America's Game* (Urbana and Chicago: University of Illinois Press, 1994).

5. James Quirk, "An Economic Analysis of Team Movements in Professional Sports," *Law and Contemporary Problems* 38 (Winter/Spring 1973), 42–45.

6. Ibid., 47–62; James Quirk and Rodney Fort, *Pay Dirt: The Business of Professional Sports* (Princeton, N.J.: Princeton University Press, 1992), 392–393.

7. Randy Roberts and James Olson, *Winning Is the Only Thing: Sports in America Since 1945* (Baltimore and London: Johns Hopkins University Press, 1989), 69. See also Quirk and Fort, *Pay Dirt*, 395–396 and James Quirk, "An Economic Analysis of Team Movement in Professional Sports," 47–62.

8. For biographies of African Americans in professional sports, see David L. Porter, ed., *African-American Sports Greats* (Westport, Conn. and London: Greenwood Press, 1995), 206–208, 284–286.

9. As quoted in Roberts and Olson, *Winning Is the Only Thing*, 135.

10. See Porter, *African-American Sports Greats*, 1–4.

11. James Quirk and Mohamed El Hodiri, "The Economic Theory of a Professional Sports League," *Government and the Sports Business*, 33–80.

12. The demand for MLB is dependent upon population, income, playing success, number of star players, sports competition, stadium age, and ticket prices. The statistical correlation of these variables and attendance is presented in Roger G. Noll, "Attendance and Price Setting," *Government and the Sports Business*, 115–157.

13. To compute population growth for an SMSA we used the U.S. Department of Commerce, Bureau of the Census, *Statistical Abstract of the United States* (Washington, D.C., 1950–1997); U.S. Department of Commerce, Bureau of the Census, *Census of Population*, Social and Economic Characteristics, Metropolitan Areas (Washington D.C., 1950–1990).

14. Riess, *Sport in Industrial America, 1850–1920*, 163; Seymour, *Baseball: The Golden Age*, 214–234.

15. See Quirk and Fort, *Pay Dirt*, 485.

16. *The Baseball Encyclopedia*, 8th ed. (New York and London: Macmillan Publishing Company, 1990), 1098.

17. See Quirk and Fort, *Pay Dirt*, 406–407, 484–485; Roberts and Olson, *Winning Is the Only Thing*, 140.

18. Quirk and Fort, *Pay Dirt*, 404.

19. For an in-depth discussion of how network television influences professional sports teams and the public see Ira Horowitz, "Sports Broadcasting," *Government and the Sports Business*, 275–323.

20. For the legal, ethical, and social influence and impact of professional sports leagues see Richard L. Worsnop, "The Business of Sports: Are Greedy Owners and Players Hurting Pro Leagues?" *CQ Researcher* (10 February 1995), 123–140.

21. See Quirk and Fort, *Pay Dirt*, 344.

22. Ibid., 338–341.

23. Roberts and Olson, *Winning Is the Only Thing*, 138.

24. For interesting incidents in the history of the NFL see Frank G. Menke, *The Encyclopedia of Sports*, 5th ed. (Cranbury, N.J.: A. S. Barnes and Company, 1975).

25. For contrasting views of the relocation of the Raiders, Colts, and other professional sports franchises see James Gattuso, "Congress and Rule-Making," *Society* (May/June 1986), 6–10; Arthur T. Johnson, "Balancing Interests," *Society* (May/June 1986), 11–16; David Meggyesy, "The National Football League Monopoly," *Society* (May/June 1986), 16–21.

26. See the *1996 Arizona Cardinals Media Guide*; Quirk and Fort, *Pay Dirt*, 414–415, 418–419, 428–429.

27. See U.S. Department of Commerce, Economics and Statistics Administration, *County and City Data Book* (Washington, D.C., Government Printing Office, 1952): 10, 26.

28. *The World Almanac and Book of Facts* (Mahwah, N.J.: World Almanac Books, 1950–1960); *Statistical Abstracts of the U.S.*, 1950–1960.

29. For a detailed history of the four AFLs see Quirk and Fort, *Pay Dirt,* 334–351. The authors also describe other professional football leagues including the All American Football Conference (1946–1949), the World Football League (1974–1975), and the U.S. Football League (1983–1985).

30. Horowitz, "Sports Broadcasting," 292.

31. Roberts and Olson, *Winning Is the Only Thing,* 138–142.

32. Ibid.

33. Frank G. Menke, *The Encyclopedia of Sports*, 464–467; Roberts and Olson, *Winning Is the Only Thing*, 138.

34. For an analysis of basketball's business operations, and the origins of professional basketball leagues, see Roger Noll, "Professional Basketball: Economics and Business Perspectives," in *The Business of Professional Sports* (Champaign: University of Illinois Press, 1991), 18–47.

35. See Quirk and Fort, *Pay Dirt,* 322–323; Roberts and Olson, *Winning Is the Only Thing*, 51.

36. Noll, "Professional Basketball: Economic and Business Perspectives," 20.

37. Leonard Koppett, *Sports Illusion, Sports Reality: A Reporter's View of Sports, Journalism, and Society*. 2nd ed. (Urbana and Chicago: University of Illinois Press, 1994), 71–72.

38. The renaming of the Kansas City team in the 1975–76 season, and the New York team in the 1977–78 season, are not considered a relocation since the teams remained in the same metropolitan areas. Also, Washington and Baltimore are in the same metropolitan area and thus are excluded from a relocation perspective.

39. See Noll, "Attendance and Price Setting," 131–140.

40. See Noll, "Professional Basketball: Economic and Business Perspectives," 22.

41. According to an attendance chart from the Public Relations staff of the NBA, regular season game attendance grew by 124 percent between 1970 and 1979, 56 percent between 1980 and 1989, and 18 percent between 1990 and 1996. Including playoffs and all-star games, the NBA's attendance increased by 117 percent in the 1970s and by 55 percent in the 1980s.

42. See Terry Pluto, "Out of Their League," *The Sporting News* (8 January 1996), 22–27.

43. See Quirk and Fort, *Pay Dirt*, 326; Steven A. Riess, *City Games: The Evolution of American Urban Society and the Rise of Sports* (Urbana and Chicago: University of Illinois Press, 1991), 247.

44. Quirk and Fort, *Pay Dirt,* 327.

45. As quoted in Koppett, *Sports Illusion, Sports Reality*, 53–54.

Chapter 2

Expansion Teams, 1950 to 1977

In the past fifty years, for cities with big-league aspirations, expansion has provided a common path to that destination. Urbanization coupled with the "continuing need of major leagues to place teams in key metropolitan and regional markets," has spurred such growth according to political affairs professor Michael N. Danielson. In his view, "The push of demographic and economic change has been reinforced by the ability of leagues to sell expansion franchises for ever-higher prices, attractive offers from places that want big-league teams, political pressures to make professional sports more accessible, and fears that rival leagues will set up business in bypassed markets."[1]

Urban affairs professor Kenneth Shropshire defines expansion as the "legitimate way for a city to obtain a franchise." He states: "Expansion involves no moving vans in the night, rarely results in lawsuits, and avoids the drastic lease concessions that are made in desperate attempts to keep an established franchise owner happy. The primary expenditure that the expansion franchise seeker must make is the franchise fee. The individual or group must show that it has sufficient operating capital to support the venture."[2]

Taking a cue from Danielson and Shropshire, this chapter focuses on why, when, and where professional baseball, football, and basketball leagues expanded between 1950 and 1977. Leagues decide whether to expand, and to which site, by having each owner vote on the issue. In reaching these decisions, sports leagues create committees to perform market research, establish criteria and guidelines, set application procedures, review bids from prospective owners, and evaluate possible sites in which to locate a new franchise. Market size, accessibility to radio and television networks, venue capacity, the ownership and management structure, and the location of other professional sports teams in a region play key roles in influencing a league's decision to expand. Along with these factors, the league may consider other issues. Interleague games or the realignment of divisions and conferences may influence league expansion inasmuch as team rivalries and competitive play determine a club's attendance, performance, and consequently, revenues and profits. In a 1997 survey of baseball fans, for example, 75 percent of those polled favored interleague games, while 44 percent preferred a geographical realignment of MLB teams. To avoid scheduling conflicts when Arizona and Tampa Bay began play, in 1998 MLB transferred the Milwaukee Brewers to the NL from the AL after the Kansas City Royals declined to change leagues.[3]

No study has extensively examined expansion within professional baseball, football, and basketball for the period 1950 to 1995. Economists Roger Noll, James Quirk, Rodney Fort, and Andrew Zimbalist have analyzed various aspects of expansion in baseball such as entry fees, franchise appreciation, attendance, ticket pricing policies, and the dilution of team quality.[4] We acknowledge and extend their work by examining a cross section of historical demographic, economic, and team-specific data and information to explain when and where expansion transpired in the three major professional sports leagues. Initially we analyze expansion in MLB, followed by the NFL, AFL, NBA, and ABA. Our analysis includes a discussion of each expansion team's success on the field and at the turnstile.

MAJOR LEAGUE BASEBALL

American League

The expansion period in the AL lasted seventeen years, from 1961 to 1977 (the NL's lasted thirty-two years, from 1962 to 1993). In 1960, AL teams played in Baltimore, Boston, Chicago, Cleveland, Detroit, Washington, New York, and Kansas City. From 1950 to 1960, total attendance grew by 1 percent (or 84,000 fans) in the AL, and over 28 percent (or 2,000,000 fans) in the NL. Eager to gain fans in urban areas and threatened by the formation of the Continental Baseball League (CBL), the AL began expanding into new and established areas in the early 1960s. Organized in 1960 by Branch Rickey and William Shea, the CBL was created to pressure the NL into bringing a team back to New York and placing other expansion franchises in Atlanta, Buffalo, Dallas, Denver, Houston, Minnesota, and Toronto. After MLB agreed to place NL expansion teams in New York, Houston, and others in the AL, the CBL disbanded on July 18, 1960, before playing a single game.[5]

The relocation of the original Senators from Washington to Minnesota in 1961, the pressures of a lawsuit by the CBL, and a congressional investigation of professional sports teams in 1960 mandated that organized ball place an expansion team in Washington in 1961. Three ownership changes would impact the Senators between that expansion year and 1969. During these years, the ownership of the team included various individuals and syndicates. In 1969, after owner Ban Johnson died, Bob Short purchased the team for $9.4 million. Short moved the franchise to Arlington, Texas, in 1971 and three years later sold his 90 percent interest in the team to another syndicate headed by Bradford Corbett for $10 million.[6]

Due to an MLB agreement allowing an AL team to occupy the Los Angeles area, a syndicate headed by former film star Gene Autry paid a $2.1 million expansion fee to admit the Angels into the league for the 1961 season.[7] Since then a syndicate headed by Autry has owned the California Angels, who moved to Anaheim in 1965. Walt Disney Company acquired 25 percent of the team in 1995 and has had an option to buy the club since Autry's death in October 1998. To earn more revenues for the team, the franchise renovated thirty-two-year-old Anaheim Stadium in 1998. According to the club's *Media Guide*, "The renovation project includes a variety of improvements and amenities designed to enhance the fan/guest experience, while bringing the stadium to a level comparable to the most popular Major League Baseball facilities in the United States."[8]

In conjunction with NL expansion, owner Ewing Kauffman and a syndicate headed by Dewey Soriano and majority stockholder William Daley each paid a $5.5 million franchise fee to the AL authorizing new franchises for Kansas City and Seattle in 1969. The Kansas City Royals began operations with a $650,000 broadcasting contract that surpassed by $250,000 the best contract that the nomadic Athletics had received while in Kansas City. On April 10, 1973, the team played its first game in 41,000-seat Royals (now Kauffman) Stadium, and two years later recorded the highest number of wins in twenty years of baseball in that Missouri city. In October 1976, the club won its first AL Championship Series game with pitcher Paul Splittorff, batting leader George Brett, and slugger Hal McRae. The next year the team set a club record with 102 victories in a single season. The Royals continued to improve. They beat the Philadelphia Phillies four games to three to win their first World Series in 1980. Owner Ewing Kauffman sold 49 percent of the Royals to Aaron Fogelman in 1983 for $11 million. After selling an additional 1 percent to Fogelman in 1988, Kauffman became sole proprietor of the team in 1991. Wal-Mart executive David Glass was one of five partners operating the Royals in 1998 due to a succession plan written by Kauffman before his death in 1993. To lower maintenance expenses, in April 1995 the owners replaced the grass field with artificial turf in Kauffman Stadium.[9]

In buying the Seattle Pilots for $5.3 million in 1969, a syndicate agreed to relinquish the club's share of national television revenues and 2 percent of its gate receipts to the AL. One year later the team went bankrupt and another syndicate, headed by Bud Selig, purchased it for $10.8 million. Selig, the current commissioner of organized baseball, then moved the franchise to Milwaukee and renamed it the Brewers in 1970.[10]

Eight years later, lawsuits resulting from the relocation of the Pilots in 1970 prompted AL expansion to Seattle. Established in 1977, the Seattle Mariners changed ownership in 1981, 1983, 1989, and 1992. Since 1976 ownership groups have included movie star Danny Kaye, George Argyros, the Emmis Broadcasting Company, Morgan Stanley and Company, and Hiroshi Yamauchi, the head of Nintendo of America. Since 1992, John Ellis, Yamauchi, and other investors have owned the Mariners. A new $363 million stadium, named Safeco Field, will be built in Seattle for the team in 1999. The sources of revenue for the stadium include a county sales tax, a special stadium sales tax, a tax on rental cars, proceeds from lottery scratch games, and $45 million from the team owners. As a result of negotiations with the state of Washington, naming rights to the stadium, worth roughly $30 million in 1998, will be awarded to the proprietors of the club.[11]

In 1977 the AL also added the Toronto Blue Jays after owners Labatts Breweries, Imperial Trust, Ltd., and the Canadian Imperial Bank of Commerce paid a $7 million expansion fee to the league. Peter Bavasi became executive vice president and general manager of the franchise. In 1977 the club finished 54–107, and 1.7 million fans attended games at Exhibition Stadium. The Blue Jays captured their first divisional title behind pitchers Jimmy Key, Dave Stieb, and Jim Clancy, and hitters Tony Fernandez, Jesse Barfield, and George Bell in 1985. Four years later, the club won their second division title, and in 1991 became the first major league team to draw four million fans in a season. In that year, Imperial Trust, Ltd. sold its interest in the team to John Labatt Limited of Canada for $60.3 million. The franchise prospered in the early 1990s. Led by pitchers Jack Morris and Juan Guzman, and key hitters Roberto Alomar, Dave Winfield, Joe Carter, and Paul Molitor the club won the 1992 and 1993 World Series, beating the Atlanta Braves and Philadelphia Phillies, respectively. In March 1998 MLB owners approved the sale of the Blue Jays to Interbrew SA, a Belgian brewery. Interbrew SA had acquired Labatts Breweries in 1995. Canadian taxpayers financed 14 percent of the $360 million Sky Dome, which the Blue Jays opened in 1989.[12]

Table 2.1 highlights the six AL expansion franchises and the demographic profile of their respective areas. Relative to the other AL franchises, the majority of expansions occurred in areas with below average total populations and above average population growth and per capita income levels. So, the AL had located its expansion clubs in medium-sized cities that had an expanding population and

Table 2.1
AL Expansion Franchises and Area Demographic Data, by Year

Year	Franchise	Population	Income	%Growth
1961	Los Angeles	6.8	3,050	16.6
1961	Washington	2.1	2,969	38.8
1969	Kansas City	1.2	4,133	14.9
1969	Seattle	1.4	4,339	28.7
1977	Seattle	2.0	9,172	12.8
1977	Toronto	2.7	–	14.0

Note: Population is the total population in millions of the Standard Metropolitan Statistical Area (SMSA) in the expansion year. Income is the per capita personal income in the SMSA in thousands of dollars. The %Growth represents the percentage growth of the SMSA population in the expansion year. In addition, our sources do not provide Income for Toronto, Canada. If located in the United States, in 1977 Toronto would have ranked tenth in population among SMSAs.

Source: The World Almanac and Book of Facts (Mahwah, N.J.: World Almanac Books, 1961–1978); U.S. Department of Commerce, Bureau of the Census, *Statistical Abstract of the United States* (Washington, D.C.,1964, 1971, 1973, and 1979); U.S. Department of Commerce, Bureau of Economic Analysis, *Survey of Current Business* (Washington, D.C., 1960–1980); U.S. Department of Commerce, Bureau of the Census, *Census of the Population*, Social and Economic Characteristics, Metropolitan Areas (Washington, D.C., 1960–1980).

high per capita incomes. As depicted in Table 2.3, the NL expansion franchise areas had demographic characteristics similar to those in the AL. Therefore, MLB owners since 1950 have adopted a strategy to locate their new teams in smaller cities containing households with more purchasing power. Large U.S. cities had sufficient MLB franchises after the 1960s and the incentive to expand in growing, prosperous areas in the Southwest and West is evident in Table 2.1.

Later in the chapter, the data on team performance and attendance show that NL expansion teams improved competitively over the first ten years, which helped increase their home attendance. This raises the question whether AL expansion teams also increased their performance and home attendance in the first ten years. Table 2.2 provides an answer to that question. When reviewing the table, keep the following in mind. The Seattle Pilots went bankrupt after the 1969 season. The owners then sold the team for $10.8 million to a syndicate led by Bud Selig, which moved the club to Milwaukee and renamed it the Brewers.

The Los Angeles Angels (renamed the California Angels in 1965 and the Anaheim Angels in 1996) was one of the better performing expansion teams in the AL during its first five seasons (see Table 2.2). The lowest performing team, the Toronto Blue Jays performed poorly by finishing between eleventh and fourteenth from 1977 to 1981. In their sixth through tenth seasons from the expansion year, the Royals won 52 percent of their games. The Angels, Blue Jays, Senators, and Mariners followed the Royals. Excluding the Angels, all expansion teams consequently improved in average win-loss percentage in the sixth through tenth seasons, especially the Blue Jays who placed second and first in the AL East Division in the 1984 and 1985 seasons, respectively.

After joining the AL in 1961, the expansion Washington Senators won less than 42 percent of their games. The team finished tenth, sixth, ninth, and eleventh between 1967 and 1970. The Senators' home attendance peaked at 918,000 in 1969 and never topped one million in the ten-year history of the franchise. Six-foot-seven, 255-pound Frank Howard played for the Senators and led the

Table 2.2
AL Expansion Franchises and Selected Data, by Seasons, by Year

Year	Franchise	Performance		Attendance	
		Five Seasons	Ten Seasons	Five Seasons	Ten Seasons
1961	Los Angeles	.470	.470	779	947
1961	Washington	.380	.420	604	726
1969	Kansas City	.480	.520	911	1,267
1969	Seattle	.395	–	678	–
1977	Seattle	.390	.410	906	944
1977	Toronto	.360	.450	1,369	1,708

Note: Performance and Attendance are, respectively, the average win-loss percentage and home attendance (in hundreds of thousands) of a team during the first five and ten seasons following expansion.

Source: *The World Almanac and Book of Facts,* 1962–1978; James Quirk, "An Economic Analysis of Team Movements in Professional Sports," *Law and Contemporary Problems* 38 (Winter/Spring, 1973), 51.

major leagues with forty-four home runs in 1968, the so-called year of the pitcher. That year Howard set a major-league record by hitting eight home runs in five games. After 382 career homers and fourteen seasons with the Dodgers, Rangers, Tigers, and Senators, he retired in 1973 and later managed the 1981 San Diego Padres and 1983 New York Mets. In 1998 Howard served as the Tampa Bay Devil Rays' bench coach and rooted for Mark McGwire and Sammy Sosa to break the single-season mark of sixty-one home runs set in 1961 by Roger Maris of the New York Yankees.[13]

The Pilots' eleventh-place finish and low attendance in the 1969 season boded trouble for the franchise in Seattle. The Mariners proved equally inept, finishing no higher than tenth in the AL from 1977 to 1986. However, the Mariners' attendance surpassed one million in 1977, 1982, and between 1985 and 1995 as the team added highly skilled players such as Randy Johnson and Junior Griffey and became a threat to the Rangers, Athletics, and Angels in the league's western division.

As an economic asset and financial investment, MLB clubs have historically increased in market value, particularly since the late 1950s when regular and post-season games were allotted prime viewing time on the national television networks. Later, during the 1960s to 1990s, the further exposure of professional baseball games on television and radio, and in the print media, undoubtedly contributed to the popularity and higher market value of these franchises.

Because of the relocation of two expansion franchises, the Seattle Pilots in 1970 and the Washington Senators in 1971, and the unstable financial position and weak demographics of the Royals in Kansas City, it seems evident that the NL dominated the AL in MLB expansion between 1950 and 1977. With six expansion teams, AL attendance increased by 93 percent (or 9.5 million fans) from 1961 to 1977. Five cities hosted new baseball teams, and fans in Los Angeles had a team to support other than the Dodgers. To discourage further expansion by the NL in the 1970s, the AL made appropriate business decisions to place expansion clubs in Seattle and Toronto. The weak fan base and ownership changes of the Senators and the financial problems of the Pilots contributed to their eventual failure in these cities.

National League

After the 1899 season, the National League successfully coped with its problems by dropping its four weakest teams and consolidating to an eight-team league. From 1900 to 1958, the NL consisted of the same eight teams—Boston, Brooklyn, Chicago, Cincinnati, New York, Philadelphia, Pittsburgh, and St. Louis. The league became notably stable and added no new teams until 1962.[14] Inspired by the profitable expansions in professional football, the threat of additional new teams in the AL, and the formation of the CBL, the NL began locating new franchises and fielding teams in baseball-hungry urban areas. Between 1962 and 1969, the NL added four new franchises. Table 2.3 lists these clubs along with pertinent demographic data about their metropolitan areas.

The commitment to build an all-weather indoor stadium with an artificial playing surface led the NL to select Houston as an expansion site. The NL's decision to expand to New York in 1962 partially stemmed from the construction of Shea Stadium (which replaced the outdated Polo Grounds), from the league's desire to quell the Big Apple's complaints about losing the Dodgers and Giants in 1958, and from the threats by the CBL to move into New York City. The owners of the Astros and Mets each paid $2 million for the franchise plus player expenses. In 1962, MLB implemented the 162-game schedule and the ten-team divisional format to boost attendance, team revenues and profits.[15]

The NL added the Montreal Expos and San Diego Padres to the league in 1969 for a $13 million franchise fee even though both areas seemed marginal locations for professional baseball. In that year, MLB adopted a best-of-five game league championship series to focus fan attention on divisional races in which teams competed for pennants.[16]

Relative to other NL sites, the data in Table 2.3 indicate that two of the new MLB sites had below-average populations and above-average per capita income levels, and three had high population growth. Since population affects attendance, scholars have estimated the drawing power of teams in various cities. Roger Noll argued in 1974 that New York, Washington, Toronto, Newark, and Dallas had populations sufficient to support an expansion team, while Miami, Denver, New Orleans, Indianapolis, Memphis, Phoenix, and Buffalo seemed unsuitable for new clubs. Noll also claimed that with an even split of gate receipts, MLB could add another seven teams that, at the time, promised to achieve financial viability and be self-supporting by the mid-1970s.[17]

Two criteria measure the success of an expansion (or relocated) franchise. One is the team's short- and long-run performance, in terms of win-loss percentage. The other is regular season home attendance. Few people expect expansion teams to contend for championships in the early years of the franchise due to the team's quality of talent. As the team matures, its performance should improve. The other measure of success, home attendance, is usually higher in the early years of the franchise and fluctuates over time as the team develops and attracts a following of loyal fans.

Table 2.3
NL Franchise Expansions and Area Demographic Data, by Year

Year	Franchise	Population	Income	%Growth
1962	Houston	1.4	2,411	39.8
1962	New York	10.9	3,424	4.5
1969	Montreal	2.1	–	30.0
1969	San Diego	1.3	3,884	31.4

Note: Population is the total population in millions in the SMSA for the expansion year. Income and %Growth are, respectively, the per capita personal income in thousands of dollars, and the percentage growth in the SMSA between 1960 and 1970. Our sources do not provide Income for Montreal. In 1969, Montreal would have been the twelfth-largest city if located in the United States.

Source: *The World Almanac and Book of Facts*, 1962–1970; U.S. Department of Commerce, Economics and Statistics Administration, *County and City Data Books* (Washington, D.C., 1962–1970); *Statistical Abstracts of the United States*, 1962–1970.

We tracked the playing records and home attendance of the four NL expansion franchises to measure their success and progress. Table 2.4 presents the success criteria. The improvement in the average performance (mean winning percentage) of the four NL expansion teams is apparent in Table 2.4. The Mets improved the most in winning percentage and the Expos the least for the seasons listed in the table. Also, if ranked by win-loss percentages, each expansion team increased their average performance from five to ten seasons following the expansion year, particularly the "amazing" Mets who posted the highest NL winning percentage in 1969.

As a group, the early newcomers in the NL realized success. With expectations high, fans in Houston, New York, and Montreal supported their new clubs, and players and coaches responded by improving the performance of their team. In spite of the moderate drop in fan attendance for the Expos during their sixth to tenth seasons, and the weak fan attendance for the Padres, team-specific and demographic factors likely increased the market value of the teams and benefited the owners and the league following expansion.

PROFESSIONAL FOOTBALL

National Football League

"Expansion has been least important in the National Football League," claims Danielson. Granting only eight new franchises since 1960, NFL growth has relied less on expansion and more on merger with ten teams arriving from the American Football League in 1970.[18]

During the 1940s and 1950s, the NFL avoided expansion despite the willingness of cities, and the ambitions of sports entrepreneurs, to invest in and operate a professional football team. Internal league disputes such as labor-management conflicts and the realignment of divisions and conferences, and external issues like the national economy, delayed the NFL from expanding into new metropolitan areas through the 1950s. But by the late 1950s, public pressure for expansion of professional football had taken root.

Table 2.4
NL Expansion Franchises and Selected Data, by Seasons, by Year

Year	Franchise	Performance		Attendance	
		Five Seasons	Ten Seasons	Five Seasons	Ten Seasons
1962	Houston	.410	.440	1,278	1,301
1962	New York	.320	.410	1,487	1,792
1969	Montreal	.430	.440	1,263	1,147
1969	San Diego	.370	.410	594	983

Note: Performance and Attendance are, respectively, five- and ten-year averages of win-loss percentages, and the regular season home attendance of the teams (in hundreds of thousands).

Source: The World Almanac and Book of Facts, 1962–1970; James Quirk, "An Economic Analysis of Team Movements in Professional Sports," 52.

Several factors led the NFL to expand in the early 1960s. These include: (a) the emergence of the AFL as an alternative professional football league, which destabilized the sports market; (b) the economic development of promising new markets in urban centers in the United States; (c) the ability and willingness of cities and municipalities to spend public funds to get into the big leagues; and (d) an enlarging pool of wealthy, prospective owners of major-league franchises. Eventually, professional sports leagues granted twenty-four expansion franchises in the 1960s, which represented 44 percent of all sports teams added between 1960 and 1998. Eight of these, or 15 percent, occurred in the NFL—four in the 1960s, two in the 1970s, and two in the 1990s.[19]

In January 1960, the NFL amended its bylaws to ease the restrictions on expansion. By a unanimous vote of existing team owners, the NFL granted franchises to Dallas and Minnesota and admitted them into the league for the 1960 and 1961 seasons, respectively. The owners of the Cowboys, Clint Murchinson and Bedford Wynne, paid a $600,000 entry fee, allocating $50,000 to the franchise and $550,000 to player contracts. In 1984, thirteen years after moving from the Cotton Bowl to Texas Stadium, a syndicate headed by H. R. "Bum" Bright purchased the team for $60 million and secured the stadium lease and other real estate for an additional $26 million. In 1988, a syndicate led by Jerry Jones, whose net worth exceeded $500 million in 1998, bought the Cowboys from Bright's syndicate for $95 million and the Texas Stadium lease for $45 million. After winning four games in two seasons, and with average seasonal attendance falling from 483,000 between 1983 and 1986 to 385,000 between 1987 and 1989, head coach Tom Landry lost his job. Landry had coached the Cowboys for thirty-two years. His teams won 61 percent of their games and two Super Bowls. Tex Schramm, the club's president and general manager since 1960, resigned in April 1989 to become the president of the new World League of American Football. To replace Landry, Jones hired University of Miami coach Jimmy Johnson. After signing first-round draft picks Michael Irvin in 1988, Troy Aikman in 1989, and Emmitt Smith in 1990, in the next five years the Cowboys won four division titles, and three NFC and Super Bowl championships. Jones and his syndicate remain owners of the Cowboys, the highest valued team in professional team sports in 1998 at $413 million.[20]

Upon receiving a franchise for Minneapolis–St. Paul, a syndicate led by Max Winter pulled its organization out of the AFL, paid a $600,000 entry fee, and joined the NFL in 1961.[21] The syndicate included five owners who each controlled the same proportion of nonvoting stock as shares of voting stock. Winter, for example, had 20 percent of the nonvoting and voting stock. Over the next three decades, several legal entanglements such as the death of owner Bill Boyer, takeover agreements, divestitures, and differences in equity interests affected the ownership structure of the Vikings. In 1972, 1975, 1977, 1985, 1987, 1989, 1991, and 1992 various syndicates and individual owners exchanged their voting and nonvoting shares and rights to the team. When disputes between competing ownership groups of the Vikings arose in the late 1980s, NFL Commissioner Paul Tagliabue offered his assistance—but to no avail. Finally, in 1991 a syndicate headed by Mike Lynn acquired an additional 51 percent of the team, bringing the syndicate's total share to 100 percent, thus satisfying a league rule that one owner must control at least 60 percent of an NFL club. One year later Lynn sold 10 percent of the franchise to other owners for an unknown price when the league lowered majority ownership requirements to 30 percent. Recently, the Vikings have been pressured by the league to select a 30 percent majority owner. Even so, in early 1998 author Tom Clancy withdrew his bid to acquire the Vikings. In August 1998, billionaire Red McCombs, former owner of the San Antonio Spurs and Denver Nuggets, bought the club for $250 million including $40 million of team debt.[22]

Along with Dallas and Minnesota, six other NFL expansions happened for various reasons. Atlanta and New Orleans, for example, joined the NFL at the same time that Miami and Cincinnati entered the AFL. Demographically, the Atlanta and New Orleans metropolitan areas ranked high in population growth in the 1960s. Both cities had a population base that could support an NFL franchise and welcomed the opportunity to do so. Rankin Smith and some minority investors bought the Atlanta Falcons for an expansion fee of $8.5 million in 1965. Twenty-three years later the Falcons value had increased to $233 million with revenues exceeding $77 million and a negative operating income.[23] Although the team is currently not for sale, and it played in the 1999 Super Bowl, weak attendance concerns owner Taylor Smith (the son of deceased owner Rankin Smith) as the club struggles in the Western Division of the NFC.

Following payment of an expansion fee of $8 million in 1966, owner John Mecom, Jr., sold the New Orleans Saints to Tom Benson in 1985 for $70.2 million. The deal included a renegotiated Superdome contract and a $15 million loan guarantee by the state of Louisiana. The Saints' performance and attendance have remained below average. Between 1970 and 1981, and from 1983 to 1986, the club finished no higher than third in their division during fifteen seasons. The team lost NFC wild card games to the Minnesota Vikings in 1987, to the Chicago Bears in 1990, to the Atlanta Falcons in 1991, and to the Philadelphia Eagles in 1992. The team's attendance averaged 525,000 from 1967 to 1969; 430,000 from 1970 to 1979; 437,000 from 1980 to 1989; and 444,000 from 1990 to 1997. In 1998 the Saints' value had risen to $243 million with over $80 million in total revenues and $18 million in operating income. Like the Falcons, the Saints have seen their winning percentage and attendance decline in recent seasons. Nonetheless, the value of the team has appreciated.[24]

In 1974 a family group headed by Lloyd Nordstrom paid a $16 million expansion fee for the Seattle Seahawks, which began playing NFL games two years later. Fourteen years later the Nordstrom family, which solely owned the team, sold the franchise to Ken Behring and Ken Hoffman for $80 million. By 1998 the value of the Seahawks had climbed to $324 million with total revenues exceeding $77 million and negative $10 million in operating income. Multibillionaire Paul Allen, a co-founder of Microsoft Corporation, currently owns the Seahawks, having bought the team for $200 million in 1997. A referendum passed in June 1997 calls for the demolition of the Kingdome in 2000 and its replacement by a $425 million high-tech, open-air football stadium and exhibition hall. Allen will chip in 25 percent of the stadium costs and receive all revenues earned from the stadium, including personal seat licenses, luxury suite sales, television rights, and advertising.[25]

A syndicate led by Hugh Culverhouse paid a $16 million expansion fee for the Tampa Bay Buccaneers in 1974. The metropolitan area then ranked twenty-fifth in population and ahead of Charlotte, Indianapolis, Jacksonville, Portland, and Phoenix. The Buccaneers played in 74,000-seat Houlihan Stadium from 1976 to 1997. Culverhouse, a real estate tycoon in Florida, had a net worth of $350 million in 1993. Malcolm Glazer, the majority owner of Houlihan's restaurant franchise, replaced Culverhouse as the owner of the Buccaneers in the mid-1990s.[26]

The NFL expansions from 1960 to 1976 appear in Table 2.5 along with a demographic profile of the metropolitan areas that hosted the teams. Since 1960, the NFL has generally placed expansion franchises in "sunbelt" cities of the United States. For the majority of expansions, the population and per capita income levels at the sites in the South fell below the league average. Additionally, most of the expansion sites were located in geographical regions that had relatively warm climates and above average population growth rates. Atlanta, Dallas, and Tampa Bay, for example, experienced more growth than Minneapolis and Seattle.

Roger Noll confirmed in 1974 that any metropolitan area with a population of one million could support an NFL team.[27] Because of this, Noll concluded that medium-sized cities such as Anaheim, Indianapolis, Newark, Phoenix, Portland, San Jose, Seattle, and Tampa–St. Petersburg could then support an NFL club. In addition, Noll claimed that large cities like Chicago, Detroit, Los Angeles, New York, Philadelphia, and possibly Boston and Washington, could host a second NFL team. To be sure, Noll's prediction rang true for Seattle and Tampa as expansion sites. But his suggestion that the other large cities could host a second or third franchise proved inaccurate. Los Angeles failed to support two NFL teams. In 1995 the Raiders returned to Oakland. After their departure, the City of Angels failed to support the Rams. The team placed last in their division from 1991 to 1994, and experienced a drop in attendance from 52,000 to 42,000 per game. In 1995, owner Georgia Frontiere moved the franchise to St. Louis.

Table 2.5
NFL Expansion Franchises and Area Demographic Data, by Year

Year	Franchise	Population	Income	%Growth
1960	Dallas	1.1	2,506	36.8
1961	Minnesota	1.5	2,825	23.0
1966	Atlanta	1.3	3,115	36.5
1967	New Orleans	1.1	3,070	15.4
1976	Seattle	1.4	8,494	12.8
1976	Tampa Bay	1.3	6,762	44.1

Note: Population is the SMSA total population in millions in the expansion year. Income is the per capita personal income level in the SMSA in thousands of dollars. The %Growth is the percentage growth of the total population in the SMSA during the decade of the expansion.

Source: See Table 2.1.

Table 2.6
Former NFL Expansion Franchise and Selected Data, by Seasons, by Year

Year	Franchise	Five-Year Season		Ten-Year Season	
		Performance	Attendance	Performance	Attendance
1960	Dallas	.256	182	.477	313
1961	Minnesota	.356	258	.456	289
1966	Atlanta	.228	406	.328	374
1967	New Orleans	.256	522	.256	460
1976	Seattle	.375	452	.450	443
1976	Tampa Bay	.278	446	.317	389

Note: Performance and Attendance are, respectively, the mean percentage win-loss record and home game attendance (in hundreds of thousands) of the teams for the first five and ten years of the franchise.

Source: The World Almanac and Book of Facts, 1960–1977; Media Guides of the teams.

Table 2.6 gives the average performance and attendance of six NFL expansion teams for the first five-year and ten-year seasons of the franchise. Except for the New Orleans Saints, the performance of all NFL expansion teams improved from the five- to ten-year period. The Cowboys improved significantly —ranking fourth in the league in 1967, and second in the next two seasons. The Vikings and Falcons also played much better as they matured. The Vikings had a winning percentage of .857 in their ninth and tenth seasons, while the Falcons won 50 percent and 64 percent of their games in their seventh and eighth seasons, respectively.

American Football League

Four teams played in each division of the American Football League (AFL) from 1960 to 1965. In that period, the league's per-game attendance grew by 95 percent, or by 107,000 per team. In addition, radio and television revenues for broadcasting AFL games increased from $1.6 million to $7.4 million, which included regular season local and national broadcasts and the playoffs.

With new NFL expansion teams in Dallas and Minnesota, and a planned expansion in Atlanta, the AFL granted a Miami franchise in 1966 to owners Joe Robbie and Danny Thomas Enterprises for a fee of $7.5 million, which reverted to the NFL under the AFL–NFL merger agreement. Over the next two years the nation's demand for professional football continued to surge as the AFL's per-game attendance rose from 31,900 to 36,500, and total network broadcasting revenues grew by 11 percent. After New Orleans joined the NFL in 1967, the AFL added a tenth franchise, Cincinnati, to play in the 1968 season. Paul Brown and other entrepreneurs paid the $7.5 million fee to the AFL to manage and operate the franchise. As coach of the Cleveland Browns in the All-American Football Conference (AAFC) in the 1940s, and the NFL in the 1950s, Brown led his club to superior performances. Between 1946 and 1949, the Browns lost only five games and won the AAFC championship each year. With quarterback Otto Graham, fullback Marion Motley, and receiver Dante Lavelli, the club won the NFL East title annually from 1950 to 1955 and in 1957. In 1950, 1954, and

1955, the Browns won NFL championships and lost the title game in 1951, 1952, 1953, and 1957.[28]

Three demographic characteristics of the Miami and Cincinnati metropolitan areas appear in Table 2.7. In 1967 Miami ranked twenty-sixth and Cincinnati seventeenth in population among Standard Metropolitan Statistical Areas (SMSAs) in the United States. From 1960 to 1967, Miami's population had grown by 19 percent, while Cincinnati's grew by 8 percent. Even though the two cities fell below the AFL average in population, the two expansions occurred in areas with above-average population growth.[29] According to Table 2.7, the Miami and Cincinnati metropolitan areas fell below the league average in per capita income. Despite these characteristics, the popularity of high school and college football and other sports in both areas may have appealed to entrepreneurs in Miami and Cincinnati seeking a site to locate a professional franchise.

In team performance, neither the Miami Dolphins nor the Cincinnati Bengals initially did well in the AFL. The Dolphins ranked ninth, seventh, sixth, and tenth in the league from 1966 to 1969. Meanwhile, the Bengals placed ninth in league standings in 1968 and 1969. Also, the home attendance of each team proved dismal. In average attendance for the league, the Bengals ranked eighth and the Dolphins seventh in 1968 and 1969. When the Houston Oilers placed first in attendance in 1968 and the New York Jets first in 1969, the New England Patriots placed last in attendance during these years.[30]

With little growth in the league's radio and television revenues from 1966 to 1969, and a small pool of talented players available from the expansion draft, Miami and Cincinnati failed to compete effectively in the AFL. In the meantime, ownership squabbles persisted in Miami between Joe Robbie and Willard Kleland over who would control the team. This dispute alienated fans, distracted players and coaches, and undoubtedly contributed to the Dolphins' four loosing seasons between 1966 and 1969.[31]

In recent years, the financial worth of the Dolphins and Bengals has improved. From 1993 to 1996, for example, the Dolphins' market value rose by 50 percent to $81 million, ranking the team fourth among all professional sports franchises in the United States.[32] Likewise, from 1993 to 1996, the Bengals increased its market value by 33 percent to $46 million, earning a rank of twenty-eighth out of all professional sports franchises, and twentieth among NFL clubs. The planned construction of a state-of-the-art stadium in Cincinnati should raise

Table 2.7
AFL Expansion Franchises and Area Demographic Data, 1966 to 1969

Year	Franchise	Population	Income	%Growth
1966	Miami	1.1	2,932	35.6
1968	Cincinnati	1.3	3,602	9.4

Note: Population is the SMSA total population in millions in the expansion year. Income is the SMSA per capita personal income in thousands of dollars. The %Growth is the percentage growth of the population in the SMSA from 1960 to 1970.

Source: See Tables 2.1 and 2.3.

additional revenues and grow the market value of the franchise from the 1999 season and beyond.

American and National Football League Merger

In 1966 the AFL and NFL agreed to merge into one league consisting of twenty-four teams and to expand to twenty-six teams by 1968.[33] To permit the merger, in 1966 Congress passed special legislation exempting the leagues from antitrust actions.[34] In 1970 ten AFL teams and the Cleveland Browns, Pittsburgh Steelers, and Baltimore Colts comprised the American Football Conference (AFC) of the NFL. The Denver Broncos, Kansas City Chiefs, Oakland Raiders, and San Diego Chargers comprised the Western Division while the Cincinnati Bengals and Houston Oilers played in the Central Division with the Browns and Steelers. The Baltimore Colts, Boston Patriots, Buffalo Bills, Miami Dolphins, and New York Jets made up the Eastern Division.

During the merger Ralph C. Wilson owned the Bills, Paul Brown owned the Bengals, Gerald and Allan Phipps owned the Broncos, K S. "Bud" Adams owned the Oilers, Lamar Hunt owned the Chiefs, and David "Sonny" Werbelin and Leon Hess owned the Jets. Syndicates owned the Dolphins, Patriots, Raiders, and Chargers.[35] One change in ownership occurred in 1970 when the Dolphins hired Don Shula as coach and gave him a minority share of the team.

With the New York Jets' 16–7 upset of the Baltimore Colts in the 1969 Super Bowl, and the Kansas City Chiefs' 23–7 triumph over the favored Minnesota Vikings in the following year's Super Bowl, AFL teams had closed any gap in quality that existed between the two leagues. The mean winning percentage (performance) and home attendance of the Patriots, Bills, Broncos, Oilers, Raiders, and Jets appear in Table 1.9 of Chapter One. Which former AFL teams have had the most and least success in the NFL? Table 2.8 gives the mean winning percentage and home attendance of the ten AFC teams during two five-year periods.

According to Table 2.8, from 1970 to 1974 the two most competitive teams were the Miami Dolphins at .825 and the Oakland Raiders at .724. The two least competitive teams were the Houston Oilers at .236 and the New England Patriots at .328. From 1970 to 1974, the Dolphins ranked no lower than second in the AFC, losing the 1971 Super Bowl to the Dallas Cowboys, 24–3, and winning back-to-back Super Bowls by beating the Washington Redskins 14–7 in January 1973, and upsetting the Minnesota Vikings 24–7 in January 1974. Quarterback Bob Griese, wide receiver Paul Warfield, and running backs Larry Csonka and Jim Kiick excelled for the Dolphins in this period. The Raiders, meanwhile, ranked no lower than fourth in the AFC and competed in the conference playoffs in 1970 and from 1972 to 1974. Besides the Oilers and Patriots, the Chargers and Bills each won less than 40 percent of their games on average during the first half of the 1970s. Collectively, the ten former AFL teams improved each season as their winning percentage increased from .426 in 1970 to .553 in 1974.

The Denver Broncos, Houston Oilers, New England Patriots, Oakland Raiders, and San Diego Chargers posted higher mean winning percentages from 1975 to 1979 than from 1970 to 1974 (see Table 2.8). Furthermore, six of the teams played above .500 from 1975 to 1979. Significant gains in winning percentage from 1970 to 1974 and from 1975 to 1979 were 150 percent by the Oilers, 76 percent by the Patriots, 42 percent by the Broncos, and 37 percent by the Chargers. On the other hand, the mean winning percentage fell by 45 percent for the Chiefs, 28 percent for the Jets, and 23 percent for the Dolphins. In the meantime, the average winning percentage of the Bengals and Raiders remained fairly constant throughout these two five-year periods.

From 1975 to 1979, grouped together the teams averaged .500 or better each year, which represented a dramatic improvement in play from the period 1970 to 1974. The teams' mean winning percentage also increased from .484 between 1970 to 1974 to .512 between 1975 to 1979.

During the 1970s, the Dolphins at .729 and the Raiders at .724 had the highest mean winning percentage of AFC teams from the old AFL. The Bills at .358 and the Jets at .392 had the two lowest mean winning percentages of the old AFL clubs during the 1970s. The winning percentages of the six other teams ranged from .540 for the Broncos, to .521 for the Bengals, to .453 for the Patriots, to .439 for the Chiefs, to .413 for the Oilers, to .412 for the Chargers. Have the mean winning percentages of the ten teams changed during the last twelve years? The majority of the former AFL teams have been competitive in the AFC since the early 1970s. The least competitive teams include the Bengals, Jets, and Chargers.

Table 2.8 also shows the mean home attendance of the teams between 1970 and 1979. From 1970 to 1974, the Dolphins and Chiefs had the highest, and the Oilers and the Chargers had the lowest, average home attendance. The Dolphins and Chiefs drew over 500,000 fans to their stadiums in 1972, as did the Bills in 1973 and 1974. The surge in attendance for the Dolphins and Bills occurred because of the team's performance. In 1972, the Dolphins went undefeated in the regular season and, as noted above, beat the Washington Redskins

Table 2.8
AFC Team Performance and Attendance, 1970 to 1979

Franchise	1970–1974		1975–1979	
	Performance	Attendance	Performance	Attendance
Buffalo	.381	388	.335	404
Cincinnati	.528	394	.514	345
Denver	.445	355	.635	499
Houston	.236	264	.591	363
Kansas City	.570	417	.309	390
Miami	.825	464	.634	416
New England	.328	382	.578	431
New York	.457	407	.328	368
Oakland	.724	382	.725	400
San Diego	.348	319	.477	318

Note: Performance and Attendance are five-year averages.

Source: *The World Almanac and Book of Facts,* 1970–1980; *Media* and *Information Guides* of the NFL teams and the league.

14–7 in 1973's Super Bowl. The Bills, led by running back O. J. Simpson, went 9–5 in 1973 and 1974, but lost 32–14 to the Pittsburgh Steelers in the 1974 playoffs.

Despite dropping from first to fifth in winning percentage in the AFC in 1972, the Chiefs' home attendance increased from 351,000 in 1971 to 509,000 in 1972 when the team began play in Arrowhead Stadium. Meanwhile, the Oilers posted a .236 winning percentage between 1970 and 1974 and the Chargers finished either third or fourth in their division during those seasons.

From 1975 to 1979, the mean attendance of the Broncos and Oilers increased over 35 percent, but fell by 6 to 12 percent for the Bengals, Chiefs, Dolphins, and Jets. The Broncos finished first or second in the AFC's Western Division between 1975 and 1979, and the Oilers coached by Bum Phillips won AFC playoff games in 1978 and 1979 as superstar running back Earl Campbell rushed for nearly four thousand yards in two seasons. The Bills and Raiders realized a 4 percent rise in average attendance between 1975 and 1979, while the Patriots realized a 12 percent rise during the same period.

In each season played during the 1970s, the mean attendance of the league (451,000) exceeded the same for the ten former AFL teams (385,000). Average attendance grew by 10 percent for the league to 465,000 during 1970 to 1974, and grew 8 percent to 378,000 for the expansion teams. But in 1975 to 1979, the league's average attendance rose merely 4 percent to 470,000 while it increased 15 percent to 443,000 for the expansion teams. In the late 1970s, the migration of people from large midwestern and eastern cities, due to the decline in manufacturing employment and the recessions of 1975 and 1979, contributed to the meager growth in attendance of the league. So during the 1970s, successful teams with large stadiums such as the Chicago Bears, Dallas Cowboys, Detroit Lions, Los Angeles Rams, Oakland Raiders, San Francisco Forty-niners, and Philadelphia Eagles kept the NFL's average attendance above the average of the AFC teams.

In the 1970s, the mean performance of five former AFL teams rose. As the seasons progressed these clubs successfully adapted their game strategies, and adjusted their player rosters and coaching staff to the NFL style of play. Combined the Dolphins, Raiders, and Steelers won seven Super Bowls during the decade. Five teams also drew more fans to their stadiums during the 1970s. Due to their exciting play and marketing expertise, the Broncos and Oilers experienced large increases in attendance despite winning only two divisional titles and no Super Bowls.

PROFESSIONAL BASKETBALL

National Basketball Association

Several franchises were admitted into the National Basketball Association (NBA) from 1947 to 1950. The sites of the expansion teams that joined the NBA during those seasons included Baltimore (1947–48), Fort Wayne, Indianapolis, Minneapolis, Rochester (1948–49), Anderson (Indiana), Denver, Sheboygan (Wisconsin), Syracuse, Tri-Cities, and Waterloo (1949–50). From a seventeen-member league in the 1949–50 season, the NBA "downsized" to eight teams by the 1960–61 season. Teams played in Boston, Cincinnati, Detroit, Los Angeles, New York, Philadelphia, St. Louis, and Syracuse.

From 1954 to 1961, NBA attendance rose by 62 percent. During these seven seasons three NBA franchises relocated. Yet large cities like Baltimore, Chicago, Cleveland, Pittsburgh, and Washington, D.C., then lacked professional basketball franchises. In the late 1950s and early 1960s, it seemed apparent that the demand for professional sports, especially basketball, was growing across the nation as television became an increasingly important revenue source for teams. With the prospect of basketball fans switching their allegiance to the American Basketball Association (formed in 1967 by Abe Saperstein), the NBA had an incentive to change team location strategies. So in the early 1960s, the NBA decided to expand after a hiatus of eleven years.

Relative to league averages, the NBA located over 50 percent of its expansion franchises in metropolitan areas that ranked below average in total population and per capita income. San Diego and Phoenix in the 1960s, and Portland and Indianapolis in the 1970s, for example, had below average demographics relative to the league in the expansion years.[36]

The NBA granted more expansion franchises from 1962 to 1977 than did MLB or the NFL. To compare strategies, three demographic features of the metropolitan areas of NBA teams appear in Table 2.9. Only five of the NBA expansions, or 35 percent, occurred in metropolitan areas that had higher per capita incomes than the league average. These sites included Chicago (twice), Denver, New York, and Seattle. For the third feature, an area's population growth, nine of the expansion franchises, or 64 percent, located in metropolitan areas that exceeded the league average. These areas included Chicago (twice), Denver, New Orleans, Phoenix, Portland, San Antonio, San Diego, and Seattle. The typical NBA expansion site, therefore, was a medium-sized city in the southern or western United States. Furthermore, the city and its surrounding area had above average population growth in the expansion year. So small cities like Denver, Phoenix, Portland, San Antonio, and Seattle appeared capable of supporting an NBA franchise based upon population growth and an expanding local and regional radio and television market.

Neither owners, fans, nor leagues expect expansion teams to contend seriously for titles against established teams before the players develop and perform as a unit. During an expansion team's inaugural year, the franchise drafts college stars and trades players in order for the team to become more competitive. Also, in this period home crowds usually fail to fill the arena unless the team performs above expectations and arouses the interest of fans. The performance and attendance of all NBA expansion teams appear in Table 2.10, which indicates that from 1961 to 1977, twelve NBA expansion franchises remained at their original home sites for at least five years. Five of the new teams—the Milwaukee Bucks, Phoenix Suns, Indiana Pacers, New Jersey Nets, and the San Antonio Spurs—declined in performance after their fifth season. During the five- and ten-year post-expansion seasons, the highest performing teams included the Bucks, Nuggets, and the Spurs. The Portland Trailblazers played

Table 2.9
Former NBA Expansion Franchises and Area Demographic Data, by Year

Year	Franchise	Population	Income	%Growth
1961–62	Chicago	6.4	3,157	12.2
1966–67	Chicago	6.7	4,066	12.2
1967–68	San Diego	1.2	3,636	31.4
1967–68	Seattle	1.3	4,232	28.7
1968–69	Milwaukee	1.3	4,282	9.8
1968–69	Phoenix	.9	3,537	46.2
1970–71	Buffalo	1.3	4,322	– 8.8
1970–71	Cleveland	2.0	4,709	– 5.5
1970–71	Portland	1.0	4,436	20.3
1974–75	New Orleans	1.1	4,484	14.2
1976–77	Denver (ABA)	1.5	9,270	29.1
1976–77	Indianapolis (ABA)	1.2	8,281	5.0
1976–77	New York (ABA)	8.9	9,366	– 3.6
1976–77	San Antonio (ABA)	1.0	6,847	20.7

Note: Population is the SMSA total population in millions in the expansion year. Income is the SMSA per capita personal income in thousands of dollars. The %Growth is the percentage growth of the SMSA population during the decade of the expansion.

Source: *The World Almanac and Book of Facts*, 1962–1977; *Statistical Abstracts of the United States*, 1961–1977; *County and City Data Books*, 1961–1977.

poorly in the first six seasons until they signed UCLA graduate Bill Walton, who led the team to an NBA title in the 1976–77 season. The Buffalo Braves (eight seasons) also had a dismal team performance after the fifth season. The Cavaliers, Bulls, and the Nets had the lowest average attendance for NBA expansion teams in their first five seasons. After their fifth season, the average home attendance of the Braves, Nuggets, Pacers, and Spurs fell. And, the attendance of the Bucks, Suns, and the Nets increased after their fifth season even though the performance of the teams declined during their sixth to tenth seasons.

In sum, between 1950 and 1976 fourteen teams joined the NBA, which placed three clubs in Chicago and New York. The populations of the areas hosting the teams had average per capita personal incomes. Following expansion, six teams played better and seven experienced growth in attendance at their arenas.

American Basketball Association

From 1967 to 1976, teams in the American Basketball Association (ABA) played at thirty-three home sites. In various seasons regional ABA franchises each played their home games at three sites within a particular state. The Carolina Cougars went to the hoop in Greensboro, Raleigh, and Charlotte. The Floridians played roundball in Miami, Tampa, and Jacksonville. Fort Worth Dallas, and Lubbock hosted the Stars in Texas. The Virginia Squires excited

Table 2.10
NBA Expansion Franchises and Selected Data, by Season, by Year

Year	Franchise	Five-Year Season		Ten-Year Season	
		Performance	Attendance	Performance	Attendance
1961–62	Chicago	.269	n.a.	–	–
1966–67	Chicago	.452	240	.510	309
1967–68	Seattle	.424	301	.442	400
1967–68	San Diego	.362	233	–	–
1968–69	Milwaukee	.663	339	.587	373
1968–69	Phoenix	.463	291	.460	292
1970–71	Buffalo	.380	354	.394	345
1970–71	Cleveland	.339	208	.415	323
1970–71	Portland	.324	325	.439	439
1974–75	New Orleans	.392	408	–	–
1976–77	Denver (ABA)	.517	582	.536	532
1976–77	Indiana (ABA)	.453	428	.383	397
1976–77	New Jersey (ABA)	.495	248	.476	384
1976–77	San Antonio (ABA)	.578	429	.550	405

Note: Performance is the mean percentage five- and ten-year win-loss record of the team following the expansion year. Attendance is the mean five- and ten-year home game attendance in hundreds of thousands during the same period. The n.a. means the data are unavailable. Chicago played two seasons, San Diego four seasons, and New Orleans five seasons in the NBA. Buffalo moved to San Diego after eight seasons.

Source: *The World Almanac and Book of Facts*, 1961–1977; *Media Guides* of the NBA teams; Quirk and Fort, *Pay Dirt*, 495–500.

fans in Roanoke, Norfolk, and Richmond. Besides Louisville, the Kentucky Colonels played several home games in Cincinnati.[37]

In the 1967–68 season, the ABA awarded eleven owners or syndicates expansion franchises for a fee of $30,000 each. The original sites of these franchises were geographically dispersed and varied economically and demographically. During various seasons, ABA teams in Oakland, Los Angeles, and New Jersey competed for fans and media publicity with NBA rivals. Over its nine-year history, most ABA teams played at sites within metropolitan areas previously unexposed to professional basketball.

We collected the total population, per capita personal income, and the population growth for the eleven metropolitan areas that originally hosted ABA franchises. This data is displayed in Table 2.11 and emphasizes the significant differences in the demographic profile between these areas and the sites of NBA expansion teams. As the table denotes, four ABA franchises represented small metropolitan areas, while four represented large U.S. metropolitan areas. The ABA placed eight franchises in areas below the league's average population of three million in 1967–68. Still, for nine seasons the metropolitan area populations of the Indiana, Kentucky, and Denver franchises proved sufficient to maintain their teams at the original site.

Table 2.11
ABA Franchises and Area Demographic Data, by Year

Year	Franchise	Population	Income	%Growth
1967–68	Indiana	1.0	3,811	17.7
1967–68	Kentucky	.8	3,497	15.0
1967–68	Minnesota	1.6	4,088	23.0
1967–68	Pittsburgh	2.4	3,555	– .2
1967–68	Oakland	3.0	4,694	17.4
1967–68	New Orleans	1.0	3,300	15.4
1967–68	Denver	1.0	3,524	32.6
1967–68	Dallas	1.4	3,760	36.8
1967–68	Houston	1.8	3,482	39.8
1967–68	Anaheim	6.8	4,331	16.6
1967–68	New Jersey	11.6	4,950	12.2

Note: Population is the SMSA total population in millions in the expansion year. Income is the SMSA per capita personal income in thousands of dollars. The %Growth is the percentage growth of the SMSA population between 1960 and 1970.

Source: *The World Almanac and Book of Facts*, 1968–1969; *County and City Data Books*, 1967 and 1972; *Statistical Abstract of the U. S.*, 1974.

In the 1967–68 season, four ABA franchise areas ranked above the league average in per capita income ($3,908) and five above the league average in Orleans lowest, in per capita income. Comparatively, the average per capita income of areas that hosted ABA teams fell marginally below the $4,100 average of NBA teams.

As stated earlier, ABA teams in Denver, Indiana, Kentucky, and New Jersey were secure franchises that remained at their original sites. The population and per capita income of the Denver, Indiana, and Kentucky metropolitan areas ranked below the league averages. Perhaps other economic and team-specific factors kept these four franchises from abandoning their original sites. Table 2.12 provides the performance of the teams in terms of winning percentages and gives home attendance for the Denver, Indiana, Kentucky, and New Jersey franchises during the tenure of the ABA. What do these data in the table reveal about these clubs? For one, the average team performance of Denver, Indiana, and Kentucky surpassed the average performance of other league teams. New Jersey finished under .500 in five seasons, achieving an average team performance of .503. Of the four teams studied, only Denver failed to win an ABA title. In contrast, Indiana won three, New Jersey won two, and Kentucky captured one league championship. On average, each team drew more fans to home games than did the league. Indiana's home attendance at 7,831 per game ranked highest among all ABA teams. Even so, NBA teams averaged 8,300 per game between 1968 and 1976. San Antonio ranked second in average seasonal attendance by drawing 7,351 fans per home game from 1973 to 1976. Among the lowest average per game attendance of ABA teams were Houston with 820 in1968–69, Los Angeles with 1,461 in 1969–70, Washington with 2,032 in

Table 2.12
Selected ABA Franchises, Performance and Attendance, 1968 to 1976

Franchise	Performance		Attendance	
	Team	League	Team	League
Denver	.555	.500	5,888	5,259
Indiana	.573	.500	7,831	5,259
Kentucky	.590	.500	6,894	5,259
New Jersey	.503	.500	6,058	5,259

Note: Performance and Attendance are, respectively, the mean win-loss percentages and per game attendance (in thousands) of the teams and league from 1968 to 1976.

Source: *The World Almanac and Book of Facts*, 1968–1977; Quirk and Fort, *Pay Dirt,* 495–500.

1969–70, Pittsburgh with 2,312 in 1970–72, and San Diego with 2,261 in 1973–76.

The average five-year home attendance of the three ABA teams prior to the 1976 merger was Denver (275,000), Indiana (341,000), and New Jersey (398,000). San Antonio's home attendance averaged 307,000 from 1973 through 1976.[38] Only the Nets suffered a decline in attendance in the five seasons following the merger despite winning nearly 50 percent of their games as an NBA team. Also, while playing against NBA teams, the performance of the Nuggets, Pacers, and Nets declined while the Spurs continued to win over 57 percent of their games. After the 1975–76 season, seven teams remained in the ABA. Four of them—the Nuggets, Pacers, Nets, and Spurs—joined the NBA. Besides paying an expansion fee of $3.2 million, each team paid $1.6 million to Kentucky and Utah to dissolve the ABA. For invading the New York area, the Nets paid compensation of $4 million to the New York Knicks. As it happened Denver, Indiana, and San Antonio acquired NBA franchises for $4.8 million, a bargain price in that the Detroit Pistons sold for $8.1 million in 1974, the Chicago Bulls for $5.1 million in 1972, and the Houston Rockets for $5.6 million in 1971.[39]

In retrospect, ABA franchises in Kentucky, Indiana, New Jersey, Denver, and San Antonio performed above the league average at the gate and on the court. The least effective ABA franchises, as measured by performance, attendance, and income earned, were Memphis, Houston, Oakland, San Diego, and Washington.

The ABA began play in eleven cities in 1967. Relative to areas of NBA clubs, the sites of ABA teams fell below average in per capita income but above average in percentage of minorities. Although four of the original ABA teams had not moved by 1977, eleven clubs had either relocated, claimed bankruptcy, or withdrew from the league. After San Diego and Utah folded, seven ABA clubs finished the final season. In June 1976, four ABA teams joined the NBA. As James Quirk and Rodney Fort put it, "Generally speaking, the ABA was not an example of a 'successful' rival league."[40]

SUMMARY

Between 1961 and 1977, the professional sports leagues expanded. MLB added ten teams, the NFL six, the AFL two, and the NBA fourteen. In organized baseball six clubs joined the AL and four the NL. Demographically, AL teams located in metropolitan areas with smaller populations and higher per capita incomes compared to their NL counterparts. New York, Los Angeles, and Houston were the largest, and Kansas City, San Diego, and Seattle the smallest cities hosting the new franchises. The majority of teams played better before more fans during their first to tenth season. As the seasons progressed, however, the Montreal Expos disappointed their fans. Following expansion the team's five- to ten-year average attendance declined (see Table 2.4).

The areas of the expansion teams in professional football were usually below the league average in population and per capita income but above average in population growth. The largest cities selected by team owners were Minneapolis and Seattle. Except for the New Orleans Saints, the teams improved in winning percentage after expansion. Surprisingly, the average attendance of only the Dallas Cowboys and Minneapolis Vikings rose in the ten seasons following the expansion year. In 1970 the NFL expanded to twenty-six teams. Four former AFL clubs joined the AFC's Western and Eastern Divisions, and two the Central Division. From 1970 to 1974, and 1975 to 1979, five of the teams played better and drew more fans to their stadiums.

Ten of the NBA's expansion franchises existed for ten years at their original sites. The Zephyrs moved to Baltimore after two seasons in Chicago, the Rockets to Houston after four years in San Diego, the Jazz to Salt Lake City after five years in New Orleans, and the Braves to San Diego after eight seasons in Buffalo. The areas of the expansion teams fell below the league average in population and above average in population growth and per capita income. From the expansion year six teams played better and seven clubs drew more fans to their arenas. In sum, over 50 percent of teams in the three sports won more games and played before larger home crowds after the expansion year. This suggests that the leagues decision to expand into untapped markets proved to be in the best interests of the owners, fans, and the respective communities hosting the teams.

NOTES

1. See Michael N. Danielson, *Home Team: Professional Sports and the American Metropolis* (Princeton, N.J.: Princeton University Press, 1997), 168.

2. See Kenneth L. Shropshire, *The Sports Franchise Game: Cities in Pursuit of Sports Franchises, Events, Stadiums, and Arenas* (Philadelphia: University of Pennsylvania Press, 1995), 1–12.

3. These results were reported in the *Charlotte Observer* (29 September 1997), 53.

4. For these issues see Roger G. Noll, "Attendance and Price Setting," in *Government and the Sports Business* (Washington, D.C.: The Brookings Institution, 1974), 115–157; James Quirk and Rodney Fort, *Pay Dirt: The Business of Professional Sports* (Princeton, N.J.: Princeton University Press, 1992); Andrew Zimbalist, *Baseball and*

Billions: A Probing Look Inside the Big Business of Our National Pastime (New York: Basic Books, 1992).

5. See Roger G. Noll and Andrew Zimbalist, eds. *Sports, Jobs and Taxes: The Economic Impact of Sports Teams and Stadiums* (Washington, D.C.: The Brookings Institution, 1997), 212; Zimbalist, *Baseball and Billions*, 16–17.

6. Quirk and Fort, *Pay Dirt*, 408.

7. Ibid., 401.

8. Foon Rhee, "Twins Sale on Agenda as Owners Talk Shop," *Charlotte Observer* (11 January 1998), 1A, 18A; *1998* Anaheim Angels *Media Guide*, 34; "Anaheim," *Charlotte Observer* (9 October 1998), 4B.

9. For the history of Kauffman Stadium see <http://www.kcroyals.com> cited 19 August 1998. See also Rhee, "Twins Sale on Agenda as Owners Talk Shop," 1A, 18A; Quirk and Fort, *Pay Dirt*, 404; Ira Horowitz, "Sports Broadcasting," in Roger G. Noll, ed. *Government and the Sports Business* (Washington, D.C.: The Brookings Institution, 1974), 299.

10. Quirk and Fort, *Pay Dirt*, 404.

11. See "Ballpark Financing," at <http://www.mariners.org> cited 6 August 1998; Quirk and Fort, *Pay Dirt*, 407. In a memo to Frank Jozsa in October 1998, James Quirk cited the fee for naming rights.

12. On 19 March 1998, major-league baseball owners approved the sale of the Blue Jays to Interbrew SA three years after the Belgian brewery took over the team as part of its purchase of the Toronto-based brewery John Labatt Ltd. See Sports Today, "Lasorda: Dodgers Sale to Murdoch Good," *Charlotte Observer* (20 March 1998), 2B; Quirk and Fort, *Pay Dirt*, 408; Rhee, "Twins Sale on Agenda as Owners Talk Shop," 18A; *1998 Blue Jays Official Guide*, 236–238.

13. See Frederick Klein, "The Big Guys' Burden," *Wall Street Journal* (14 August 1998), W5.

14. Steven A. Riess, *Sport in the Industrial Age, 1850–1920* (Wheeling, Ill.: Harlan Davidson Inc., 1995), 163.

15. See Quirk and Fort, *Pay Dirt*, 394–396.

16. *The Baseball Encyclopedia,* 9th ed. (New York and Toronto: Macmillan Publishing Company, 1993), 10; Quirk and Fort, *Pay Dirt*, 396–398.

17. Noll, "Attendance and Price Setting," 130–131.

18. Danielson, *Home Team,* 170.

19. Ibid.

20. Scott Fowler, "List Puts Panthers Among Most Valuable Pro Teams," *Charlotte Observer* (25 May 1997), 1A, 18A; Quirk and Fort, *Pay Dirt*, 414; *1998 Dallas Cowboys Media Guide*, 234–242; Michael Ozanian, "Selective Accounting," *Forbes* (14 December 1998), 125.

21. In *Pay Dirt*, Quirk and Fort vividly describe the "The Great Football Wars" involving the NFL, AFL, WFL, and the USFL during the last half of the twentieth century.

22. Tagliabue said there were no commitments from any Vikings' owner to be part of Clancy's group and that the selling partners had agreed to sell 100 percent of the club. The sale is subject to approval by twenty-three of the thirty NFL owners. See "Tagliabue Says Sale of Vikings to Tom Clancy May Proceed," available at the Worldwide Web site <http://football.yahoo.com> cited 24 March 1998. For the requirement that NFL teams have a majority owner with a 30 percent share see "Clancy Buys Majority Share of Vikings. Novelist, Investor Group Will Dish Out Over $200 Million," at the Web site <http://www.cnnsi.com> cited 3 February 1998. The sale of the Vikings is discussed in "Sold! Vikings Accept Red McCombs' Bid for Ownership," at <http://www.cnnsi.com> cited 6 July 1998.

23. See Tushar Atre, Kristine Auns, Kurt Badenhausen, Kevin McAuliffe, Christopher Nikolov, and Michael K. Ozanian, "Sports, Stocks, and Bonds," *Financial World* (20 May 1996), 58; Ozanian, "Selective Accounting," 132.

24. See Atre, et al., "Sports, Stocks, and Bonds," 58; Quirk and Fort, *Pay Dirt*, 425, 492; Wire memo from the New Orleans Saints' Media Relations (17 December 1997), 2; Ozanian, "Selective Accounting," 132.

25. See "Seahawks Get Land for Open-Air Stadium. Proposed Park Would Open in 2002, Seat 72,000," at <http://www.cnnsi.com> cited 7 July 1998; "Ballpark Financing," at <http://www.mariners.org> cited 6 August 1998; Tom Farrey, "Too Much of a Good Thing," *Business Week* (11 May 1998), 70; Rhee, "Twins Sale on Agenda as Owners Talk Shop," 1A, 18A; Ozanian, "Selective Accounting," 132. For a brief history of the Seahawks, see Quirk and Fort, *Pay Dirt*, 432.

26. Quirk and Fort, *Pay Dirt,* 432; John Steinbreder, "The Owners," *Sports Illustrated* (13 September 1993), 68.

27. Noll, "Attendance and Price Setting," 145–146.

28. See Quirk and Fort, *Pay Dirt*, 240, 392–395; Frank G. Menke, *The Encyclopedia of Sports*, 5th ed. (Cranbury, N.J.: A. S. Barnes and Company, 1975), 869.

29. U.S. Department of Commerce, Bureau of the Census, *Census of Population*, Social and Economic Characteristics, Metropolitan Areas (Washington, D.C., 1960, 1970).

30. See Quirk and Fort, *Pay Dirt,* 488–494; *The Oakland Raiders: The Team of the Decades 1996*, 176.

31. Quirk and Fort, *Pay Dirt*, 421–422.

32. See Fowler, "List Puts Panthers Among Most Valuable Pro Teams," 1A, 18A.

33. Menke, *The Encyclopedia of Sports*, 467; Quirk and Fort, *Pay Dirt*, 346–353.

34. Menke, *The Encyclopedia of Sports*, 467; Quirk and Fort, *Pay Dirt*, 349.

35. Quirk and Fort, *Pay Dirt,* 409–434.

36. See U.S. Department of Commerce, *Census of Population*, 1960, 1970.

37. For a discussion of rival leagues in professional basketball see Quirk and Fort, *Pay Dirt*, 320–326, 459–463. See also Terry Pluto, *Loose Balls* (New York: Simon & Schuster, 1990); Steve Hall, "HBO Explains How the Wacky ABA Revolutionized the Game," at <http://www.starnews.com> cited 18 November 1997.

38. See Quirk and Fort, *Pay Dirt*, 495–500.

39. Ibid., 327, 446–463.

40. Ibid., 327.

Chapter 3 _____

Franchise Relocation since 1977

In 1976 an investment group negotiated a deal to buy the San Francisco Giants with the intention of moving the club to Toronto. Even though the team had nineteen years remaining on its lease of Candlestick Park, the investors were eager to spend $8 million for the franchise. The investment group sweetened its offer with another $5 million to terminate the Giants' lease. Not wanting to go down as the mayor who lost the Giants, George Moscone sought a court order to delay the sale long enough to secure a buyer who would keep the team in San Francisco. Moscone argued that if the club migrated elsewhere, the city stood to lose roughly $175 million a year. Because the parties had agreed to a pending price of $8 million for the team, someone suggested to the mayor that San Francisco could buy the team and save $167 million. Although Moscone and other city officials ignored the advice, local buyers came forth, put up the cash, and the Giants stayed in San Francisco.[1]

Yet controversy continued, plaguing the team. For example, Candlestick Park was constructed in 1959 as part of the package used to lure the Giants west from New York and ward off similar offers coming from Minneapolis. After choosing the Golden Gate City, the Giants had a 42,000-seat baseball stadium strictly to themselves, and the Giants became a major commercial success in California. But San Francisco decided to enlarge Candlestick Park's capacity by 18,000 to accommodate the NFL FortyNiners. Consequently the city installed artificial turf to "simplify changing the configuration of the stands and to better equip the stadium to withstand wear and tear that would result from more frequent use." To pay for the enlargement San Francisco placed a fifty-cent tax surcharge on baseball tickets, which the baseball promoters had opposed from the start. Several years later the FortyNiners decided that the artificial playing surface caused too many injuries and began pushing for a return to natural grass. The Giants opposed this proposal because it would revive the problems of infield dust blowing about by the force of strong prevailing winds. As it turned out, the FortyNiners prevailed and groundskeepers sodded the playing field again. In 1981 a new campaign was launched to build a dome for Candlestick Park.[2] The San Francisco Giants released a report declaring Candlestick Park unfit for baseball. Either build a new $100 million domed stadium, or place a $60 million dome on Candlestick were offered as options in the report. Due to the estimated cost, however, neither option was adopted by the club or city.[3]

"Similar sequences of events," Leonard Koppett has noted, "have occurred in a dozen other cities." If the terms of a lease seem too favorable to a ballclub, "the city soon comes under political pressure to tighten them. If the landlord does well, the tenant feels he's paying too much. No matter what happens, conflicting forces abound."[4] Koppett's observation in 1981 seems particularly germane to franchise relocation since 1977. Indeed, whenever ballclubs consider changing locations, an array of interests enter the fray. For instance, after exploring all options, professional sports leagues ultimately have the authority to approve the relocation of a franchise. Before the team's owners and league announce whether a club will relocate, the local fans and media—and perhaps the team's players, coaches, and staff—express uncertainty about the future of the franchise and question the necessity to move. Upon learning that a team will move, some hometown fans become disillusioned or embittered, and local newspapers might denounce the decision. Given those conditions, players and coaches will clearly hope that the team improves its performance at the new site.

Once the season concludes, the team abandons its current site, leaving behind die-hard fans, a vacated ballpark, arena, or stadium, and the community's sense of itself as a major-league city diminishes. The emotional turmoil that the fans and the community suffer from such moves may linger for years. But the opportunity to host a team has a positive impact on the new site. Local newspapers publish articles about the team thereby adding readers and generating interest. Concurrently, the community that receives the franchise realizes psychic or economic spillover benefits from the business activities accruing from the team.[5]

Numerous articles and several books question the economic benefits and development derived from professional teams. Economists James Quirk, Rodney Fort, Roger Noll, Andrew Zimbalist, and Robert Baade claim that the use of public funds to finance renovation and construction of venues for professional sports teams is inefficient and a waste of taxpayer dollars. Mark Rosentraub's *Major League Losers: The Real Costs of Sports and Who's Paying for It* explores this issue and concurs with many scholars who claim that the economic rewards to a community for hosting a professional team are minimal to nonexistent.[6]

A goal of this chapter is to measure and analyze the short- and long-term effects that relocation since 1977 has had on teams that moved in MLB, the NFL, and NBA. We apply available information such as win-loss percentages, home game attendance, television and radio revenues, and estimated market values to determine whether a team's relocation proved successful from the viewpoints of the franchise owner and the league. In doing so, this chapter addresses four questions. First, did the team's short- and long-term performance and attendance improve at the post-move site? Second, which factors—economic, team-specific, or demographic—explain the changes in team performance and attendance at the post-move site? Third, do team results differ among and between the four leagues studied? Fourth, did each relocation benefit both the franchise owner and the league? In responding to these questions, the chapter reveals the consequences of teams shifting from one metropolitan area to another.

PROFESSIONAL BASEBALL

National League

As discussed in Chapter One, between 1952 and 1966 four National League (NL) franchises relocated. The league unanimously approved each move.[7] With relocation, ownership remained intact for each NL team that moved. The Perini brothers, for example, continued to own the Milwaukee Braves. Walter O'Malley, Ann Branca, and Bud Mulvey controlled 92 percent of the Los Angeles Dodgers. Horace Stoneham retained majority ownership of the San Francisco Giants, and a syndicate headed by William Bartholomay and Donald Reynolds had controlling ownership of the Atlanta Braves.[8]

Changes in the ownership of these relocated NL teams since the mid-1970s deserves mention. Media mogul Ted Turner purchased the Atlanta Braves for $11 million in 1976 and controlled the club until 1998 when Time Warner became the principal owner of the team. In 1977 Turner acquired 55 percent of the Atlanta Hawks for $4 million. By 1998 the estimated value of the Braves had neared $300 million, the fifth highest in organized ball, and Turner's net worth was $5 billion.[9]

Since 1992 Safeway Stores executive Peter Magowan has served as the managing general partner of the San Francisco Giants. Magowan, whose net worth is estimated to be $60 million, owns about 10 percent of the Giants with the remainder of the team equally shared by other Bay Area business leaders, such as real estate mogul Walter Shorenstein, the Fischer family from the Gap, Charles Schwab, and money manager Michael Steinhardt.[10]

In March 1998 Rupert Murdoch and Fox Sports acquired the Los Angeles Dodgers from the O'Malley family for $350 million. Peter O'Malley and his sister Terry Seidler inherited the team, Dodger Stadium, and the spring training facilities in Vero Beach, Florida, from their late father, Walter. As of March 1998, Peter had served twenty-seven years as president of the Dodgers, longer than anyone in major league baseball history. For personal and business reasons the O'Malleys sold the Dodgers to Murdoch's Fox Group in 1998. Seventy-five percent of the NL and a majority of the AL owners approved the sale. Fearing that Murdoch would escalate player salaries, Ted Turner and John Moores, the owners of the Atlanta Braves and San Diego Padres, voted against the sale.[11]

Have the trends in performance and attendance of these teams changed in the 1990s? From 1990 to 1998, the Braves had the highest winning percentage in the NL followed by other league rivals such as the Dodgers and Giants. In those seasons, the Dodgers' average attendance was 2.9 million, the Braves 2.6 million, and the Giants 1.7 million. Since the tenth season following relocation, the Braves have increased attendance the most, and the Giants the least. Furthermore, the attendance of the Braves and Dodgers exceeded the NL mean of 2.1 million from 1990 to 1998.

Based on franchise values reported in *Financial World*, the two NL teams least likely to change residences are the Atlanta Braves and the Los Angeles Dodgers.[12] Table 3.1 lists the two least and most vulnerable NL franchises to relocate predicated on the team's win-loss record (performance) and home attendance over six years. The data in Table 3.1 indicate the wide gap in attendance between large and small market teams in the NL. In addition, the table denotes that even when the team significantly improves its performance, attendance for small market teams usually changes little. Given these figures, the San Diego Padres and Pittsburgh Pirates should consider relocating to either Salt Lake City, Charlotte, Indianapolis, or the research triangle of Raleigh-Durham-Chapel Hill, North Carolina. *The Sporting News* rates these sites highest among sports cities that lack a major-league baseball franchise.[13] According to *Financial World*, the Padres and Pirates are high-risk franchises, meaning that they will probably generate insufficient operating income to compete with other teams in the NL as the 1990s come to an end. On the other hand, the Braves represent a low-risk franchise and the Dodgers a moderate-risk organization. Hence, the Braves and Dodgers should sustain their historical growth in value and remain competitive in the NL through the turn of the century.

Intersport competition (that is, the presence of other MLB, NFL, and NBA teams at a given team's site) may influence a proprietor's decisions when and where to relocate. Roger Noll contends that cities with more sports interest have more teams and higher home attendance per team. In addition, he suggests that team attendance in the average MLB city is about 21 percent lower because of intersport competition.[14]

Mark Kreider has argued that the baseball market of San Francisco and Oakland will fail to support two big-league franchises in the near future. According to Kreider, the Bay Area market has not yet rebounded from the baseball strikes of 1993 and 1994. Our analysis of the facts supports his thesis. From 1994 to 1996 the home attendance of the Giants fell 17 percent, from ninth to thirteenth place in the NL. The Athletics' attendance declined 8 percent, from twelfth to fourteenth place in the AL. From 1994 to 1996, NL attendance grew

Table 3.1
Selected NL Franchises, Performance, and Attendance, 1992 to 1997

Franchise	Performance						Attendance					
	1992	1993	1994	1995	1996	1997	1992	1993	1994	1995	1996	1997
Atlanta	.605	.642	.596	.625	.593	.623	3.1	3.9	2.9	2.6	2.9	3.4
Los Angeles	.389	.500	.509	.524	.556	.543	2.5	3.2	2.3	2.7	3.2	3.3
San Diego	.506	.377	.402	.486	.562	.469	1.7	1.4	1.0	1.0	2.2	2.1
Pittsburgh	.593	.463	.465	.403	.451	.488	1.8	1.6	1.2	.9	1.3	1.6

Note: For the years listed, Performance is the final standing of the team in the NL based on win-loss percentage. Attendance is the team's home game attendance in millions.

Source: The World Almanac and Book of Facts (Mahwah, N.J.: World Almanac Books, 1992–1996); Memo from American League of Professional Baseball Clubs (New York 1997), 1.

by 18 percent and the AL by 23 percent. In June 1997 the Giants ranked four-teenth in NL attendance averaging over fifteen thousand per home game, and the Athletics placed twelfth in AL attendance averaging over sixteen thousand per home game. From May 1994 to May 1996 the value of the Giants increased by 31 percent, and that of the Athletics decreased by 15 percent. In 1995 and 1996 the road attendance for the Giants averaged 2.03 million and for the Ath-letics 1.16 million. By season's end 1998, the Giants' and Athletics' average home and away attendance was twenty-four and thirty-two thousand, and fifteen and twenty-eight thousand, respectively. In other words, the Giants represent a high-risk franchise and the Athletics typify a moderate-risk franchise.[15]

Given the criteria studied, the Atlanta Braves and the Los Angeles Dodgers are the most successful relocated NL franchises. Despite trading slugger Matt Williams and losing in the 1997 NL playoffs, the performance and attendance of the Giants has increased in recent seasons due in part to manager Dusty Baker and the outstanding performance by superstar Barry Bonds. To illustrate the point, on 23 August 1998, Bonds became the first major-league player to hit four hundred home runs and steal four hundred bases. The previous record of three hundred homers and three hundred stolen bases was held by Willie Mays and Barry's father, Bobby. Consequently, such performance has added market value to the franchise and solidified the team's status in San Francisco. If the Athletics are sold and the team's owners decide to relocate from the Bay Area in the next few years, we recommend that the Giants stay put and exploit the op-portunities offered by being the only MLB team in a large market.

In December 1997, the Giants broke ground on a new $360 million ballpark in downtown San Francisco. When it opens in April 2000, Pacific Bell Park will be the first privately financed stadium to be built in more than thirty-five years. Along with luxury suites and club seats, the Giants sold over twelve thousand charter seat licenses to finance the stadium. With the new ballpark, the debt of the Giants should reach 164 percent of the team's 1997 estimated market value.[16] The franchise has committed its future cash flows to debt reduction and also to player salaries and other operating expenses. Because of this strategy, the Giants' future in San Francisco seems secure.

Table 3.2 gives a benchmark value and sales price of a team in a given year and the inflated market value of the relocated NL and AL teams that played in the 1998 season. Of the teams listed in the table, since 1953 the Baltimore Ori-oles appreciated 10,666 percent; since 1976 the San Francisco Giants appreci-ated 2,250 percent; since 1963 the Texas Rangers appreciated 4,980 percent; and since 1950 the Los Angeles Dodgers appreciated 5,800 percent. The Minne-sota Twins have more than doubled in value since 1984, but appreciated only 13 percent from 1993 to 1998. Other teams such as the Oakland Athletics and Mil-waukee Brewers have also appreciated little in value in recent years. The Brew-ers should earn more revenue from a new ballpark in Milwaukee in 2000 and that should help increase the value of the team in the future. On the other hand, unless the Athletics perform above expectations or acquire more revenues from its ballpark or the league, relocation may represent the best option available for the team to pursue. In retrospect, the moves by the NL teams since 1950 have

Table 3.2
NL and AL Relocated Franchises, Sales Prices, and Market Values for Selected Years

			Market Value		
Franchise	Sales Price (Year)		1993	1998	%Change
NL					
Los Angeles	4	(1950)	138	236	71
San Francisco	8	(1976)	93	188	102
Atlanta	4	(1951)	96	299	211
AL					
Baltimore	3	(1953)	129	323	150
Minnesota	35	(1984)	83	94	13
Oakland	3	(1950)	114	118	4
Milwaukee	11	(1970)	96	127	32
Texas	5	(1963)	132	254	92

Note: Sales Price is the sales price of the team in millions of dollars in the given year. Market Value is the estimated market value of the team in millions of dollars in 1993 and 1998 as reported in the table's sources. The %Change is the percentage change in the value of the franchise from 1993 to 1998.

Source: James Quirk and Rodney Fort, *Pay Dirt: The Business of Professional Sports* (Princeton, N.J.: Princeton University Press, 1992), 391–409; Tushar Atre, Kristine Auns, Kurt Badenhausen, Kevin McAuliffe, Christopher Nikolov, and Michael K. Ozanian, "Sports, Stocks, and Bonds," *Financial World* (20 May 1996), 56; *Information Please Sports Almanac* (New York: Houghton Mifflin Company, 1996), 573; Scott Fowler, "List Puts Panthers Among Most Valuable Pro Teams," *Charlotte Observer* (29 May 1997), 1A, 18A; Michael K. Ozanian, "Selective Accounting," *Forbes* (14 December 1998), 124–134.

benefited each team and the league. When considering this, other moves should have occurred. If the league had allowed the San Diego Padres and Pittsburgh Pirates to relocate to non-MLB cities with a population greater than a million, such as Indianapolis, San Antonio, or New Orleans, then a more rational geographic dispersion of NL franchises would exist. Historically owners and league rules restrict teams from moving. That distorts sports industry resources and perpetuates the inequality in revenues and profits between franchises located in small and large markets.

American League

In 1955 Clark Griffith died, leaving 50 percent of the Washington Senators to his nephew, Calvin Griffith. Given a 6–2 favorable vote by the AL, Griffith moved the team to Minnesota in 1961 and renamed it the Twins. Billionaire Carl Pohlad, a banking executive, purchased the Twins in 1984. To generate greater revenues Pohlad wants either a new stadium to replace the Metrodome, which the Twins share with the Minnesota Vikings, or to sell his club to interested buyers, hoping to lure the team to the Triad region of North Carolina.[17] But after voters in the Triad region rejected tax increases on food and tickets to finance a stadium for the team, Pohlad's proposal to sell the Twins remains uncertain. In 1998 business leaders in Charlotte formed the Regional Baseball Partnership to bring organized baseball to the Charlotte area. They negotiated with Pohlad and perhaps with other owners who would consider relocating to North Carolina. In 1998 Pohlad signed a new lease committing the Twins to Minnesota for three years, while they search for a local buyer.[18]

In 1993 Walter A. Haas, Jr., a descendant of Levi Strauss, owned 75 percent of the Athletics while his son and daughter owned the other 25 percent of the team. Real estate developer Scott Schott bought the team in 1995. Schott instituted a $100 million renovation and expansion of the Oakland Coliseum in 1996. The Oakland Football Marketing Association raised $460 million of the renovation cost by selling permanent seat licenses. However, when the actual cost of the coliseum rose to $130 million because the financial plan excluded a scoreboard, seat covers, and a field drainage system, the stadium renovation was $70 million in the red in the first year. In Quirk and Fort's view, "It would be optimistic to believe that most of the cost of the stadium renovation will not be paid out of increased taxes and reduced public services." In October 1998 the Oakland Athletics triggered a clause giving it a year-to-year lease at the coliseum, increasing the likelihood the club will be sold or moved. This occurred because the Oakland City Council failed to agree on a settlement of a $48 million suit the club filed against public officials from damages on the coliseum's renovation in 1995–1996.[19]

Besides owning Selig Executive Leasing Company and 25 percent of the Brewers, Bud Selig serves as the commissioner of Major League Baseball. To avoid a conflict of interest, Wendy Selig-Prieb replaced her father in operating the club. Former Oakland Athletics infielder Sal Bando will continue as general manager and Phil Garner as manager. The Brewers will play in $250 million, 43,000-seat Miller Park in 2000.[20]

The Milwaukee Brewers with an estimated worth of $127 million (ranked twenty-fourth in MLB), and the Kansas City Royals, valued at $108 million (ranked twenty-eighth in MLB), represent two low-valued franchises in 1998 as reported in *Forbes*. The two highest valued AL franchises in 1998 were the New York Yankees at $362 million and the Baltimore Orioles at $323 million.[21] From 1993 to 1998 the value of the Yankees and Orioles increased over 118 percent, while that of the Brewers and Royals rose by 32 percent and 15 percent, respectively.

The team's past performance and home attendance helped determine these changes in franchise values. Table 3.3 shows, for example, that the Yankees' team performance dominated the AL between 1993 and 1997, while the Orioles drew capacity attendance from 1992 to 1997. Interestingly, even though the Yankees had the best win-loss record, the Orioles had the highest home attendance over the six years of the survey. Undoubtedly, the Orioles' fan base extends to the Washington D.C., area, giving the team a boost in home attendance. Meanwhile, dismal team performance and low home attendance partially account for the decline in the value of the Brewers. Likewise located in a small city, the Royals ranked at or near the AL's top 50 percent in team performance from 1993 to 1995, but placed in the league's lower half for attendance throughout the period. With insufficient home attendance and operating income, it seems likely that the Brewers and Royals will appreciate little in value. Mind-

Table 3.3
AL Franchises, Performance, and Attendance, 1992 to 1997

	Performance						Attendance					
Franchise	1992	1993	1994	1995	1996	1997	1992	1993	1994	1995	1996	1997
New York	.469	.543	.619	.549	.568	.593	1.7	2.4	1.7	1.7	2.3	2.6
Baltimore	.549	.525	.563	.493	.543	.605	3.5	3.6	2.5	3.1	3.6	3.7
Milwaukee	.568	.426	.461	.451	.494	.484	1.8	1.6	1.2	1.1	1.3	1.4
Kansas City	.444	.519	.557	.486	.466	.416	1.8	1.9	1.4	1.2	1.4	1.5

Note: Performance is the final mean win-loss percentage of a team in the AL for the years listed. Attendance is the team's home game attendance in millions for the same period.

Source: *The World Almanac and Book of Facts*, 1993–1997; Memo received from the AL of Professional Baseball Clubs (New York 1997), 1–5.

ful of this, the Royals, Twins, and Athletics appear destined to depart from their current sites in the next several years. If sold to local proprietors, the Royals will probably remain in Missouri as a condition of sale mandated by the current owners, the Greater Kansas City Community Foundation. The succession plan for the club was established by Ewing Kauffman prior to his death in 1993.[22]

Between 1992 and 1997 the mean winning percentage and home attendance of the Pirates and Padres fell below that of the St. Louis Cardinals and Cincinnati Reds, both small-city NL teams. During the same period in the AL, the winning record and attendance of the Cleveland Indians, another small city club, exceeded the Royals, Twins, and Athletics. Interestingly, one large-market team, the Detroit Tigers, played worse and drew fewer fans, on average, than the Brewers and Royals.

As suggested above two NL franchises, Pittsburgh and San Diego, and three AL franchises, Kansas City, Minnesota, and Oakland, should relocate from their current sites. Due to several demographic and team-specific factors, the value of these five franchises should remain constant or increase marginally. As their value stagnates, the teams should generate insufficient revenues for hiring the talented players necessary to compete successfully in organized ball.

Along with below average home attendance, the road attendance of the five franchises has faired poorly. When teams are ranked according to road attendance respectively for the 1995 and 1996 seasons, Pittsburgh placed eleventh and fourteenth, San Diego placed thirteenth and sixth, Kansas City placed twelfth and ninth, Minnesota placed fourteenth and thirteenth, and Oakland placed ninth and eighth. Prospects for a turnaround for any of these teams failed to materialize by 1996, since each of these franchises ranked in the bottom third of the league in value and for the future remained moderate to high risk investments. Even though the teams played competitively in 1997, the Pirates ranked twelfth and the Padres seventh in home attendance at the season's end. In the AL, only the Tigers ranked lower in home attendance, and the Mariners and Rangers in road attendance, than the Royals, Brewers, Twins, and Athletics.

As of 1998, it appears that one in five MLB franchises has a bleak economic future. MLB, moreover, needs effective proposals to resolve the issue of inequality in team performance, attendance, and revenues between large, medium, and small-city franchises. In principle, we favor a market solution to remedy the dilemma with each owner deciding when and where to relocate. Such a scenario assumes that the league will approve any relocation that increases the profits of the league. The freedom of proprietors to exit a site, the choice to share revenue among teams in the league, and utilization of a competitive labor market for players represent key components of this principle.

Interleague play, which was introduced for the 1997 season, increased gate attendance at each MLB site. Initially, 38 percent more fans attended games featuring interleague competition.[23] For instance, a three-game series between the Royals and the Pirates drew over 108,000 fans. Still, the largest attendance increases occurred at Atlanta, Chicago, and New York—that is, the big-city teams. In our view, the novelty of interleague play will wear thin and fail to produce a long-run panacea for the inequality that exists between financially weak and strong franchises. The leagues need a better long-term solution to the problem.

MLB has considered realigning the NL and AL along geographic lines as a way of increasing gate attendance and television ratings. One plan proposes two fifteen-team leagues, with each league containing three divisions, comprising five teams per division. A second proposal calls for a sixteen- and fourteen-team league, with each league consisting of two or more divisions. The Major League Baseball Players Association and baseball traditionalists adamantly oppose realignment. They fear that realignment would blur the historic lines between the NL and AL and that realignment would detach baseball fans from their long-standing support of, and identification with, a particular home team.[24]

In December 1996, MLB adopted a luxury fee that required the thirteen wealthiest teams to redistribute over $5.3 million to each of the thirteen poorest teams in the 1997 season. In addition, the players agreed to contribute 2.5 percent of their annual salary to a revenue sharing pool. For the marginal NL and AL clubs identified above as candidates for relocation, the five teams would realize an approximate annual percentage increase in revenues of 22 percent for the Pirates, 19 percent for the Padres, 17 percent for the Twins, 15 percent for the Royals, and 13 percent for the Athletics.[25]

In the meantime, we advise against any major-league team relocating to Chicago, Los Angeles, New York, or Washington. It seems unlikely that these four cities could, or would, support another MLB franchise. In 1991, Buffalo, Charlotte, Columbus, Greensboro, Hartford, Indianapolis, Memphis, Nashville, New Orleans, Norfolk, Orlando, Portland, Providence, Rochester, Sacramento, Salt Lake City, and San Antonio, each had a metropolitan population in excess of one million and lacked a MLB franchise. These seventeen cities would likely welcome a major-league team. If these American sites seem unappealing to MLB, then the leagues should consider foreign cities such as Tokyo or Mexico City. Locating a franchise in Mexico's capital would be a bold and innovative move by organized baseball to initiate an international strategy of developing emerging baseball markets beyond the United States and Canada.

In 1996 MLB planned other innovations to boost revenues such as forming partnerships with brand-name companies, building an international strategy, implementing programs that appeal to minority groups, and marketing the league's film division. In 1997, the Chicago Cubs introduced a Beanie Baby giveaway. Beloved by children, and held as a collector item by adults, the "stuffed critters" have become a powerful tool for teams trying to attract younger fans. Even with these ploys, the inequalities in team playing strengths between large- and small-market teams will persist. The league should consider other measures for addressing this matter, such as easing rules that restrict owners from moving their clubs to higher-valued sites.[26]

If local citizens refuse to subsidize a MLB team with public money, fans should expect to pay higher prices for game tickets, team merchandise, and for food and beverages at the venue. Perhaps a franchise owner will demand a new ballpark with amenities. This may require the public's approval of a bond referendum and a local tax increase to share in the financing of the venue. To be sure, the Brewers, Mariners, and Pirates have new facilities under construction that will increase the revenues and value of their franchises, as well as provide an opportunity for the three teams to compete better in the next three to five years. Still, it will take a generation to retire the public debt that subsidized the construction of these new facilities. Unless the long-term stadium leases prevent the teams from moving within two decades, the Brewers, Expos, Mariners, Padres, Pirates, and Padres may be playing elsewhere in different home cities.

From 1975 to 1996 MLB realized annual operating profits only during the years 1987 to 1993. Between 1993 and 1996 MLB's operating losses totaled $839 million and the league averaged $2 million in operating income in 1997.[27] So for the last quarter century, MLB has become an increasingly high cost, risky, and unprofitable industry. This is especially true for individual franchise owners in the smaller and medium-sized markets. With operating expenses rising faster than operating revenues, teams must seek other sources of financing. In addition to corporate money one option is public ownership, that is, the sale of stock to investors in the financial markets. Such sales would provide additional revenues for the controlling owners to finance team operations and to hire skilled players. Also, this financial scheme would allow fans in the smaller markets to invest in their hometown team and share the risk of owning a franchise.[28]

PROFESSIONAL FOOTBALL

National Football League

In 1976 Wayne Valley, a limited partner of the Oakland Raiders, sold his shares to the team, at an unknown price, with Al Davis, the managing general partner maintaining control of the franchise. After a federal district court jury ruled against the NFL on an antitrust count and bad faith charges, Davis moved the team to Los Angeles in 1982. On 2 November 1982, after a fifty-seven-day strike by NFL players, the Raiders beat the San Diego Chargers, 28–24, in the Raiders' first home game in Los Angeles. The next season the Raiders won the AFC Championship and defeated the heavily favored Washington Redskins, 38–9, in the Super Bowl. After the Raiders finished second in the Western Division and sixth in the AFC in the 1994 season, Al Davis returned the team to Oakland and drew crowds below the league average. Davis, with a net worth estimated at $60 million in 1993, owned about 30 percent of the team to complement his various real estate holdings.[29]

The Baltimore Colts drew less than forty thousand people in 75 percent of their home games in 1983. Given the court's ruling in the Oakland Raiders case, and due to weak home game attendance, owner Bob Irsay moved the Colts to Indianapolis in 1984. Worried that Baltimore would condemn his property, Irsay packed the team's equipment in the middle of the night and departed the city.[30]

Phoenix tried to lure the Eagles from Philadelphia in 1984 with a sweetheart deal that included an array of economic incentives. But after local, state, and federal government pressure, and the threat of a lawsuit by Philadelphia interests, the Arizona city withdrew its proposal to the Eagles. Four years later, and sixteen years after buying his brother's 45 percent interest in the St. Louis Cardinals for $6.5 million, Bill Bidwell moved the team to Phoenix. The NFL had arrived in the Southwest. Bidwell has remained majority owner of the franchise in Phoenix, and in 1994 he changed the team's name from the Phoenix to the Arizona Cardinals.[31]

Besides the Raiders, the Rams also had little success in Los Angeles. In 1988, for example, the attendance at home games for the Rams was 55,000 per game (in a coliseum that seated 100,000) when the team finished in a first-place tie in the Western Division of the NFC but lost 28–17 to the Minnesota Vikings in a wild card playoff. By 1995, Georgia Frontiere, who inherited the team from her late husband, Carroll Rosenblum, in 1979, decided to move the Rams. After finishing twenty-third in the NFL in 1993 at .313, and twenty-fifth at .250 in 1994, and with attendance averaging a mere 50,000 per game, the Rams moved to St. Louis in 1995. The move proved to be a wise choice for the team. Playing in the TWA Dome and in a new city, the media and stadium revenues of the Rams significantly increased in St. Louis. Even with the dome's 113 luxury boxes and 6,500 club seats, and $1 million per year from naming rights, the Rams are allowed to move from St. Louis after ten years if the stadium does not remain among the most lavish in football. In retrospect, a combination of poor team performance, weak home attendance, and a more lucrative television contract and stadium deal, were key factors in the Rams and Raiders leaving Los Angeles. In 1994, for example, the media revenues of the Rams and Raiders averaged $39 million in Los Angeles. One year later these revenues increased to $41 million, then to $44 million in 1996 in St. Louis and Oakland, respectively. So as of 1999, the second and fifth largest cities in the United States lack an NFL franchise. In a January 1998 survey of Southern Californians, almost 60 percent said having a pro football team was unimportant, and 66 percent opposed using public funds to build the new stadium the league says it will require before returning. That notwithstanding, because of stadium opportunities in Los Angeles and the size of the television market, the California city should have an NFL team in the near future.[32]

The Cleveland Browns began play in 1946 in the All-American Football Conference (AAFC). Between 1946 and 1949 the team won four AAFC titles. After the AAFC and NFL merged in December 1949, the club dominated the NFL beginning in 1950. From 1950 to 1965 the Browns won nine league championships led by all-pro quarterback Otto Graham and fullback Jim Brown. In

1961 a syndicate headed by Art Modell, a former television and advertising executive, acquired the club for $4.5 million. Modell contributed $250,000 of his own money for the franchise. Between 1966 and 1995 the team won four Central Division titles but no AFC Championships. So the Browns failed to appear in a Super Bowl. By the 1990s Modell owned 52 percent of the club.[33]

Although attendance at Cleveland's Municipal Stadium exceeded seventy thousand per season from 1986 to 1994, and despite a $175 million commitment from the city to upgrade its stadium, in 1996 Modell moved the team to Baltimore and renamed it the Ravens. After playing two seasons at Memorial Stadium, the team began the 1998 season in 68,400-seat Ravens Stadium, an open-air, natural grass facility in Camden Yards, a warehouse district near Baltimore's revitalized business district and Inner Harbor tourist attractions. Besides the two biggest scoreboards in the NFL, the stadium has 7,900 club seats and 108 suites, and neither pillars nor columns obstruct views of the field. Club seats quickly sold out in 1998, leaving fans who wished to see a Ravens' game live the option of buying seat licenses, which start at $250. The licenses require the purchase of season tickets. These tickets cost between $20 and $60 per game.[34]

After analyzing the economics of the sports facilities at Camden Yards, Bruce W. Hamilton and Peter Kahn conclude, "With respect to football in Baltimore, . . . in terms of direct impact, the state and it[s] subdivisions lose approximately $13 million a year on the Ravens' stadium, depending on the amount of non-NFL activity generated at the new stadium, and on the fraction of such activity that would not have happened but for the stadium. And because the Ravens play many fewer games, the state has fewer opportunities to recoup tax revenue from out-of-state fans than the Orioles."[35]

In September 1998 NFL proprietors unanimously approved billionaire Alfred Lerner as the owner of the new Cleveland Browns. In doing so, the league handed him the job of restructuring one of its brand-name franchises. Lerner, who had assisted Art Modell in relocating the original Browns to Baltimore, paid $530 million for the expansion team, of which $54 million will go toward stadium costs. Claiming he "wants to produce the best football team for Cleveland," Lerner hired former FortyNiners president Carmen Policy to make the football decisions. Because of operating costs, the Browns will probably not generate excess economic returns for Lerner, a multibillionaire and the chief executive officer of MBNA Corporation and the chairman of Town and County Trust located in Baltimore. According to Terry Pluto, a columnist for the *Akron Beacon Journal*, "I really believe buying the Browns was a way for Al Lerner to get back his honor in the community." Apparently Lerner seeks the trust of Browns fans to promote his team and to compete for a division title. The price he paid significantly exceeded the previous record of $140 million for an expansion team established by Jacksonville and Carolina in 1993. By surpassing the $350 million that Rupert Murdoch spent for the Los Angeles Dodgers in 1998, Lerner has become the owner of the most expensive sports team in history.[36]

The expansion Browns will begin play in 1999 in a $280 million football-only facility constructed on the site where old Cleveland Stadium stood. Lerner should earn millions in revenue from luxury boxes, club seats, and the sale of fifty-two thousand personal seat licenses. The portion of money that the Browns will receive from the league's $17.6 billion television contract remains undetermined. Despite such lucrative sources for earnings, some experts doubt that the Browns will yield handsome returns considering its high start-up price. Richard Jacobs, owner of the Cleveland Indians, and Thomas Murdough, an Ohio toy manufacturer, both dropped out of the bidding war. They claimed that if the price went above $450 million, the club would realize little or no profit.[37] (Because of the Ravens' brief history, the relocation of Modell's team from Cleveland to Baltimore is excluded in the tables that follow.)

The history of ownership described above highlights the justification and impetus for the NFL's approval of an owner's request to relocate a team. Media attention and controversy surround such moves. Consider, for example, the relocation of the Colts from Baltimore to Indianapolis in 1984 and the Raiders from Oakland to Los Angeles in 1982. In hindsight, to stay in an area where the team is struggling and attendance is dwindling economically burdens other owners and results in a loss of status for the sport. So in the last analysis, all NFL moves between 1977 and 1995 were optimal decisions made by the franchise owners and in the long-term interest of the league. Yet without a franchise in Los Angeles since 1995 or in Houston since 1997, the NFL should approve an expansion at one of those cities.

Due to limited stadium capacity, most NFL teams sell out home games, making it difficult to determine how a franchise move affected attendance at the post-move site. In his article, "Attendance and Price Setting," Roger Noll proved that attendance in the current year, and the record of the team in the previous year, relate positively. Other factors Noll considered to influence attendance include the team's ticket prices, weather conditions (at stadiums without domes), number of competing professional teams, quality of players on the team, the size and racial composition of the city's population, and the per capita income in the metropolitan area.[38]

Of these moves, only the relocation of the Raiders from Los Angeles to Oakland seemed unjustified because of poor team performance (see Table 3.4). The majority of teams that moved had ranked in the lower half of the NFL in win-loss record at the pre-move site. Three clubs improved, and two did worse in average winning percentage at the post-move site. The Indianapolis Colts, Oakland Raiders, Phoenix Cardinals, and St. Louis Rams continued to lose the majority of their games at the post-move location. This raises two questions. First, what effect did the franchise relocation and the subsequent change, if any, in team performance have on home attendance at the post-move site? Second, did differences in population, per capita income, and population growth between the pre-move and post-move sites encourage the owners to move their franchises?

For each NFL franchise in our study we calculated the home site attendance in the final season (prior to its relocation) and in the year preceding the final season, along with the league attendance. As expected, home attendance declined for two moving franchises over the final seasons and averaged between 50 and 75 percent of the league's attendance (see Table 3.5). Of the five teams, the Raiders in 1980–1981 and 1993–1994, and the Rams in 1993–1994 had

Table 3.4
NFL Franchise Relocation and Performance for. Three-Year Pre-Move and Post-Move Intervals

Year	Franchise Move	Pre-Move Performance			Post-Move Performance		
1981–82	Oakland to Los Angeles	.563	.688	.438	.889	.750	.688
1983–84	Baltimore to Indianapolis	.125	.063	.438	.250	.313	.188
1987–88	St. Louis to Phoenix	.313	.281	.483	.438	.313	.313
1994–95	Los Angeles to St. Louis	.375	.313	.250	.438	.375	.313
1994–95	Los Angeles to Oakland	.438	.625	.563	.500	.437	.250

Note: Table entries are the team's final regular season win-loss percentages for three seasons prior to and following relocation. The table lists the Los Angeles Rams followed by the Raiders in 1994–1995.

Source: The World Almanac and Book of Facts, 1981–1996.

home attendance at or above 79 percent of the league average. With a large population to draw from in Southern California, the Raiders and Rams apparently managed to maintain parity in attendance with the league despite fan dissatisfaction with the demeanor and behavior of owners like Al Davis. In contrast, the attendance of the Cardinals plummeted by 30 percent in 1987, their final season in St. Louis. When it is known that a team is planning to move, attendance falls, so final season attendance is not an unbiased measure of fan support.

From 1990 to 1996, the NFL experienced little growth in attendance at games. Several reasons explain the low growth rates, including the glut of other professional teams at NFL sites, ineffective marketing campaigns, poor bonding with fans, a surplus of low-performing teams, and high ticket prices. Furthermore, if most teams are close to capacity, the only way that league attendance rises is through expansion. Through the first five weeks of the 1996 season, eighteen teams had fewer fans watching their home games than during a similar period in 1995. The attendance ranged from 40 percent below capacity in Houston to 1 percent below capacity in San Diego.

Escalating ticket prices may have contributed to lower attendance. NFL ticket prices averaged $36 in the 1996 season. At $25 a seat, the New York Jets offered the cheapest tickets in the league. Meanwhile, the New York Giants, who play in the same stadium as the Jets, set ticket prices on average at $35. Fan support was affected as the Jets realized a 6 percent increase, and the Giants a mere 1 percent increase, in home attendance for the 1995 season to the first five home games of the 1996 season. The Oakland Raiders charged the highest average ticket price at $51. The average NFL ticket price increased by 4.7 percent, or from $41 in 1997 to $43 in 1998. In that year the Washington Redskins charged the highest average ticket price at $74, up from $36 in 1996, and the Atlanta Falcons the lowest at $32. Thirteen clubs boosted their price from 1997 to 1998 with the Tampa Bay Buccaneers posting an 82 percent increase. League revenues from club seating rose by nearly 21 percent in 1998 as the average club seat price increased from $109 to $110 and twenty-five thousand additional seats became available in Baltimore and Tampa Bay.[39]

Table 3.5
NFL Franchise Home and League Attendance at the Pre-Move Site, by Year

Year	Franchise	Year Preceding Final Season		Final Season	
		Home	League	Home	League
1980–81	Oakland	392	480	384	480
1982–83	Baltimore	208	467	336	474
1986–87	St. Louis	280	485	203	407
1993–94	Los Angeles	393	496	392	500
1993–94	Los Angeles	392	496	416	500

Note: Unlike MLB and the NBA, the NFL provided only the league's regular season, post season, and total paid attendance (in hundreds of thousands) from 1934 to 1995. Home attendance was acquired from the team's *Media Guides.*

Source: The World Almanac and Book of Facts, 1980–1995; Memo from the NFL Public Relations Department (New York, 1997), 1; Quirk and Fort, *Pay Dirt*, 488–494.

To combat this trend in attendance, the Seahawks, Colts, and Broncos implemented new marketing approaches. One goal of these efforts was to inject excitement into game day with high-profile activities, more fan participation, and price discounts to boost attendance. Consistent winners like the FortyNiners, Cowboys, Bills, and Packers fill their stadiums to capacity with or without an intense marketing campaign. Mediocre teams such as the Saints and Buccaneers can no longer count on the capacity crowds they drew prior to 1990. These and other teams must now offset their weak performance with new marketing and promotional ploys.[40]

The size, composition, and wealth of the market in which the team is located affects a professional sports team's performance, home attendance, and profitability. In MLB, teams tended to move to areas with above average population growth and similar per capita income levels than at the pre-move site. This raises the question of whether NFL franchises relocate for reasons similar to moves in MLB. Also, do demographic and economic differences exist between the pre-move and post-move sites in the NFL?

Table 3.6 reveals how these characteristics vary at the NFL sites. Data in the table indicate that the majority of NFL teams departed to some areas that had (a) a smaller population, (b) a lower rate of population growth, and (c) a moderately lower per capita income level than the areas at the pre-move sites. These results underscore that owners make rational decisions given the demographic and economic trends that they anticipate to occur across markets and the public's demand for professional football.

The period between the first and most recent NFL relocation covers forty-three years. In contrast, all MLB moves occurred within two decades. Because of a dynamic economy and changing demographic conditions, any observations and inferences regarding NFL moves must be based on individual franchises. The population, per capita income, as well as percentage growth data in Table 3.6, therefore, provide insight concerning how to evaluate the quality of a site from the perspective of a professional sports owner.

Table 3.6
NFL Franchise Relocation and Area Demographic Data, by Site, by Year

Year	Franchise Move	Pre-Move Site			Post-Move Site		
		Pop	Income	%Growth	Pop	Income	%Growth
1981–82	Oakland to LA	2.7	13,431	16.5	5.9	12,376	26.4
1983–84	Baltimore to Indianapolis	3.0	12,254	8.3	1.3	12,458	7.1
1987–88	St. Louis to Phoenix	2.4	16,176	2.8	2.1	15,279	40.6
1994–95	LA to St. Louis	7.7	21,661	5.3	2.5	20,671	1.8
1994–95	LA to Oakland	7.7	21,661	5.3	3.2	29,179	4.2

Note: We divided the total population in these Metropolitan Statistical Areas (MSAs) by the number of teams in the same sport to determine the population per franchise (Pop) per year. We used statistical interpolation to calculate population between the census years. Population is in millions. Income is the per capita personal income in thousands of dollars in the MSAs. The percentage growth of the MSAs' population during the decade the relocation occurred is represented by %Growth.

Source: U.S. Department of Commerce, Economics and Statistics Administration, *County and City Data Books* (Washington, D.C., Government Printing Office, 1980–1995); U.S. Department of Commerce, Bureau of Economic Analysis, *Survey of Current Business* (Washington, D.C., 1980– 1995); *World Almanac and Book of Facts*, 1998; U.S. Department of Commerce, Bureau of the Census, *Statistical Abstract of the United States* (Washington, D.C., 1992).

So far we have analyzed the performance, attendance, total population, population growth and the per capita income of NFL franchises that have relocated since 1950. Another matter that relates to relocation decisions is the number of professional sports teams at a site. Since the football season overlaps the baseball, basketball, and hockey seasons, NFL owners have an incentive to choose areas that lack other professional teams. In MLB, the pre-move sites generally contained more professional teams than the post-move sites. This raises the question: Did NFL clubs relocate to sites where other professional teams existed?

According to Table 3.7, eleven other professional sports teams (excluding hockey) existed at the pre-move sites and eight at the post-move sites. Only the moves by the Raiders in 1982 and 1995 involved another NFL team at the pre-move and post-move sites. With no NFL club situated in the Los Angeles area, it seems likely that Al Davis will probably consider moving his franchise to that area at the earliest opportunity. Touted as the "Team of the Decades," the Raiders' have performed impressively. Besides winning 65 percent of their games from 1963 to 1995 (which is the top professional sports win-loss record), and winning 62 percent of games played between 1960 and 1995 (which is the best among NFL teams), the Raiders had a winning percentage of 71 percent for Monday night games from 1970 to 1995, also the best in the league. Between 1979 and 1981 the Raiders' home attendance averaged 407,000 per season. After the NFL players strike in the 1982 season, the Raiders averaged 472,000 per season from 1983 to 1994 in Los Angeles. At the same time, the team's away-game attendance exceeded 500,000 per season from 1983 to 1994. In 1995, over 423,000 fans attended the Raiders' eight home games at the Oakland-Alameda County Coliseum.[41]

Table 3.7
NFL Franchise Relocation and Intersport Competitors, by Site, by Year

Year	Franchise Move	Pre-Move Site			Post-Move Site		
		MLB	NFL/AFL	NBA/ABA	MLB	NFL/AFL	NBA/ABA
1981–82	Oakland to LA	1	1	0	1	1	1
1983–84	Baltimore to Ind	1	1	0	0	0	1
1987–88	St. Louis to Phoenix	1	0	0	0	0	1
1994–95	Los Angeles to SL	2	1	2	1	0	0
1994–95	LA to Oakland	2	1	2	2	1	1

Note: The table contains the number of professional baseball, football, and basketball teams located at the Pre-Move and Post-Move Sites for the years listed.

Source: The World Almanac and Book of Facts, 1981–1996.

As the new millennium approaches the Oakland area has a smaller population, higher per capita income level, as well as lower population growth than the Los Angeles area. Still, with fewer professional sports teams in the region, Davis may want to keep his team in Oakland. To express his community's dismay with losing the Raiders, in 1984 Mayor Lionel J. Wilson of Oakland said, "Oakland needs the pride and identity it gets from the Raiders and, in return, we have taken the team into our hearts. It is difficult for me to convey the sense of abandonment, of loss, and yes, of outrage with which East Bay residents greeted the Raiders' announcement that they were leaving Oakland for Southern California merely because a larger California community had offered them a candy store of supposed financial goodies."[42] If the Raiders can improve their team performance, then home attendance should rise above 500,000 in Oakland. Davis may assess his franchise's economic performance after the 1998 season and then decide if Los Angeles or elsewhere offers an optimal site for the Raiders. But with the lease of Oakland Alameda Coliseum valid until 2010, the Raiders are contractually committed to play in the Bay Area unless escape clauses exist in the lease that would free the team to move.

According to Michael Ozanian, in 1998 the three highest valued teams in the NFL were the Dallas Cowboys at $413 million, the Washington Redskins at $403 million, and the Carolina Panthers at $365 million. The Indianapolis Colts at $227 million, the Arizona Cardinals at $231 million, and the Atlanta Falcons at $233 million, represented the three lowest valued teams in the league. Of the 113 professional sports teams listed by Ozanian, the Cowboys ranked first and the Colts forty-third in estimated market value. Since 1993, the valuations of these teams have appreciated as follows: Cowboys 117 percent, Redskins 155 percent, Colts 60 percent, Cardinals 58 percent, and the Falcons 57 percent. The other NFL teams that ranked in the bottom 20 percent in value were the Minnesota Vikings at $233 million, the Oakland Raiders at $235 million, and the Chicago Bears at $237 million. To be sure, in 1997 *Financial World* ranked the Broncos twenty-sixth in the league at $182 million and at high risk. Perhaps aroused by such figures, the Broncos went on to win the AFC title and Super Bowl after the 1997 season. As a result, in 1998 the Broncos value rose by 76 percent to $320 million, placing the franchise tenth in the league.[43]

The six low-valued NFL teams remain high-risk business enterprises, that is, a majority of these teams will probably generate insufficient revenues to compete with other NFL clubs over the next few years. An analysis of these teams reveals an array of financial deficiencies. Along with below-average gate receipts, each team earned inadequate venue revenues and insufficient operating income. Since 1990 a majority of the six low-rated franchises lost more games than they won thus undermining their support from fans.[44]

Table 3.8 measures the mean performance and attendance during various seasons for the five NFL teams that relocated between 1977 and 1997. Did the mean performance and attendance of the teams change after relocation? How do these changes compare with those of the relocated teams in MLB? To answer these questions we averaged the winning percentages and home attendance of the teams for three, six, and ten seasons following the team's moves.

According to Table 3.8, the Los Angeles Raiders had the highest, and the Phoenix Cardinals the lowest, winning percentages (performances) averaged over six and ten seasons dating from the relocation year. The most improved team over ten seasons was the Indianapolis Colts. The club improved its winning percentages by more than 48 percent, in the decade following relocation. The Los Angeles Raiders and Phoenix (now Arizona) Cardinals won fewer games and declined in performance as the seasons progressed. Yet, the Los Angeles Raiders achieved the highest average winning percentage of the relocated NFL teams.

During the fourth to sixth seasons following relocation, the Indianapolis Colts played better. In the three seasons played from 1987 to 1989, the Colts ranked seventh, twelfth, and fifteenth respectively in the NFL in winning percentage after finishing twenty-fourth, twenty-second, and twenty-seventh from 1984 to 1986, respectively. In contrast, the Raiders ranked first, second, and fifth, then second, fourteenth, and twenty-third in winning percentage in their first six seasons, that is from 1982 to 1987, respectively. Thus between the fourth and sixth seasons following relocation, one relocated NFL team improved and two played worse at their new sites.

During the seventh to tenth seasons following relocation, the Los Angeles Raiders and the Indianapolis Colts declined in performance, while the Phoenix Cardinals improved in performance. The Raiders finished at or below .500 twice in the seventh to tenth season in Los Angeles. The Colts faded after the sixth season, ranking fifteenth, twenty-eighth, twelfth, and twenty-sixth in winning percentage between 1990 and 1993, respectively. The Phoenix Cardinals, whose winning percentage peaked at .438 in the 1988 and 1993 seasons, won 50 percent of their games in the 1994 season and over 40 percent in the 1996 season. The recently relocated teams, the St. Louis Rams and Oakland Raiders, have continued playing poorly at their post-move sites. In retrospect, the Colts improved the most for NFL teams during the first decade following relocation.

Did the attendance of the relocated teams change at their new sites? The Indianapolis Colts had the highest and the Phoenix Cardinals had the lowest average attendance of the NFL franchises listed in Table 3.8. The Los Angeles

Table 3.8
NFL Relocated Franchises, Performance and Attendance for Selected Seasons

Franchise	Three Seasons		Six Seasons		Ten Seasons	
	Performance	Attendance	Performance	Attendance	Performance	Attendance
Los Angeles	.775	355	.651	407	.622	423
Indianapolis	.250	465	.402	461	.372	444
Phoenix	.354	388	.333	361	.340	380
St. Louis	.375	497	–	–	–	–
Oakland	.395	412	–	–	–	–

Note: Performance and Attendance are, respectively, averages of the final percentage win-loss record and home attendance (in hundreds of thousands) of the team for three, six, and ten seasons following relocation.

Source: The World Almanac and Book of Facts, 1977–1997; Media Guides provided by the NFL and the teams.

Raiders increased their average attendance in the fourth to sixth season at the post-move site by 24 percent, 17 percent, and 15 percent, respectively. Meanwhile the Colts' average attendance fell by 1 percent, and the Cardinals' by 7 percent, in their fourth to sixth seasons respectively at home. After the sixth season only the average attendance of the Colts continued to decline. The Raiders attendance rose by 4 percent and the Cardinals by 5 percent in the seventh to tenth seasons.

The information in Table 3.8 reveals that winning teams in the NFL usually draw more fans to home games. The attendance of the Indianapolis Colts declined less than 5 percent whether the team played better or worse. In the seventh to tenth seasons, the performance of the Los Angeles Raiders declined, yet attendance increased. The Phoenix Cardinals played better and drew more fans in the fourth to sixth seasons following relocation, while the Colts played worse and drew fewer fans in the seventh to tenth seasons. In sum, the percentage changes in performance and attendance per season for the Cardinals, Colts, and Raiders proved minor for the years studied at the post-move sites.

The Rams and Raiders continued to play at or under .500 in St. Louis and Oakland in their first three seasons following relocation. Even so, home attendance rose for both teams in the 1995 season. The Rams averaged 392,000 per season and the Raiders 404,000 per season in their final two seasons in Los Angeles. In the 1995 season, the first year at their post-move sites, the Rams drew 496,000 and the Raiders 424,000. Whether the Rams can sustain its growth in attendance at St. Louis in the future appears doubtful unless the team wins more games and competes for division and conference titles.[45]

The future of the Colts in Indianapolis remains uncertain. The team won 41 percent of its games between 1984 and 1996 and averaged only 446,000 in attendance per season. In 1997 the mayor of Indianapolis joined other local and regional corporate leaders to negotiate a new lease with the Colts owner Jim Irsay to increase the team's revenues from the RCA Dome. They agreed to allow the prices of luxury suites in the dome to rise from an average of $32 thousand to $80 thousand per season, and the franchise would offer thirty-five hundred club seats in the Dome for sale to corporate customers. In 1999 each club seat will sell for $990, an increase of 100 percent from 1997. Irsay claims that the funds are necessary for the Colts to compete in the league. Currently the team earns 50 percent of its revenues from the suites, or $1.6 million per season. At $80 thousand per suite, they should generate $4 million in incremental stadium revenues for the team to spend on operations. In 1996 the Colts ranked twenty-fourth with $22.4 million in gate receipts, twenty-ninth with $16.8 million in media revenues, twenty-first with $4.7 million in stadium revenues, and twenty-fourth with $114 million in franchise value among NFL teams. This indicates the financial distress of the team in Indianapolis.[46]

Other long-term problems hinder the Colts' ability to compete in the NFL. Indiana is corporate headquarters for only six Fortune 500 companies, and fewer than 2 percent of the households in the Indianapolis area earn more than $150 thousand in income. So, besides marketing luxury suites and club seats, the Colts should try expanding the fan base of the team throughout Indiana. Meanwhile, the stadiums of the other Eastern Division teams in the American Football Conference earn revenues from luxury suites and have capacities as follows: Buffalo Bills ($3.3 million, 80,024); Miami Dolphins ($21.5 million, 74,916); New England Patriots ($3.3 million, 60,292); and the New York Jets ($8.3, 78,024). Should the robust economy of the Indianapolis area and the state slow down, or the Colts continue to play mediocre football, the future revenue stream of the team will likely diminish. If so, it will further weaken the Colts' ability to compete in the league. Then the team's relocation to another city may be inevitable.[47]

Table 3.9 reports the sales price of a team in a given year and the changes in the value of the relocated NFL franchises that played in the 1998 season. The data underscore how lucrative the financial returns have been for the four NFL franchise owners over time. Moreover, the growth in the market value of these four teams has skyrocketed, particularly since the 1993 season. In 1997 the operating income of these four franchises varied between $400 thousand for the Indianapolis Colts to $17 million for the St. Louis Rams.[48] The enhanced value of the Rams and Raiders stems from the stadium amenities and the television and radio networks available in St. Louis and Oakland. If the Colts earn an additional $15 million in revenues from premium seats in the 1999 season, the

Table 3.9
NFL Relocated Franchises, Sales Prices and Market Values for Selected Years

Franchise	Sales Price	(Year)	Market Value		
			1993	1998	%Change
Indianapolis	19	(1972)	141	170	60
Phoenix	13	(1972)	146	186	58
St. Louis	7	(1962)	148	243	117
Oakland	7	(1962)	146	210	60

Note: Sales Price, Market Value and %Change were derived as in previous tables. Sales Price and Market Value are in millions of dollars for the designated years.

Source: Scott Fowler, "List Puts Panthers Among Most Valuable Pro Teams," 1A, 18A; Quirk and Fort, *Pay Dirt,* 409–434; Michael Ozanian, "Selective Accounting," 124–134.

team should rank among the top fifteen NFL teams in total revenues—up from a twenty-eighth ranking in 1997. With the league signing a new eight-year contract with the national television and cable networks for $17.6 billion, in 1999 each team will receive an estimated $75 million annually to operate and upgrade their franchises and offer higher salaries and perquisites to attract skilled players and talented coaches. We expect player salaries to escalate, forcing team owners to renovate their stadiums in order to earn more revenues and ensure greater profits.[49]

Given the above, the Cardinals and Colts appear as the most likely NFL teams destined to relocate in the next three to five years. With inadequate stadium revenues and insufficient income from home game attendance, it seems unlikely that these franchises will remain at their current sites. These teams need to increase cash flows from (1) local, regional, and national broadcasting, (2) concessions and parking, (3) the sale of merchandise, and (4) their stadiums. Otherwise the value of these franchises should continue to appreciate only marginally, or at worst, decline.

Mindful of this analysis, Columbus, Houston, Las Vegas, Los Angeles–Anaheim, Salt Lake City, and San Antonio represent the six optimum sites for a relocating NFL franchise to choose. Because of a $530 million expansion fee, however, the league would likely veto a relocation to Los Angeles–Anaheim. We established four criteria to evaluate each site's ability to support a team. Table 3.10 lists and ranks the sites based upon this criteria. The optimal sites ranked from first to last relative to the four criteria are Los Angeles–Anaheim, Houston and Las Vegas (tie), Columbus, San Antonio, and Salt Lake City. Other potential NFL sites omitted in the table, but with a population greater than one million in 1994 include Portland, Hartford, and San Jose.

Earlier we identified six financially unstable NFL teams. They seem destined to fail at their current locations. Considering their stadium leases, two of the teams should relocate as follows: Indianapolis, after 2014 when their lease

Table 3.10
Selected Characteristics of Potential NFL Sites, 1997

Site	Population	% Males	Income	Growth
LA-Anaheim	15.3	Above Average	Average	Average
Houston	4.1	Above Average	Average	Average
Las Vegas	1.1	Average	Average	Above Average
Columbus	1.4	Average	Average	Average
San Antonio	1.4	Average	Below Average	Average
Salt Lake City	1.2	Below Average	Below Average	Average

Note: In the MSA, Population is the total population in millions, the %Males is a ranking of the percent of males, Income is a ranking of the per capita personal income, and Growth is a ranking of the area's population growth rate.

Source: The World Almanac and Book of Facts, 1997; Ty Ahmad-Taylor, "Who Is Major Enough for the Major Leagues," *New York Times* (2 April 1995), 5.

expires on the RCA Dome, and Arizona after 2002 when their lease and renewal options expire on Sun Devil Stadium in Tempe.

For those teams looking to move, they should seriously consider Columbus, San Antonio, Salt Lake City, or Las Vegas. Despite attractive demographics, neither the Los Angeles–Anaheim nor Houston areas seem suitable sites in view of the league's decision to expand in Los Angeles, the recent departures of the Raiders to Oakland, the Rams to St. Louis, and the Oilers (now Titans) from Houston to Nashville.[50]

PROFESSIONAL BASKETBALL

National Basketball Association

After they traded the Boston Celtics to John Brown and Harry Mangurian and acquired the Buffalo Braves, Irving Levin and Harold Lipton moved the Braves to San Diego in 1978 and changed its name to the Clippers. From 1979 to 1984 the Clippers averaged 236,000 fans per season at home and finished sixth in the NBA between 1982 and 1984. Donald Sterling's syndicate, which purchased the team from Levin and Lipton for $13.5 million in 1981, moved it to Los Angeles in 1984. In Los Angeles, the Clippers improved in performance finishing fourth, third, and sixth in the seasons played between 1985 and 1987 respectively. The team, valued at $102 million in 1998 (ranked twenty-eighth in the league), plays in the 16,000-seat Los Angeles Sports Arena built in 1959 for $7 million.[51]

From 1975 to 1979 the New Orleans Jazz averaged 408,000 fans per season as superstar Pete Maravich set scoring records and baffled opponents with his ball-handling skills. However, after back-to-back fifth-place finishes, and finishing sixth in the NBA between 1977 and 1979, the Jazz's owners moved the team to Utah. The club retained its name and Sam Battistone assumed control of the franchise in Salt Lake City. Some owners and league officials questioned the strategy of taking a team named the Jazz into the staid atmosphere of Salt Lake City. In addition, some worried whether the club could win the affection of fans previously loyal to the ABA's Utah Stars. In any case, by the mid-1980s coach Tom Nissalke and general manager Frank Layden had reformed the Jazz into consistent winners. By replacing Pete Maravich with Adrian Dantley in 1979 and drafting a NCAA Player of the Year, Darrell Griffith, in 1980, the Jazz became a better team. Larry Miller, the current owner of the Jazz, also owns the Golden Eagles hockey team of the International League, the Delta Center, the television station KXIV, and nineteen automobile dealerships. Miller had a net worth estimated at $120 million in 1993.[52]

Due to pressure by activists who associated the team's name with inner city violence, in 1997 the Washington Bullets became the Wizards. Owner Abe Pollin made the decision as part of the team's antiviolence campaign and after reviewing a poll taken to select a new name for the club. The franchise also adopted a new logo and uniform as the team prepared to move from suburban Landover, Maryland, to the 20,000-seat, $200 million MCI Center in downtown Washington for the 1997–98 season. Pollin, the owner of the NHL's Washington Capitals and the MCI Center, doubled the average price of Wizard individual tickets to $75 in two seasons to pay for star players such as Juwan Howard and Chris Webber who together earned 50 percent of the team's $40 million annual payroll. With the second highest ticket prices in the NBA, and $7,500 for a club seat and $100,000 to $175,000 for an executive suite, Washington has become one of the most expensive sports entertainment cities in the nation.[53]

Tables 3.11 and 3.12 presents team-specific and demographic data about the relocated NBA teams at their pre-move and post-move sites. These numbers partially explain why the teams relocated. They also show the most and least important factors to the owner and league in deciding to move a franchise from a given city between 1978 and 1986.

In three seasons after relocating, the Clippers played better in Los Angeles (1985–1987) than in San Diego (1982–1984), and the Clippers and Kings played worse in San Diego (1982–1984) and Sacramento (1986–1988) than in Buffalo (1976–1978) and Kansas City (1983–1985), respectively (see Table 3.11). After trading Bob McAdoo in 1976, Adrian Dantley in 1977, and Nate Archibald in 1978, the Clippers fell in performance. But the team improved after acquiring Earl Cureton from Detroit in 1987, Gary Grant from Seattle in 1988, and Ron Harper from Cleveland in 1989. Meanwhile, the Jazz's average winning percentage fell by 23 percent in Salt Lake City (1980–1982) after relocating from New Orleans in 1979.

In Table 3.12, the population and per capita incomes in San Diego (1978–79) and Los Angeles exceeded the same for Buffalo and San Diego (1984–85). However, New Orleans and Kansas City had greater populations and households with higher per capita incomes than did Salt Lake City and Sacramento. Thus in the 1970s and 1980s, two teams moved to cities with smaller populations and lower per capita incomes. Additionally, two teams migrated to, and one within, California as the population and economy of the region grew.

When the teams moved, no NBA clubs existed in San Diego, Utah, and Sacramento. While organized baseball and NFL teams played in San Diego and Los Angeles, neither sport had a franchise in Utah. Therefore, intersport competition at the post-move sites influenced the decision by the team owners and

Table 3.11

NBA Franchise Relocation and Team Performance for Three-Year Pre-Move and Post-Move Intervals

Year	Franchise Move	Pre-Move Performance			Post-Move Performance		
1978–79	Buffalo to San Diego	.561	.366	.329	.524	.427	.439
1979–80	New Orleans to Utah	.427	.476	.317	.293	.341	.305
1984–85	San Diego to Los Angeles	.207	.305	.366	.378	.390	.146
1985–86	Kansas City to Sacramento	.549	.463	.378	.451	.354	.293

Note: Performance is the final regular season win-loss percentage of a team in the league in the three seasons prior to and following relocation.

Source: The World Almanac and Book of Facts, 1978–1987.

Table 3.12
NBA Franchise Relocation and Area Demographic Data, by Site, by Year

		Pre-Move Site			Post-Move Site		
Year	Franchise Move	%Growth	Pop	Income	%Growth	Pop	Income
1978–79	Buffalo to San Diego	– 7.9	1.3	7,763	37.1	1.8	8,908
1979–80	New Orleans to Utah	14.2	1.2	8,605	33.1	.9	8,354
1984–85	San Diego to Los Angeles	34.2	2.1	12,998	2.0	6.5	14,891
1985–86	Kansas City to Sacramento	1.2	1.4	14,188	34.7	1.3	13,130

Note: The %Growth is the MSA's percentage population growth during the decade of the relocation. Pop is the MSA's total population per team in millions. Income measures the per capita personal income in the MSA in thousands of dollars.

Source: The World Almanac and Book of Facts, 1978–1987; *County and City Data Books,* 1952,
1967, and 1972; *Census of Population,* 1970–1990; U.S. Department of Commerce, Bureau of
Economic Analysis, *Survey of Current Business,* May 1974.

league to relocate franchises between 1978 and 1986. From 1986 to 1997, the
nine NBA teams that had relocated since 1950 played in the following conferences and divisions: Philadelphia SeventySixers (Eastern, Atlantic); Detroit
Pistons and Atlanta Hawks (Eastern, Central); Utah Jazz and Houston Rockets
(Western, Midwest); and the Los Angeles Lakers, Los Angeles Clippers, Sacramento Kings, and Golden State (formerly San Francisco) Warriors (Western,
Pacific). How have these teams performed since 1985 when the latest relocated
franchise, the Sacramento Kings, began play in the NBA? Did the mean performance and attendance of the franchises increase in these seasons? How do
the results compare to those in previous seasons? Table 3.13 suggests answers to
these questions. The table lists the teams according to relocation year, beginning
with the Pistons in 1957 and ending with the Kings in 1984. The data in the table are grouped in three periods, four seasons in length, to detect any trends in
performance and attendance of the teams between 1986 and 1997.

The Los Angeles Lakers had the highest, and Los Angeles Clippers had the
lowest, mean winning percentage of the nine teams listed in Table 3.13. The
Golden State Warriors, Los Angeles Clippers, and Sacramento Kings had a
lower winning percentage than the nine-team average of .525 for the seasons
presented.

From 1986 to 1993, the mean performance of four teams increased and for
five teams decreased. The winning percentage fell by 9 percent for the Detroit
Pistons, by 18 percent for the Los Angeles Lakers, by 13 percent for the Philadelphia SeventySixers and Sacramento Kings, and by 21 percent for the Atlanta
Hawks. The Los Angeles Clippers improved the most (79 percent), playing at or
above .500 in 1992 and 1993. The Golden State Warriors and Utah Jazz increased their mean performance by 26 percent and 15 percent, respectively,
from 1986 to 1993. During these eight seasons (1986–1993) the average winning percentage of the nine teams decreased from .525 to .521, due primarily to
the deteriorating performances of the Atlanta Hawks and Los Angeles Lakers.
After the 1992–93 season, the performances of the Detroit Pistons, Philadelphia

Table 3.13
NBA Relocated Franchises, Performance and Attendance for Selected Seasons

Franchise	1986–1989 Seasons		1990–1993 Seasons		1994–1997 Seasons	
	Performance	Attendance	Performance	Attendance	Performance	Attendance
Detroit	.655	887	.600	879	.451	769
Los Angeles	.750	700	.618	685	.579	620
Golden State	.411	469	.518	616	.433	617
Philadelphia	.552	543	.481	574	.271	533
Atlanta	.637	538	.502	526	.612	533
Houston	.561	656	.579	602	.640	650
Utah	.561	495	.643	663	.707	812
Los Angeles	.249	367	.447	510	.332	431
Sacramento	.356	486	.309	700	.427	709

Note: Performance and Attendance are the mean winning percentage and home attendance (in hundreds of thousands) of the teams for the three grouped seasons. The Los Angeles Lakers, then the Los Angeles Clippers, are listed in the table.

Source: The World Almanac and Book of Facts, 1987–1997; NBA Public Relations Department, 1997; *Media Guides* of the teams.

SeventySixers, and Los Angeles Lakers continued to decline. Meanwhile, the play of the Golden State Warriors, which had improved in the previous four seasons, also worsened between 1994 and 1997. Regarding the four teams that improved after 1993, between 1995 and 1997 the Sacramento Kings finished above .400, a winning percentage last achieved by the franchise in 1986.

So from 1986 to 1993, the mean performance of the Detroit Pistons, Los Angeles Lakers, and Philadelphia SeventySixers declined, while the average performance of the Houston Rockets and Utah Jazz rose. The play of the Atlanta Hawks and Los Angeles Clippers varied more than the other seven teams. The Hawks' performance fell from .634 in 1989 to .463 in 1992 due to player injuries, trades, and retirements. In the meantime, the Los Angeles Clippers finished below .205 in the 1987 through 1989 seasons and above .500 in the 1992 and 1993 seasons as a result of trading veteran players like Cedric "Cornbread" Maxwell in 1987 and Michael Cage in 1988, and acquiring talented players such as Olden Polynice and Glen Rivers in 1991 and Mark Jackson and Stanley Roberts in 1992.[54]

Despite the improved play of the Atlanta Hawks, Houston Rockets, Utah Jazz, and Sacramento Kings, the mean winning percentage of the nine teams in Table 3.13 declined from .521 to .494 between 1990 and 1997. The winning percentage of the Philadelphia SeventySixers, Los Angeles Clippers, and Detroit Pistons fell by more than 25 percent. The SeventySixers experienced their worst seasons in recent history from 1994 to 1997. The club's difficulties seemed insurmountable. It won less than twenty-seven games each season from 1993 to 1996. The team traded Charles Barkley, their leading player in points scored and rebounds, after the 1991–92 season. The club placed no players on the all-star squad in 1993, 1994, and 1996. The franchise terminated head coach John Lucas's contract after he compiled a 42–122 record over two seasons. Owner Harold Katz sold the SeventySixers to Comcast Corporation and to Pat Croce, who became the president of the organization in March, 1996. In contrast to the underachievement of the Seventy- sixers, the average performance of the Atlanta Hawks rose by 22 percent, and the Houston Rockets and Utah Jazz by 10 percent, from 1990 to 1997.[55]

In the 1993–94 and 1996–97 seasons the Atlanta Hawks won more than 60 percent of their games. The sixty-nine victories in the 1993–94 season are attributed to coach Lenny Wilkens and the skilled play of NBA All-Stars Dominque Wilkins and Mookie Blaylock. Acquiring high-caliber players like Christian Laettner, Steve Smith, and Dikembe Mutumbo boosted the Hawks to a second-place finish in the Central Division for the 1996–97 season, highlighted by a 36–5 home court record, the third best in the league after the Chicago Bulls (39–2) and the Utah Jazz (38–3).[56]

From 1986 to 1997, the Los Angeles Lakers won 65 percent of their games while the Los Angeles Clippers and Sacramento Kings won 34 and 36 percent of their games, respectively. The other teams' mean winning percentage in these seasons were the Utah Jazz at .637, Detroit Pistons at .568, Houston Rockets at .593, Atlanta Hawks at .583, Golden State Warriors at .454, and Philadelphia SeventySixers at .434. As a group the nine teams' mean winning percentage was .513 during the seasons played between 1986 and 1997, which was marginally above the league average of .500. Collectively the mean performance of the relocated NBA teams was relatively stable in the twelve seasons studied.

What was the mean attendance of the relocated teams at their post-move sites? From 1986 to 1989, the nine relocated teams averaged 571,000 fans per season in their home arenas (see Table 3.13). The Detroit Piston, Los Angeles Lakers, and Houston Rockets had the highest, and the Los Angeles Clippers, Golden State Warriors, and Sacramento Kings had the lowest, average attendance of the relocated franchises. What is more, the mean attendance of the Pistons, Lakers, and Rockets exceeded the league average of 544,000 fans per season from 1986 to 1989.

Comparing the 1985–86 season to the 1988–89 season, the attendance of the Atlanta Hawks and Sacramento Kings increased over 59 percent, while that of the Los Angeles Lakers, Philadelphia SeventySixers, and Utah Jazz increased by less than 10 percent. Between 1986 and 1989 the Pistons respectively drew 695,000, 908,000, 1,066,000 and 879,000 fans to games. These numbers represent the highest attendance of the nine relocated teams in those seasons. The attendance of the Sacramento Kings increased by 254,000 people, or 60 percent, from 1988 to 1989 despite the Kings winning less than 33 percent of their games. Meanwhile, the attendance of the Warriors, Hawks, and Jazz increased each season during this period.

The Pistons, Lakers, Hawks, and Rockets drew less fans to their home games in 1990 to 1993 than in 1986 to 1989. Excluding the Rockets, the mean winning percentage of the Pistons, Lakers, and Hawks also had declined from 1986 to 1993. Concurrently, as the Golden State Warriors, Utah Jazz, and Los Angeles Clippers won more games, and the Philadelphia SeventySixers and Sacramento Kings won less games, each team attracted more fans to home games from 1986 to 1993. Averaging the eight seasons played from 1986 to

1993, attendance increased from 549,000 to 642,00 fans or 18 percent, for the league, and from 571,000 to 639,000 fans or 12 percent, for the nine relocated teams. These differences in attendance occurred largely because of the drawing power of established teams like the Chicago Bulls, Cleveland Cavaliers, and New York Knicks, and expansion teams like the Charlotte Hornets and Orlando Magic.

In the seasons played between 1994 and 1997, the mean attendance of the Jazz, Pistons, and Kings exceeded 700,000 per season, and less than 535,000 per season for the Hawks, Clippers, and SeventySixers. From 1990–1993 to 1994–1997, the mean attendance increased for five relocated teams and declined for four teams. Since their average winning percentage dropped, the Pistons, Lakers, Clippers, and SeventySixers drew fewer fans to their arenas in the mid-1990s than in the early 1990s.

The mean seasonal attendance of the Hawks, Rockets, Kings, and Jazz increased between 1990 and 1997, along with the mean performance of the teams. In contrast, the average attendance of the Golden State Warriors increased slightly during the same period, but the average performance of the club declined from .518 to .433. Despite inconsistent seasonal performances, the Warriors and Kings played before capacity crowds from 1989 to 1997. In total, the mean attendance of the nine relocated teams stood at 630,000 per season, or 59,000 fewer fans per season than the mean attendance of the league between 1994 and 1997.

From 1986 to 1997 the Lakers and Jazz won more than 63 percent of their games, while the Clippers, Kings, SeventySixers, and Warriors won less than 50 percent of their games. The low and high winning percentages of each relocated team from 1986 to 1997 were: Detroit Pistons (.244–.768), Los Angeles Lakers (.402–.793), Golden State Warriors (.244–.671), Philadelphia SeventySixers (.220–.659), Atlanta Hawks (.463–.695), Houston Rockets (.512–.707), Utah Jazz (.512–.780), Los Angeles Clippers (.146–.548), and the Sacramento Kings (.280–.476). In sum, the lowest winning percentage of the Lakers, Rockets, and Jazz never fell below .402, reflecting the superior players and coaches employed by these teams.

The mean winning percentage of the Pistons, Lakers, and SeventySixers fell, while that of the Rockets and Jazz rose throughout the twelve seasons. The average winning percentage of the Warriors and Clippers increased between 1986 and 1993, then decreased between 1994 and 1997. Moreover, the Kings won fewer games between 1990 and 1993, and more games between 1994 and 1997, than during the seasons played between 1986 and 1989. To improve their future performance, the Kings hired Rick Adelman as the nineteenth head coach in the franchise's fifty-year history. Between 1988 and 1997 Adelman posted a 357–252 record while coaching the Portland Trail Blazers and Golden State Warriors. He ranks thirteenth in the league, winning over 58 percent of his games as a head coach. "I'm excited to be in Sacramento," said Adelman, and "I look forward to the challenge that lies ahead." Candidates eliminated for the position were Charlotte Hornets assistant coach Paul Silas, former Laker forward Kurt Rambis, and assistant coaches Scott Skiles of the Phoenix Suns and Rick Carlisle of the Indiana Pacers.[57]

Unless they perform better in the next three to five years, the Golden State Warriors or Sacramento Kings, and the Los Angeles Clippers should relocate for the good of the league. In the long-run, fans in northern California will not support two weak NBA franchises. The prospect of the Warriors and Kings improving in their performance and increasing their attendance in the future seems unlikely given the competitiveness of the other teams in the league. In Los Angeles the play of the Lakers makes headlines in the daily sports pages and they dominate the Clippers at the gate. Thus, the Warriors or Kings, and the Clippers could enhance their survival as franchises and strengthen themselves economically by relocating to a city such as Baltimore, St. Louis, or Pittsburgh, where no NBA team currently exists. These cities were sites of former NBA or ABA teams and have populations above two million.

Forbes reported that the three highest-valued NBA franchises in 1998 were the Chicago Bulls at $303 million, New York Knicks at $296 million, and the Los Angeles Lakers at $268 million. Of 113 professional sports franchises surveyed in the report, the Milwaukee Bucks at $94 million, the Los Angeles Clippers at $102 million, and the Denver Nuggets at $110 million had the lowest estimated value of NBA teams. The same report placed the value of the Dallas Mavericks, the Sacramento Kings, and the Minnesota Timberwolves each at under $120 million.[58] Whether these last six teams can continue to exist at their current sites and remain competitive over the next three to five years is open to debate. To examine this question we analyzed an array of economic, demographic, and team-specific data and report the results in Table 3.14.

As evident in Table 3.14, the relocation of the Los Angeles Clippers and perhaps the Dallas Mavericks and Milwaukee Bucks appears inevitable given the financial outlook of these franchises. In the 1997–98 season, each team's total revenues and operating income were between 50 and 80 percent of the league average ($64.6 million and $6.6 million). Sites for these franchises to relocate to and worthy of a look include St. Louis, Cincinnati, Memphis, and San Diego. The other franchises listed in Table 3.14 are either superior in performance (Denver), will be playing in a new venue (Denver), are located in a relatively large market (Minnesota), or have significantly appreciated in value (Denver, Minnesota, and Sacramento). Thus these clubs possess little inclination toward relocating.

Five NFL and four NBA teams moved after 1976. The post-move areas of the relocated NFL clubs in the majority had smaller populations, higher population growth rates, and households with lower per capita incomes than in the pre-move areas (see Table 3.6). Also, fewer organized baseball and NBA teams existed in the post-move areas. The Raiders played better in Los Angeles than in Oakland, while the team performances of the Cardinals, Colts, and Rams remained poor in Phoenix, Indianapolis, and St. Louis, respectively. However, the value of each relocated NFL team appreciated between 1993 and 1997, even when their performance and attendance fell. For most relocated NBA teams, the pre-move and post-move areas had similar populations and per capita incomes.

Table 3.14
NBA Franchises and Selected Data

Franchise	%Value	Risk	Performance	Attendance	Population
Dallas	13	High	.268	14.7	4.3
Denver	59	Moderate	.404	14.4	2.2
Los Angeles	6	High	.396	10.9	7.6
Milwaukee	22	Moderate	.347	15.4	1.6
Minnesota	29	High	.286	16.4	2.7
Sacramento	41	Moderate	.393	16.9	1.6

Note: The %Value is the percentage change in the value of the franchise from 1993 to 1996. Risk is a rating assigned by *Financial World*. The rating is based on a team's ability to generate sufficient revenues to remain competitive in the league. Performance is the mean win-loss percentage of a team during 1990 to 1996. Attendance is the average home per game attendance in thousands of a team during 1990 to 1995. Population is the MSA population in millions, per team in 1990.

Source: The World Almanac and Book of Facts, 1990–1997; Tushar Atre, Kristine Auns, Kurt Badenhausen, Kevin McAuliffe, Christoper Nikolov, and Michael K. Ozanian, "Sports, Stocks, and Bonds," *Financial World* (20 May 1996), 57, 63; *Statistical Abstract of the United States*, 1993.

The Clippers played better after relocating to Los Angeles, and the Jazz and Kings continued to record losing seasons in Utah and Sacramento following their move. Between 1986 and 1997, the attendance of the Clippers, Jazz, and Kings increased in their home arenas. Therefore, for nine departures by professional football and basketball teams between 1977 and 1995, on average the post-move area's population was smaller, the per capita income was less, and the population growth was greater than at the pre-move site. Despite this, the estimated market value of each team rose because of higher ticket prices, the expansion of radio and television coverage, a boom in merchandise sales, and profits from the team's stadium or arena.

SUMMARY

Our analysis of sports franchise relocation since 1977 suggests that several teams are weak and financially unsustainable at their current sites. Unless they become more competitive in their divisions and conferences, then, without voluntary or mandated restructuring of league revenues, league officials should enable team owners to abandon their site for more lucrative locations. We have offered several alternative sites for moribund teams to consider. Each location offers appealing demographic amenities that could be exploited by a struggling franchise, especially one situated in a small city like Indianapolis, Milwaukee, or Kansas City. However, with new sources of revenue from renovated or newly constructed venues, or from a more equitable sharing of gate receipts and national broadcasting rights, even the small-city teams may co-exist and compete with teams located in large and medium-sized cities. It is in the best economic interests of all owners in a league to provide competitive performances and rivalries throughout the divisions and conferences, thereby maximizing attendance and league profits. The freedom to relocate must remain a viable and ongoing option for each franchise owner. Otherwise an inefficient and nonoptimal number of teams and sites will exist to the detriment of fans, cities, and all participants in the sport.

NOTES

1. Leonard Koppett, *Sports Illusion, Sports Reality: A Reporter's View of Sports, Journalism, and Society*, 2nd ed. (Urbana and Chicago: University of Illinois Press, 1994), 68–69.

2. Ibid.

3. See Roger G. Noll and Andrew Zimbalist, eds., *Sports, Jobs, and Taxes: The Economic Impact of Sports Teams and Stadiums* (Washington, D.C.: The Brookings Institution, 1997), 389.

4. Ibid.

5. See Charles C. Euchner, *Playing the Field: Why Sports Teams Move and Cities Fight to Keep Them* (Baltimore: Johns Hopkins University Press, 1993), 104–130.

6. Mark S. Rosentraub, *Major League Losers: The Real Costs of Sports and Who's Paying for It* (New York: Basic Books, 1997).

7. See James Quirk, "An Economic Analysis of Team Movements in Professional Sports," *Law and Contemporary Problems* 38 (Winter–Spring 1973), 42–66. Also Tables 1.1–1.3 contain the mean winning percentages and home site attendance of four NL teams, and the population and per capita income of the metropolitan areas, at the post-move sites.

8. See James Quirk and Rodney Fort, *Pay Dirt: The Business of Professional Sports* (Princeton, N.J.: Princeton University Press, 1992), 391–393, 399.

9. See Foon Rhee, "Twins Sale on Agenda as Owners Talk Shop," *Charlotte Observer* (11 January 1998), 1A, 18A; Scott Fowler, "List Puts Panthers Among Most Valuable Pro Teams," *Charlotte Observer* (25 May 1997), 1A, 18A; Quirk and Fort, *Pay Dirt*, 447; Michael Ozanian, "Selective Accounting," *Forbes* (14 December 1998), 126.

10. For a ranking of all the owners in the four major sports leagues, with each owner listed according to his or her net worth, see John Steinbreder, "The Owners," *Sports Illustrated* (13 September 1993), 64–87.

11. The Fox Group is expected to market the Dodgers more aggressively and increase ticket prices at Dodger Stadium. Currently, Fox is entering the third year of a four-year, $575 million deal to televise baseball nationally. Also, Fox has local broadcasting agreements with thirty-two major-league teams and owners. See "Baseball Owners Approve Sale of Dodgers to Fox Group," at the Web site <http://baseball.yahoo.com> cited 15 March 1998.

12. Tushar Atre, Kristine Auns, Kurt Badenhausen, Kevin McAuliffe, Christopher Nikolov, and Michael K. Ozanian, "Sports, Stocks, and Bonds," *Financial World* (20 May 1996), 53–64.

13. Salt Lake City was ranked 19th, Charlotte 21st, Indianapolis 31st, and Raleigh-Durham-Chapel Hill 34th. For further details see Bob Hille, "TSN's Best Sports Cities," *The Sporting News* (30 June 1997), 14–23. The owner of the Houston Rockets, Les Alexander, has expressed an interest in Las Vegas for his two-time world champions. One of the fastest growing cities in the United States, Las Vegas could finance a new stadium with casino revenues. Even so, Las Vegas ranked 70th in *The Sporting News's* "TSN's Best Sports Cities."

14. Roger G. Noll, "Attendance and Price Setting," in Roger G. Noll, ed., *Government and the Sports Business* (Washington, D.C.: The Brookings Institution, 1974), 124. In the statistical model, the total number of teams in major-league professional sports

located in the city indicated sports competition. The population of the metropolitan area was used as a rough index of nonsports competition.

15. Atre, et al., "Sports, Stocks, and Bonds," 62. The other NL teams with high risk include the Houston Astros, Montreal Expos, and the Pittsburgh Pirates. The other AL teams with moderate risk are the New York Yankees, Boston Red Sox, Texas Rangers, Seattle Mariners, California Angels, Kansas City Royals, and the Minnesota Twins. Team attendance was reported in a memo received by Frank Jozsa on 7 April 1998, from the AL headquarters in New York.

16. See Laura Jereski, "Take Me Out to the Ball Game," *Wall Street Journal* (17 December 1997), B12.

17. See Quirk and Fort, *Pay Dirt*, 405; Rhee, "Twins Sale on Agenda as Owners Talk Shop," 18A.

18. A survey of six hundred business people and others in a fifty-mile radius of Charlotte concluded that a big-league baseball team could draw twenty-five thousand fans per game, attendance would grow by 4 percent with a reasonably competitive team, and if everything fell into place, attendance could reach three million per season. In a poll taken by the *Charlotte Observer* of residents in Mecklenburg and six neighboring counties, 64 percent opposed using public money for a baseball stadium, yet 55 percent felt that the Charlotte area could support a team. For a complete discussion of the results of the poll, see Foon Rhee, "Triad's Big No Puts Area Group Into the Game," *Charlotte Observer* (7 May 1998), 1A; Ames Alexander, "Poll: Few Back Ballpark Taxes," *Charlotte Observer* (7 May 1998), 1A; and Foon Rhee, "Baseball Study Can't Answer All Questions," *Charlotte Observer* (20 May 1998), 1C.

19. Rhee, "Twins Sale on Agenda as Owners Talk Shop," 18A; Quirk and Fort, *Pay Dirt*, 24–25.

20. Rhee, "Twins Sale on Agenda as Owners Talk Shop," 18A; John Shea, "Selig's Daughter to Keep Brewers on Same Course," *Charlotte Observer* (14 July 1998), 4B.

21. Atre, et al., "Sports, Stocks, and Bonds," 53–64; "What Major League Franchises Are Worth," *Information Please Sports Almanac* (1993), 573; Michael Ozanian, "Selective Accounting," 126.

22. See "Royals Leaning Toward Prentice Bid," at <http://www.cnnsi.com> cited 21 August 1998; "Hunt Looks Into Buying Royals," at <http://www.kcstar.com> cited 19 November 1997; "A Royal Deal. Kansas City Approves Sale of Team to Prentice Group," at <http://www.cnnsi.com> cited 19 November 1998.

23. This percentage was reported in the *San Antonio Express News* (17 June 1997), 9C.

24. In 1998, the Milwaukee Brewers finished fifth in the NL's Central Division at .457. An average home game attendance of 17,955 placed the team fifteenth in the NL. The per game attendance of the Brewers at road games was 29,933, the third highest among NL teams and following the Atlanta Braves and Chicago Cubs at 33,000 per game. Due to realignment, the Brewers attracted more fans at away games than at home. See *San Antonio Express* (9 June 1998), 7C. In January 1999, commissioner Bud Selig reported that all teams will remain in their division for the 2000 season. See "Realignment Postponed. Leagues Will Remain the Same Through 2000," at the Web site <http://www.cnnsi.com> cited 14 January 1999.

25. The distribution of revenues from rich to poor clubs is reported in Stephen Baker, "Baseball's Losers Still Lose," *Business Week* (16 December 1996), 42. We calculated the percentage increase in revenues for the five MLB teams likely to relocate. In 1999, the Orioles paid a luxury fee exceeding $3.1 million based on their 1998 payroll of $79 million. The fees for the Red Sox, Yankees, Braves, and Dodgers ranged from $50,000 to $2 million in 1999. See "Orioles Top List at $3.1 million," at <http://www.cnnsi.com> cited 12 January 1999.

26. For how baseball will restore its image see David Leonhardt, "A Marketing Slugger Steps Up to the Plate," *Business Week* (4 November 1997), 84. Also by studying demographic trends new marketing campaigns may benefit teams. For example, to attract more women and children the Toronto Blue Jays are running public-service announcements on the charitable contributions of their players, starting home games earlier, and having players recite poems about baseball in Toronto radio ads. See Solange DeSantis, "Blue Jays Pitch Poems to Draw Women, Kids," *Wall Street Journal* (9 April 1998), B1. The impact of the Beanie Babies at baseball games is discussed in "McGwire's a Top Draw, But So Are Beanie Babies," *Charlotte Observer* (23 August 1998), 2H.

27. As reported in the *Charlotte Observer* this loss may be overstated because teams rarely disclose their financial statements. The article criticized MLB commissioner Bud Selig for his lack of leadership and recognition of MLB's financial record despite being awarded monopoly rights. See also Editorial, "Selig Presents Wrong Face for Game's Future," *Charlotte Observer* (2 June 1998), 4H; Michael Ozanian, "Selective Accounting," 126.

28. In April 1998 Richard Jacobs, the owner of the Cleveland Indians, filed a proposal with the Securities and Exchange Commission to sell four million shares to raise $62 million for the team. He sold the shares and the Indians became owned directly by public stockholders. Public companies already own the Anaheim Angels, Atlanta Braves, Chicago Cubs, and Los Angeles Dodgers. See Observer News Services, "Indians Seek Chance to Sell Public Shares," *Charlotte Observer* (4 April 1998), 6B; Associated Press, "Cleveland Indians Plan Stock Offerings, First in Big Leagues," *Charlotte Observer* (28 March 1998), 6C.

29. The annual winning percentage and attendance of the Raiders appears in *The Oakland Raiders: The Team of the Decades 1996*. See also Steinbreder, "The Owners," 80.

30. Johnson, "Balancing Interests," 11–16.

31. Quirk and Fort, *Pay Dirt*, 428–429.

32. The Rams ranked third in stadium revenues and fourth in total revenues and franchise value in the NFL in 1996. The team's financial status is rated low risk. The team's value increased by $90 million, or nearly 60 percent, from 1994 to 1997. See Atre, et al., "Sports, Stocks, and Bonds," 58, 62. Performance and attendance were extracted from Quirk and Fort, *Pay Dirt*, 420–421, 488–489; *The Oakland Raiders: The Team of the Decades 1996*, 177–184; Frederick Klein, "Why L.A. NFL Doesn't Need the NFL," *Wall Street Journal* (4 September 1998), W4.

33. See Quirk and Fort, *Pay Dirt*, 341–345, 413; *The Oakland Raiders: The Team of the Decades 1996*, 177–184.

34. See Rosentraub, *Major League Losers*, 17. For the history and other information about the Ravens see the Web site <http://www.nfl.com> cited 14 September 1998.

35. For an economic and historical analysis of public stadium subsidies in Baltimore, see Bruce W. Hamilton and Peter Kahn, "Baltimore's Camden Yards Ballparks," in Roger G. Noll and Andrew Zimbalist, eds. *Sports, Jobs and Taxes: The Economic Impact of Sports Teams and Stadiums*, 245–281.

36. See Associated Press Report, "NFL Picks Browns Owner," *Daytona Beach News Journal* (9 September 1998), 3B. Al Lerner's $530 acquisition of the Browns was topped in January 1999 when New York banker Howard Milstein bid $800 million for the Washington Redskins and Jack Kent Cooke Stadium.

37. See Associated Press Report, "NFL Picks Browns Owner," 3B.

38. See Noll, "Attendance and Price Setting," 115–157.

39. John Helyar, "More NFL Fans Stay at Home," *Wall Street Journal* (4 October 1996), B4; *Media Guides* of the teams; "NFL Ticket Prices Up 4.7 Percent for '98. Bucs

Lead 13 Teams Who Raised Cost of Attending Games," at the Worldwide Web site
<http://www.cnnsi.com> cited 3 September 1998.

40. See Helyar, "More NFL Fans Stay at Home," B4.

41. See *The Oakland Raiders: The Team of the Decades 1996*.

42. Lionel J. Wilson, "Statement," U.S. Congress, House Committee on the Judiciary, *Oversight Hearings: Antitrust Policy and Professional Sports* (Washington, D.C.:
Government Printing House, 1984), 416–418.

43. For these values see Michael K. Ozanian, "Selective Accounting," *Forbes* (14
December 1998), 124–134.

44. Atre, et al., "Sports, Stocks, and Bonds," 62.

45. After twenty-one days of trial spread over five weeks, on 10 November 1997, a
U.S. District Judge ruled in favor of the NFL and threw out St. Louis' $130 million anti-
trust suit. Judge Hamilton decided that the arguments made by the St. Louis Convention
and Visitors Commission were too weak for a jury to evaluate. In the decision Hamilton
made no mention of relocation fees. See William C. Lhotka, "Judge Throws Out Suit
Against NFL; St. Louis Will Appeal," at the Web site <http://www.stlnet.com> cited 13
November 1997. On 3 September 1998, in a 10–2 vote for the plantiffs, a federal appeals
court in St. Louis upheld the previous decision. The court ruled that a sports league has
the right to have reasonable rules relating to the operation of its business partnership. See
"St. Louis Loses Conspiracy Lawsuit Against NFL," at the Worldwide Web site at
<http://www.sportsline.com> cited 3 September 1998.

46. The RCA Dome ranks eleventh in seating capacity in the AFC at 60,272. See
page 100 of the *1996 Indianapolis Colts Media Guide* for a listing of the stadium capacities of NFL teams. Other information on the Colts was obtained from Sean Horgan,
"Mayor, Colts Sign Lease Agreement," at the Web site <http://www.starnews.com> cited
21 January 1998.

47. See Sean Horgan, "Corporate Community Has Central Role in Colts' Future,"
Indianapolis Star (26 October 1997), E2. NFL stadium capacities and revenues were
obtained from the team's *Media Guides* and various issues of *Financial World* and the
Wall Street Journal.

48. Tushar Atre, et al., "Sports, Stocks, and Bonds," 53–64.

49. For the negotiations between the NFL and the networks see Stefan Fatsis, "NFL
Players May Help Get Fatter TV Deal," *Wall Street Journal* (2 January 1997), 3; Kyle
Pope and Stefan Fatsis, "TV Networks Rush to Splurge on NFL Deals," *Wall Street
Journal* (15 December 1997), B1; Richard Turner, "NBC: The Road to Tap City,"
Newsweek (26 January 1998), 42–44; Joseph Dubow, "It's a Wonderful World for NFL's
TV," *Charlotte Observer* (14 January 1998), 1B, 3B; Stefan Fatsis, "For Pro Football,
Giant TV Pacts May Carry a Price," *Wall Street Journal* (15 January 1998), B1, B6;
Kyle Pope, "Networks' Big Play for NFL May End in Fumble," *Wall Street Journal* (5
February 1998), B10.

50. Michael Ovitz, the former president of Walt Disney Company, met with Ed
Roski, co-owner of the Los Angeles Kings hockey team to locate an NFL franchise in the
Los Angeles area. Ovitz presented his plans for a $350 million stadium, to be financed
privately, to the NFL in November 1998. The stadium would be built in Carson, Califor-
nia, as a component of a $750 million sports and entertainment complex. Richard Rior-
dan, mayor of Los Angeles, proposed to the NFL a plan to allow a team to play in the
Los Angeles Memorial Coliseum. See Bruce Orwall, "He's Ba-ack! Ovitz Returns as a
Mall Developer," *Wall Street Journal* (27 March 1998), B1; Roger G. Noll and Andrew
Zimbalist, eds. *Sports, Jobs, and Taxes: The Economic Impact of Sports Teams and Stadiums*, 42–49.

51. See the *1996–1997 Los Angeles Clippers Information Guide*; Fowler, "List Puts Panthers Among Most Valuable Pro Teams," 1A, 18A; Martin Tarango, *Basketball Biographies* (Jefferson, N.C. and London: McFarland & Company, 1991), 192; Quirk and Fort, *Pay Dirt*, 453; Ozanian, "Selective Accounting," 130.

52. Quirk and Fort, *Pay Dirt*, 458; "Malone Chides Jazz Owner Miller. The Mailman Says He Is Underpaid and Underappreciated," at <http://www.cnnsi.com> cited 17 March 1998; "Mailman May Not Stick in Salt Lake City. Agent Wants to Make Mountain Out of Malone's Money," at <http://www.cnnsi.com> cited 21 August 1998; Steinbreder, "The Owners," 76.

53. Quirk and Fort, *Pay Dirt*, 458–459; Thomas Heath, "Pollin: Player Salaries Cause Increases in Ticket Prices," *Washington Post* (27 November 1997), B7; "Washington Wizards History" available at the Web site <http://www.nba.com> cited 5 February 1998.

54. See the *Atlanta Hawks Media Guide 1996–97*, 189–196; *1996–97 Los Angeles Clippers Information Guide*.

55. Featuring a theme of "New Spirit. New Attitude," the *1996–97 Philadelphia Seventy Sixers Media Guide* gives the history of the team since 1949 when the Syracuse Nationals joined the NBA from the Midwest-based National Basketball League.

56. The data are based on a memo received from the Charlotte Hornets on 9 October 1997.

57. See the Observer News Services, "Silas Among Sacramento Candidates," *Charlotte Observer* (22 August 1998), 9B; "Rick Adelman Hired as Coach," at the Web site <http://www.nba.com> cited 28 September 1998.

58. The total revenues of the Clippers and Nuggets were the lowest in the league at $40 million in 1998, and excluding the Timberwolves, each team had a negative operating income. See Atre, et al., "Sports, Stocks, and Bonds," 57, and Ozanian, "Selective Accounting," 130. Another valuation model estimates the three most valuable NBA franchises—the Knicks, Lakers, and the Bulls—at $288 million each.

Chapter 4 ————————————————————

Expansion Teams since 1977

After owning the Florida Marlins for five seasons and winning the World Series in 1997, Wayne Huizenga placed his team on the market for $165 million. Although home attendance had improved by 36 percent in its championship season, Huizenga claimed that the team needed a new retractable-roof stadium to break even or earn a profit. Without public financing of a new stadium the Marlins traded players to reduce salaries from $53 million in 1997 to $19 million in the 1998 season. As a result, in 1998 the Marlins ended the season 54–108, the worst performance ever for a defending champion and the poorest record in the NL since 1969. After investing over $200 million in the team and incurring operating losses exceeding $70 million between 1993 and 1997, Huizenga decided to sell the Marlins in 1999 for $150 million but retain his ownership of the NHL's Florida Panthers, Pro Player Stadium, and the Miami Dolphins. Even so, the Marlins have appreciated over 96 percent in value between 1993 and 1998.[1]

In Chapter Two we identified and analyzed a combination of demographic, economic, and team-specific factors affecting expansion in professional baseball, football, and basketball. In doing so, we found that ten expansion teams joined MLB, six the NFL, two the AFL, fourteen the NBA, and eleven the ABA between 1950 and 1977. This chapter explores the ownership history, playing performance, home attendance, and estimated market value of expansion teams in the three sports since 1977. Furthermore, it analyzes the recent history of the former expansion teams relative to each other and to the league. Pursuing that goal, this chapter lists and compares the expansion teams in the three sports in winning percentage, attendance, and economic value. This information provides a better understanding of the operations and business aspects involved in professional sports.

Along the way, this chapter evaluates four important questions: Which expansion teams have realized the most and least success on the field and at the gate since the late 1970s? Were the leagues justified in expanding since 1977? How did the expansion teams compare competitively within, and between, sports? Finally, what factors influenced the decision by leagues to expand the number of teams in professional baseball, football, and basketball?

MAJOR LEAGUE BASEBALL

National League

We described the demographics of the metropolitan area and the mean winning percentage and home attendance of the four expansion teams in the NL using Tables 2.3 and 2.4. Specifically, Table 2.3 provides three attributes of the metropolitan area surrounding the expansion site. Table 2.4 lists the mean winning percentage and home attendance of the teams for five and ten seasons from the expansion year. Before extending the data in Table 2.4 to encompass the late 1980s to the mid-1990s, we provide a description of the ownership histories of the NL expansion teams to evaluate the stability of these franchises from an investment perspective.[2]

After assuming complete ownership of the Houston Colts (now Astros) in 1963 from the Houston Sports Association, Roy Hofheinz went bankrupt in 1976. The team's two creditors, General Electric and Ford Motor Credit Corporations, assumed control of the Astros until 1979 when they sold it for $19 million to a syndicate headed by John McMullen. Thirteen years later Drayton McLane, Jr., bought the team from McMullen, who earned approximately $50 million in profits from the sale. In 2000, a $250 million, 42,000-seat ballpark will open in downtown Houston replacing the three-decades-old Astrodome and improving the revenue stream of the Astros as a business enterprise. Of the ballpark's cost, 68 percent—$170 million—will come from hotel and rental-car taxes. Thirteen corporations and eleven thousand season-ticket holders have the opportunity to buy twenty-three hundred Charter Seat Licenses (CSLs) at the ballpark. Valued at $2,000 to $20,000 per license, the owners expect to raise $12 million from the CSLs. Additionally, they will place sixty-three luxury suites priced between $75,000 and $130,000 per suite up for sale. Game tickets are expected to cost between $1 and $200 per ticket (in 1998 seats at the Astrodome cost between $1 and $23). The revenues from the taxes, cash from the club's owners, and a zero interest rate loan will liquidate the debt on the ballpark.[3]

Joan Payson, the head of a syndicate that owned the New York Mets, died in 1975 and bequeathed her majority ownership of the team to her relatives. In 1980, her spouse sold the team for $21 million to a syndicate led by Doubleday and Company. Six years later Nelson Doubleday and Fred Wilpon bought 95 percent of the team for $95 million and assumed control of the club. They remain owners of the franchise as of 1999. Doubleday and Wilpon plan to replace Shea Stadium with a modern 45,000-seat facility strictly for baseball. When the Mets conclude a financial agreement with New York City, a $500 million retractable-roof stadium, resembling Ebbets Field will be built on the parking lot next to Shea Stadium. The owners intend to sell naming rights to the ballpark and begin play there in 2003. In 1998 New York mayor Rudolph Giuliani proposed diverting money collected from a commercial tax in Manhattan to a Sports Facilities Corporation that would oversee the stadium's construction in Queens. The mayor's plan should provide $600 million over three years to build stadiums for the Mets and Yankees.[4]

Majority owners Charles Bronfman and John McHale sold the Montreal Expos for $86 million in 1990 to a syndicate headed by Charles Brochu. Seven years later the proprietors of the team began selling seat licenses and seeking public money to help finance a proposed ballpark in downtown Montreal to replace Olympic Stadium, which was built in 1976. To pay for the $250 million ballpark, by December 1998 the team had sold more than five-thousand seat licenses, which represent 12 percent of the stadium's cost. Additionally, a study reported that a nonprofit stadium authority could issue $150 million of government-guaranteed bonds and repay the debt with taxes on player salaries. Quebec's finance minister Bernard Landry, however, told the *Montreal Gazette* the province would not guarantee any debt for the stadium. To refinance the club and build a new downtown stadium, in January 1999 Brochu agreed to sell his 8 percent ownership share for $10 million to investors. With the lowest attendance in the NL in 1998, vacating Montreal is an appealing option for the Expos.[5]

After earning a fortune with McDonalds restaurants, Ray and then Joan Kroc purchased the San Diego Padres in 1974. In 1990, three years after Ray died, his heirs sold the team for $75 million to a syndicate led by Tom Warner. John Moores bought the team from Warner in 1994 and three years later renovated the Padres' ballpark, Qualcomm (formerly Jack Murphy) Stadium, to boost the operating income and profits of the team. The renovation of the stadium was done by the city at the behest of the Chargers and the NFL so that San Diego could host a Super Bowl in 1999. The Padres opposed this strategy and demanded a new stadium to replace the expanded Qualcomm. In November 1998, San Diego voters approved Proposition C, which will authorize a $411 downtown redevelopment project providing shops, restaurants, hotels, and a baseball-only field for the Padres.[6]

In the early 1990s, the populations of Denver and Miami failed to rank in the top ten U.S. cities. Even so, each area contained over two million people and represented untapped markets for professional baseball. Besides Denver and Miami, in 1990 the *Sporting News* ranked Buffalo, Charlotte, Honolulu, New Orleans, Phoenix, St. Petersburg, San Antonio, Tampa, Vancouver, and Washington as viable sites for MLB expansion.[7]

In 1991, for $95 million, MLB awarded the Colorado Rockies franchise to an investment group—Colorado Baseball Partnership—that included Coors Brewery and was headed by John Antonucci. Jerry McMorris, a magnate in the trucking industry, owned the team as of 1998. Opened in 1995, Coors Field contributes 24 percent, or $25 million from suite rentals, tickets, concessions, parking, advertising, naming rights, and other events to the team's annual revenues.[8]

Table 2.4 in Chapter Two reveals how each NL expansion team's winning percentage and home attendance changed during the first five and ten seasons following the expansion year. Table 4.1 shows the mean winning percentages and home attendance of the four pre-1993 NL expansion teams for the 1987 to 1996 seasons. The table also contains the same for the two post-1992 expansion teams for the 1993 to 1996 seasons. This information indicates that the group performance of the pre-1993 NL expansion teams fell from .505 between 1987 and 1991, to .497 between 1992 and 1996. From 1987 to 1991, the best and worst performing NL expansion teams were the New York Mets at .553 and the Houston Astros at .474. The Mets ranked first in winning percentage in the NL in 1988 and second in the 1987 and 1990 seasons. Nonetheless, the Mets' performance plummeted after the 1991 season. The team finished no higher than sixth in winning percentage among all league teams between 1992 and 1996. The mean performance of the San Diego Padres, meanwhile, fell by 5 percent (.489 to .466) over the ten seasons. Additionally, the mean performance of the Houston Astros and Montreal Expos each rose over 10 percent (.474 to .526 and .505 to .553) from 1987 to 1996.

During 1992 and 1996, the Montreal Expos ranked fourth in winning percentage in the NL in 1992, 1993, and 1996. But the winning percentage of the two newest expansion franchises proved bleak. The Colorado Rockies ranked eleventh, eleventh, fourth, and sixth respectively, and the Florida Marlins placed twelfth, twelfth, tenth, and ninth respectively in winning percentage during the 1993 to 1996 seasons. In 1997, however, the play of the Rockies and Marlins improved. The teams ranked seventh and second, respectively, in winning percentage in the NL, and the Marlins won the 1997 World Series, beating the Cleveland Indians in a dramatic seven-game series that was climaxed by a run-scoring, ninth-inning single by Edgar Renteria, Florida's second baseman.

In 60 percent of the seasons designated in Table 4.1, the mean winning percentage of the six former expansion teams exceeded .500. During 1987 to 1996,

Table 4.1
Post-1960 NL Expansion Franchises, Performance, and Attendance for Selected Seasons

Franchise	1987–1991 Seasons		1992–1996 Seasons	
	Performance	Attendance	Performance	Attendance
Houston	.474	1.6	.526	1.6
New York	.553	2.8	.442	1.5
Montreal	.505	1.4	.553	1.5
San Diego	.489	1.7	.466	1.4
Colorado	–	–	.478	3.7
Florida	–	–	.450	2.1

Note: Performance and Attendance are, respectively, the mean winning percentage and home game attendance (in millions) of the teams during the seasons indicated in the table. The mean winning percentage and attendance of the Colorado Rockies and Florida Marlins are for the 1993 to 1996 seasons.

Source: The World Almanac and Book of Facts (Mahwah, N.J.: World Almanac Books, 1987–1997); James Quirk and Rodney Fort, *Pay Dirt: The Business of Professional Sports* (Princeton, N.J.: Princeton University Press, 1992), 479–483; Wire memo from American League of Professional Baseball Clubs (New York, 1997), 1–3.

the highest average winning percentage of the expansion teams was .536 in the 1988 season when the New York Mets ranked first in the NL. The lowest average winning percentage of the teams was .442 in the 1993 season when the Colorado Rockies ranked eleventh, the Florida Marlins twelfth, the San Diego Padres thirteenth, and the Mets fourteenth in the league. The Rockies and Marlins, moreover, played more competitively between 1995 and 1997 than in the previous two seasons, illustrating that expansion franchises need a few years to develop before they can successfully compete with the established teams. After the development period ends, an expansion team matures and gains in performance vary based on the talents of the players and coaches.

The demand to attend these teams' games has increased since 1987. Table 4.1 shows that for those teams listed, the Mets had the highest average home attendance from 1987 to 1991. Furthermore, the Rockies and Marlins dominated the four expansion teams and the other league teams in home attendance between 1993 and 1996.[9]

Over three million fans attended the Mets' home games in 1987 and 1988 as the team ranked first and second respectively in attendance, and second and first respectively in winning percentage in the NL. Less than one million fans watched the Montreal Expos play at home in the 1991 season when the team finished eleventh in the league in winning percentage. During the 1987 and 1989 seasons, the home attendance of the four expansion teams exceeded the league average by roughly 2 percent.[10]

The winning percentage and attendance of the Houston Astros and Montreal Expos rose during 1987 to 1996. However, attendance declined by 45 percent for the Mets and 15 percent for the San Diego Padres because these teams played poorly. From 1993 to 1996, the home attendance of the Rockies and Marlins also declined even though the teams played better during 1995 and 1996 than they did in their first two seasons.

Even with huge hometown fan support for the Rockies from 1993 to 1996 and for the Marlins in 1993, the mean attendance of the league exceeded the mean attendance of the six former expansion teams from 1993 to 1995. The Rockies drew over 4.4 million fans in the 1993 season and between 3.2 and 3.9 million fans per season from 1994 to 1996. On the other hand, the home attendance of the Marlins fell from 3.1 million in 1993 to 1.7 million in 1996, despite the team's 25 point increase in winning percentage.[11]

Wayne Huizenga's asking price of $165 million for the Florida Marlins in 1997 represented a 34 percent increase in the estimated market value of the team from 1996. Given the team's negative operating income, the $100 million debt on Pro Player Stadium, and Huizenga's effort to cut costs by trading veteran star players, the Marlins have depreciated to less than $150 million. The Marlins' estimated value falls somewhere between $125 and $150 million. In August 1998, Huizenga put his team up for sale and announced he would accept no offers for the club below $165 million. For the sale to occur, Huizenga stipulated that the new owner must accept a twenty-seven-year contract to televise Marlin games on SportsChannel Florida, which Huizenga also planed to sell. After Huizenga lowered his price from $165 to $150 million in September 1998, Boca Raton commodities trader John Henry agreed to purchase the club. In addition,

Henry wants the owner of the Miami Heat, Micky Arison, to be a limited partner in the deal. But before he will commit himself to the deal, Arison wants the team to build and finance a state-of-the-art stadium in downtown Miami without his participation. In January 1999, the league approved the sale of the club to Henry for $150 million.[12]

MLB franchises have appreciated over 75 percent in market value from 1993 to 1998. According to *Financial World*, the six NL expansion clubs have experienced the following growth in market values: Houston 123 percent, New York 31 percent, Montreal 16 percent, San Diego 89 percent, Colorado 175 percent, and Florida 96 percent. In 1998, the Expos at $87 million, the Brewers at $127 million, the Phillies at $131 million, the Pirates at $133 million, and the Reds at $136 million were the five lowest valued NL teams. Additionally Pittsburgh, Montreal, and San Diego remain high-risk financial investments and therefore should generate insufficient operating income over the next three to five years to compete with league rivals. Unless these latter three teams improve their performance and receive more revenues from their home stadiums, local and national broadcasting rights, or other sources, we predict that at least one of them will relocate by 2002.[13]

American League

The demographics of the metropolitan areas of the six American League (AL) franchises, that expanded between 1961 and 1977, appear in Table 2.1. The mean winning percentage and home attendance of the teams for five and ten seasons following the expansion year, appear in Table 2.2. Like the NL expansion teams, their AL counterparts tended to improve in performance as the seasons progressed and play to larger home crowds in the sixth to tenth seasons after expansion. Did these and other trends exist for the AL teams between 1987 and 1996?

Two-thirds of the league's expansion franchises still played at their original sites in 1998. Table 2.2 reveals the changes in the mean winning percentage and home attendance of the teams after the expansion year. Since the late 1980s, these teams have performed better and at times worse, than other AL teams and compared to the NL expansion teams (see Tables 4.1–4.2).

The former AL expansion teams had a higher mean winning percentage from 1987 to 1991, and the same mean winning percentage from 1992 to 1996, than their counterparts in the NL. From 1987 to 1991, the Toronto Blue Jays at .554 had the best winning percentage of the expansion teams. Following the Blue Jays, the Kansas City Royals played at .514, the Anaheim Angels at .496, and the Seattle Mariners at .468. Taken together, the expansion teams' winning percentage equaled .508. Moreover, the Blue Jays ranked second in winning percentage in the AL between 1987 and 1991 and fourth in the 1989 and 1990 seasons. Of the other teams, the Angels ranked third in 1989, the Royals ranked second in 1989, and the Mariners ranked eighth in 1987, 1990, and 1991. During 1987 to 1991, the highest and lowest mean winning percentage of the four teams was .532 in 1989 and .486 in 1988.

From the 1987 to 1991 seasons to the 1992 to 1996 seasons, the mean winning percentage of the Mariners increased by 3 percent. Meanwhile, the winning percentage of the Angels, Royals, and the Blue Jays fell by 7 percent, 4 percent, and 10 percent, respectively. After ranking first in the 1992 and 1993 seasons, the Blue Jays fell to sixth, thirteenth, and twelfth between 1994 and 1996. The other AL expansion teams, from 1992 to 1996, varied in rank from fifth to thirteenth for the Angels, fifth to eleventh for the Royals, and fourth to fourteenth for the Mariners. This data denotes the wide deviation in performances for the Angels, Royals, Mariners, and Blue Jays between 1992 and 1996.

Collectively, the former AL expansion teams won 4 percent fewer games on average between 1992 to 1996, than between 1987 to 1991. Also, as a group they won 51 percent of their games in 1993 and 47 percent in 1994. These represent the best and worst seasons for the teams combined.

Did the performance of the teams affect their home attendance? Table 2.2 indicates that the mean attendance of the Angels, Royals, Mariners, and Blue Jays increased between the first to fifth and the sixth to tenth seasons following the expansion year. Did the average attendance of these teams increase during 1987 to 1996? Table 4.2 shows that the Blue Jays finished first and the Mariners last in average attendance between 1987 and 1991 for the expansion teams. The Blue Jays drew over 4 million fans in the 1991 season and less than 2.6 million fans in the 1988 season when the team ended fifth in winning percentage in the league. The attendance of the Angels and Royals fell during the seasons played between 1987 and 1991, and the attendance of the Mariners increased by 89 percent during these years.

Unlike that of NL expansion teams, the mean attendance of AL expansion clubs exceeded the league average during each season from 1987 to 1991. In the NL, the attendance of the expansion teams exceeded the league average in 1987 and 1989. But if we exclude the Blue Jays from Table 4.2, the mean attendance of NL expansion teams equaled their AL counterparts between 1987 and 1991.

The mean attendance of the Mariners rose by 29 percent between 1987 and 1996. During these years the Angels and Royals experienced significant drops in average attendance as their winning percentages fell. Moreover, from 1992 to 1996, the mean attendance of the Blue Jays declined by 2 percent. From 1994 to

Table 4.2
Post-1960 AL Expansion Franchises, Performance and Attendance for Selected Seasons

Franchise	1987–1991 Season		1992–1996 Season	
	Performance	Attendance	Performance	Attendance
Anaheim	.496	2.5	.462	1.8
Kansas City	.514	2.3	.494	1.5
Seattle	.468	1.4	.482	1.8
Toronto	.554	3.3	.500	3.2

Note: We calculated Performance and Attendance as in Table 4.1.

Source: The World Almanac and Book of Facts, 1988–1997; Quirk and Fort, *Pay Dirt*, 483–488; Wire memo from the AL, 30 August 1997; *Media Guides* of the teams.

1996, less than 3 million fans saw home games each season in the Toronto SkyDome.[14] This reflects, in part, fan dissatisfaction with the 1994–1995 players strike and the cancellation of the 1994 World Series.

Again, unlike the former NL expansion teams, the post-1960 AL expansion teams outdrew the league in attendance from 1992 to 1996. The mean attendance of the NL teams exceeded the mean attendance of the league's expansion teams from 1992 to 1995. Yet, in 1996, the attendance of the Padres at Qualcomm Stadium in San Diego exceeded 2 million fans for the first time, raising the mean of the expansion teams above the NL average.

To summarize, Tables 4.1 and 4.2 reveal that during 1987 to 1996 two post-1960 NL expansion teams, the Houston Astros and Montreal Expos, and one post-1960 AL expansion team, the Seattle Mariners, improved in winning percentage and drew more fans to their ballparks for those years. In addition, the mean winning percentage of expansion clubs in the AL surpassed those in the NL in the period 1987 to 1991. But for 1992 to 1996, the NL and AL expansion clubs tied at .485. We also determined the mean home attendance for the teams and leagues in this period. The mean attendance of AL expansion teams exceeded the league average in each season 1987 to 1996. The mean attendance of NL expansion clubs exceeded the league average only during the 1987, 1989, and 1996 seasons. In three of the ten seasons studied, the NL expansion franchises had a higher mean attendance, and in four of the ten seasons, a lower mean winning percentage, than the expansion teams in the AL.

This means that even though the post-1960 expansion teams in the NL and AL had similar winning percentages, AL expansion teams drew larger crowds to home games and thereby earned higher gate receipts than NL expansion clubs. Furthermore, if the seasonal winning percentage and home attendance of the Blue Jays, Angels, and Royals continues to decline, and the attendance of the Rockies and Marlins rises, NL expansion teams should soon overtake the rival league's expansion teams in average attendance. Considering the poor performance of the Marlins in 1998, we doubt that this will occur.

Table 4.3 shows the growth in the market value of MLB's former expansion franchises from 1993 to 1996. All but three expansion teams—the New York Mets, Los Angeles (now Anaheim) Angels, and Kansas City Royals—increased in market value. Although mediocre in team performances, the Rockies and Marlins ranked first and third in average attendance from 1993 to 1996, which partially explains their appreciation in value. Also, the Rockies and Marlins have gradually improved in performance since 1993, ranking sixth and ninth, respectively, in the NL in the 1996 season.

In the NL, the Expos and Astros ranked the highest in team performance over the four seasons. Interestingly, the attendance of the Expos increased by 200,000, while that of the Astros decreased by 200,000 during those seasons. Yet the market value of the Astros increased by 34 percent, and the Expos by just 3 percent, even though both organizations remain high-risk investments.[15] Perhaps Houston's large population and lucrative broadcasting market, in addition to economic advantages in gate, media, and stadium revenues, help explain the differences in the market value of these two clubs.

Table 4.3
Post-1960 NL and AL Expansion Franchises and Selected Data, 1993 to 1996

Year	Franchise	Performance	Attendance	Change in Franchise Value $	Change in Franchise Value %
	National League				
1962	Houston	.533	1.7	29	34
1962	New York	.442	1.4	– 3	– 2
1969	Montreal	.557	1.5	2	3
1969	San Diego	.456	1.4	1	1
1993	Colorado	.478	3.8	74	67
1993	Florida	.450	2.1	42	52
	American League				
1961	Los Angeles	.455	1.8	0	0
1969	Kansas City	.507	1.5	– 6	– 7
1977	Seattle	.504	1.9	27	34
1977	Toronto	.477	3.1	5	3

Note: Performance is the final regular season average win-loss percentage of a team, and Attendance is the team's average home attendance (in millions), from 1993 to 1996. Change in Franchise Value represents in dollars ($) and percentages (%) how the franchise values changed from 1993 to 1996.

Source: *World Almanac and Book of Facts,* 1962–1978; Tushar Atre, Kristine Auns, Kurt Baden-hausen, Kevin McAuliffe, Christopher Nikolov, and Michael K. Ozanian, "Sports, Stocks, and Bonds," *Financial World* (20 May 1996), 53–64; *Information Please Sports Almanac* (New York: Houghton Mifflin, 1996), 573; *Media Guides* of the teams and leagues; Scott Fowler, "List Puts Panthers Among Most Valuable Pro Teams," *Charlotte Observer* (25 May 1997), 1A, 18A

The Mets and Padres ranked low in team performance and appreciated the least in market value in the NL. Both clubs averaged 1.4 million in home attendance per year. But, while the home attendance of the Mets declined by 300,000 from 1993 to 1996, that of the Padres increased by 800,000 due to their second-place finish in the 1996 season. In 1996 the Mets earned $21 million in operating income, while the Padres incurred an operating loss of $5 million, which represents the $58 million gap in the total market value between the two franchises.[16]

For the AL expansion franchises, Seattle experienced the greatest appreciation in market value from 1993 to 1996. Of the four AL teams listed in Table 4.3, only Seattle's home attendance increased by at least 700,000 from 1993 to 1996. What is more, the Mariners led the AL expansion team ranking by placing eighth in 1993, fourth in 1995, and fifth in 1996. With a new ballpark under construction and continued improvement in team performances, the $251 million Seattle franchise should appreciate in market value over the next several years.

Despite posting a .507 average winning percentage, the Royals declined in value by $6 million, or 7 percent, from 1993 to 1996. During the same seasons, the Angels played poorly while the Blue Jays' team performance fell from first to twelfth in the league. Despite earning over $30 million in gate receipts, low ancillary revenues and high operating expenses prevented the Blue Jays from significantly appreciating in value. Similarly, the Angels and Royals received less than $15 million per year in media revenues and $10 million per year in other revenues during the four-year span. This contributed to their operating losses and limited gain in market value during those four seasons and bodes unfavorably for future earnings of the teams.

In recent years the NL has experienced more success than the AL by adding new franchises. NL teams in Houston, New York, Denver, and Miami ranked among the top two-thirds in market value in 1996. On the other hand, AL clubs in Anaheim, Kansas City, and Seattle ranked in the bottom third in estimated market value in 1996. Also, two of the four AL expansion teams, Seattle and Kansas City, reported the lowest local radio and television revenues in MLB for the 1996 season.[17]

PROFESSIONAL FOOTBALL

National Football League

The NFL expanded by four teams in the 1960s, two in the 1970s, and two more in the 1990s. Table 2.5 shows the population, per capita income, and the population growth in the metropolitan areas of these expansion teams. Table 2.6 contains the mean winning percentage and home game attendance of the clubs for five and ten seasons from the expansion year. Before exploring how each NFL expansion team has performed and prospered since the late 1980s, we revisit the ownership histories and control of the eight new NFL teams. Subsequently, we analyze the attendance and economic status of the franchises for recent seasons.

After several years of meticulous preparation and planning, representatives from Charlotte and Jacksonville outbid prospective ownership groups from Baltimore, St. Louis, Memphis, and other areas to acquire the twenty-ninth and thirtieth NFL franchises, which began play in the 1995 season. The reasons the NFL granted Charlotte a team in 1993 are noteworthy. In September 1989, Jerry Richardson announced the formation of Richardson Sports. A fifteen-member partnership group, the company believed ownership was "a key element in obtaining a franchise, and [felt] extremely pleased with the quality of [the] group." Not only do the partners reflect the strength needed to achieve their goal, Richardson added, the group also includes "people with a mutual and demonstrated interest in the growth, progress, and improved quality of life in this region."[18] By late 1993, Richardson Sports had developed a financing plan involving NationsBank (renamed Bank of America in 1998) and a $60 million commitment from the city of Charlotte to assist in the improvement of the land and the infrastructure surrounding the stadium. The financing plan called for the sale of Permanent Seat Licenses (PSLs) to raise funds to construct the stadium. These plans served as essential components for Richardson Sports acquiring the franchise and entering the small, exclusive cartel of NFL team proprietors.

Earlier attempts to establish a professional football team in Jacksonville had failed. The World Football League (WFL) placed the Sharks in Jacksonville in 1974. Before long the team went bankrupt. The league then assumed control of the Sharks. A year later, league officials sold the team (for an unknown price) to Earl Knabb, who renamed his property the Express, which disbanded when the

WFL folded. In 1983 Fred Bullard located his United States Football League (USFL) expansion team, the Bulls, in Jacksonville. The Bulls merged with the Denver Gold in 1985, but terminated operations in 1986 when the league ceased to exist. Three years later, Jacksonville boosters began lobbying the NFL for an expansion franchise. Millionaire shoe-retailer Wayne Weaver joined the campaign in 1993. Focused on a mutual goal, the city of Jacksonville spent $121 million in refurbishing the Gator Bowl, and an ownership group led by Weaver contributed another $19 million for upgrading the stadium. The NFL awarded an expansion franchise to Jacksonville in 1993. The short histories of the Panthers and the Jaguars reveal that Jerry Richardson and Wayne Weaver both applied economics to professional football by conducting business, and coordinating financial plans, in a way that would enable them to establish a site and to acquire competitive players to ensure success in the 1995 season.[19]

Prior to 1993, restricted free-agency precluded NFL expansion team owners from readily acquiring or drafting highly skilled players from established teams. Before 1993, moreover, NFL teams had no salary caps. But in 1993, according to journalist John Helyar, "the NFL adopted unrestricted free-agency, and in 1994 salary caps, allowing the newest expansion teams, the Carolina Panthers and Jacksonville Jaguars, to acquire veteran free agents from established teams and to obtain extra picks in the 1995 and 1996 drafts."[20] Consequently, NFL expansion clubs now compete better in league play by employing an optimal combination of players and coaches. Before these rule changes, in the early years of a franchise, home attendance usually fell below stadium capacity due to the team's poor performances.

With the departure of general manager Bill Polian (to the Indianapolis Colts in December 1997), assistant general manager Joe Mack, and director of player personnel Dom Anile, head coach Dom Capers (in 1999 replaced by former San Francisco FortyNiners head coach George Seifert) received more decision-making authority within the Panthers' organization. In 1998, Mark Richardson, son of owner Jerry Richardson, oversaw business operations as president of the club. Jack Bushofsky served as director of player personnel, and Marty Hurney negotiated player contracts and managed the salary cap as director of football administration. With these changes the front office of the Panthers appears to be similar in structure and management style to the organization of the Jaguars. Neither franchise has a general manager, and their coaches have complete responsibility and authority over team operations.[21]

In 1998 the Panthers ranked third in value at $365 million, and the Jaguars fourteenth at $294 million, of professional sports franchises in the United States and Canada. In the NFL, only the Dallas Cowboys at $413 million and the Washington Redskins at $403 million had higher estimated market values than the Panthers.[22]

Table 4.4 shows the mean winning percentage and home attendance of six former NFL expansion teams for 1987 to 1996 and of two teams for 1995 and1996. These seasonal data for the NFL clubs have similarities to data compiled for expansion teams in MLB and the NBA.

Table 4.4
Former NFL Expansion Franchises, Performance and Attendance for Selected Seasons

	1987–1991 Season		1992–1996 Season	
Franchise	Performance	Attendance	Performance	Attendance
Dallas	.368	426	.737	513
Minnesota	.544	439	.587	457
Atlanta	.305	314	.387	447
New Orleans	.647	503	.462	451
Seattle	.520	465	.375	404
Tampa Bay	.291	391	.364	419
Carolina	–	–	.594	495
Jacksonville	–	–	.406	543

Note: Performance and Attendance are the mean winning percentage and home attendance of the teams, respectively, for the seasons listed. Attendance is in hundreds of thousands. The 1995 and 1996 seasons are included for the Carolina Panthers and Jacksonville Jaguars.

Source: World Almanac and Book of Facts, 1987–1997; Quirk and Fort, *Pay Dirt,* 488–494; Media and Public Relations departments of the NFL teams.

The New Orleans Saints at .647, and the Minnesota Vikings at .544, performed the best for expansion teams in the NFC during the 1987 to 1991 seasons. In winning percentages, the Saints finished no lower than eighth, and the Vikings no lower than ninth, in their conference during this period.

Only two non-AFL (post-1975) expansion teams, the Seattle Seahawks and Jacksonville Jaguars, play in the American Football Conference (AFC). With a mean winning percentage of .520 during 1987 to 1991, the Seahawks ranked third in the AFC at .600 in the 1987 season, and fifth at .563 in the 1988 and 1990 seasons. Taken together, the mean winning percentage of the NFL expansion teams varied from a low of .365 in the 1989 season to a high of .531 in the 1991 season. The expansion teams had a mean winning percentage of .445 from 1987 to 1991. Also, the Seahawks ranked no higher than fourteenth in the NFL during 1992 to 1996.

Two-thirds of the pre-1995 NFL expansion teams played better in 1992 to 1996 than in 1987 to 1991. In the NFC, the Dallas Cowboys ranked first in winning percentage in the 1993 and 1995 seasons and second in the 1992 and 1994 seasons. Renowned players such as quarterback Troy Aikman, running back Emmitt Smith, and wide receiver Michael Irving led the Cowboys to a 52–17 win over the Buffalo Bills in the 1993 Super Bowl, a 30–13 win over the Bills in the 1994 Super Bowl, and a 27–17 win over the Pittsburgh Steelers in the 1996 Super Bowl.[23] Other NFC expansion teams that improved in winning percentage from 1992 to 1996 were the Minnesota Vikings, Atlanta Falcons, and the Tampa Bay Buccaneers. Meanwhile, the New Orleans Saints saw its winning percentage fall from third in the NFL in 1992 to twenty-seventh in 1996.

Led by second-year quarterback Kerry Collins and all-pro veteran linebackers Sam Mills, Lamar Lathon, and Kevin Greene, the Panthers tied the San Francisco FortyNiners for the Western Division title of the NFC in 1996. Likewise, with inspirational play by quarterback Mark Brunnell and running back

Natrone Means, the Jacksonville Jaguars upset the Denver Broncos and super-star John Elway in the divisional playoffs, but lost the 1996 AFC title game to the New England Patriots.

In short, the NFL expansion teams played at or above .500 in 1992, 1994, and 1996. Moreover, the mean winning percentages of the clubs increased from .445 in 1987 to 1991, to .485 in 1992 to 1996. These winning percentages demonstrate that the league rules adopted in 1993 have enabled expansion teams to compete better against their established rivals.

Table 2.6 indicates that, from the expansion year, the mean attendance of the Dallas Cowboys and Minnesota Vikings increased in their first ten seasons. Has the attendance of the Cowboys, Vikings, and the other former expansion teams changed significantly during the 1987 to 1996 seasons? If so, why? During 1987 to 1991, the mean seasonal attendance of the Saints exceeded 500,000, and the Seahawks, 460,000. The Vikings at 439,000, Cowboys at 426,000, Tampa Bay Buccaneers at 391,000, and Atlanta Falcons at 314,000 followed the Saints and Seahawks with the highest average seasonal attendance (see Table 4.4). The mean attendance of the six former expansion clubs grew by 30 percent from 1987 to 1991, while the league averaged 47,000 more fans per season.[24]

Between 1992 and 1996 the Cowboys at 513,000 and the Vikings at 457,000 had the highest, and the Seahawks at 404,000 and the Buccaneers at 419,000 had the lowest, attendance of the pre-1995 expansion teams. In 1995 and 1996, the Jaguars led expansion teams in attendance with 554,000 and 533,000, respectively. Also, the Panthers placed fifth in attendance at 441,000 in 1995 and second at 550,000 in 1996. Even with the attendance of the Jaguars and Panthers, and an improvement in winning percentage of .445 to .485, the mean attendance of the expansion teams fell by 3 percent from 467,000 in 1992 to 452,000 in 1996. The steep drop in attendance of the Falcons from 506,000 in 1992 to 392,000 in 1996, and the Saints from 548,000 in 1992 to 301,000 in 1996, overwhelmed the gains in attendance of the Jaguars and Panthers, and thus lowered the mean for expansion teams.

So for the periods 1987 to 1991 and 1992 to 1996, the mean percentage changes in attendance of each pre-1995 NFL expansion team fell as follows: Cowboys, 23 to 20 percent; Vikings, 8 to 4 percent; Falcons, 66 to 42 percent; Saints, 19 to negative 11 percent; Seahawks, 13 to 2 percent; and the Buccaneers, 22 to 7 percent. Several factors explain the change in attendance for the expansion teams and the league between 1987 and 1996. For one, NFL attendance growth was restricted in this period due to capacity constraints at stadiums. Teams responded to these conditions by raising ticket prices reflecting blackout rules imposed by the television networks. The inferior performance and weak drawing power of the Falcons, Saints, and, until 1995, the Buccaneers, also partially explain the gap in attendance among the NFL teams studied. Furthermore, although the NFL's mean attendance expanded to 500,000 per season between 1994 and 1996, other teams such as the Arizona Cardinals, Cincinnati Bengals, Indianapolis Colts, and Tennessee Oilers (now Titans) will likely depress attendance and gate receipts for the league in the foreseeable future.

The Cowboys, Vikings, Falcons, and Buccaneers won more games and drew more fans to their stadiums between 1987 to 1991 and 1992 to 1996.

During this period, the Cowboys and Falcons experienced the most improvement in winning percentage. The Falcons with 42 percent and the Cowboys with 20 percent realized the largest mean increases in attendance. But from 1987 to 1991, and from 1992 to 1996 the mean winning percentage of the Saints and Seahawks each fell by 28 percent, and the teams' mean attendance dropped by 10 and 13 percent, respectively.

The historical relationship between the winning percentage and attendance of the post-1959 NFL expansion teams proved consistent with the relationship of the post-1960 MLB expansion clubs. The Houston Astros and Montreal Expos of the NL, and the Toronto Blue Jays of the AL, won more games and had greater attendance between 1992 and 1996 than between 1987 and 1991. Conversely, the New York Mets, San Diego Padres, Anaheim Angels, Kansas City Royals, and Toronto Blue Jays lost more games and their average attendance fell in the period 1992 to 1996. Obviously, a strong, positive relationship existed between winning percentage and attendance for MLB and NFL expansion teams between 1987 and 1996.

Which NFL expansion franchises are secure investments? Data reported in *Financial World* and other publications show that all NFL franchises have increased in value during the 1990s.[25] Two reasons explain why this happened. Due to profitable television contracts and new, or recently renovated, stadiums, many NFL owners have reaped windfall gains from their investment in players and sites. In light of that, we calculated the changes in market value for the NFL expansion franchises from the 1993 to 1996 season. The results appear in Table 4.5 along with the expansion fees, franchise risk, and performance of the teams during that period.

Led by the Cowboys, all former NFL expansion franchises increased in market value in the mid-1990s averaging over 7 percent per year (see Table 4.5). The Cowboys ranked first in performance in the 1993 season, and second in the 1994 and 1995 seasons, which contributed to their 68 percent appreciation in market value. Even the high-risk Seattle and Tampa Bay franchises increased market value in the 1990s despite both teams winning less than 44 percent of their games. Also, neither the Seahawks nor the Buccaneers ranked higher than fourteenth in the league during the seasons played between 1993 and 1996. The most recent expansion clubs, Carolina and Jacksonville, increased in market value by 80 percent and 64 percent, respectively, from 1995 to 1996, based on total revenue and operating income for two years.[26] The Panthers ranked eighteenth and the Jaguars twenty-ninth in performance in the NFL in the 1995 season, but improved to third and ninth respectively in the following season.

The percentage increase in franchise fees, unadjusted for inflation, is useful in estimating the appreciation in the market value of NFL clubs. These fees, paid by the teams, rose by 219 percent per year from 1960 (Dallas and Minnesota) to 1965 (Atlanta), by 12 percent per year from 1966 (New Orleans) to 1974 (Seattle and Tampa Bay), and by 41 percent per year from 1974 to 1993 (Carolina and Jacksonville).[27]

The gap in the market value of the NFL expansion franchises widened in the mid-1990s, increasing from $42 million to $186 million. The highest valued expansion team in 1998 was the Cowboys at $413 million, the lowest valued the

Table 4.5
Post-1960 NFL Expansion Franchises and Selected Data, 1993 to 1996

Franchise	Fee	Risk	Performance	Change in Franchise Value	
				$	%
Dallas	.6	Moderate	.765	130	68
Minnesota	.6	Moderate	.594	39	26
Atlanta	8.5	Moderate	.437	43	29
New Orleans	8.0	Low	.531	45	34
Seattle	16.0	High	.343	23	15
Tampa Bay	16.0	High	.359	45	31
Carolina	140.0	Moderate	.593	107	80
Jacksonville	140.0	Moderate	.406	94	64

Note: Fee is the expansion fee in millions of dollars, paid to the NFL by the franchise owner. Risk measures the ability of the franchise to generate sufficient operating income to compete in the NFL as reported in *Financial World*. Performance is the final regular-season mean win-loss percentage of the team. Change in Franchise Value represents the dollar ($) and percentage (%) increment for a team between 1993 and 1996. The data for the Carolina Panthers and Jacksonville Jaguars are based on the 1995 and 1996 seasons.

Source: *The World Almanac and Book of Facts, 1960–1997;* Scott Fowler, "List Puts Panthers Among Most Valuable Pro Teams," 1A, 18A; *Information Please Sports Almanac, 573;* Atre et al., "Sports, Stocks, and Bonds," 58; Quirk and Fort, *Pay Dirt,* 409–434.

Colts at $227 million.[28] With total revenues exceeding $118 million, and the highest operating income in the NFL in 1997 at $41 million, the Cowboys spent roughly $70 million annually for players to compete for the league championship.

The market value of a typical NFL club increased from approximately $170 million to over $288 million from 1995 to 1998. Because of $1 billion (1990–1993) and $1.2 billion (1994–1997) from television contracts, coupled with profits from stadium amenities, the average net worth of an NFL franchise has increased above those in MLB ($194 million) and the NBA ($167 million).

Newly constructed stadiums, or proposals to build one at a later date, in Baltimore, Cincinnati, Denver, Detroit, Hartford, Nashville, Pittsburgh, Seattle, and possibly Chicago, Miami, Minneapolis, Phoenix, San Diego, and San Francisco should add future value to these and other league franchises.

In contrast, from 1993 to 1996, the former NL and AL expansion teams increased in value by 26 and 8 percent, respectively. The differences in the values of post-1950 NFL and MLB expansion teams suggest that sports markets and demographic and economic conditions supported professional football more than baseball in the mid-1990s. Perhaps the 1994 and 1995 player strikes and higher ticket prices in MLB curbed the growth in the value of baseball teams. Only the Rockies and Marlins managed to significantly appreciate in value as expansion teams in baseball during the mid-1990s.

New NFL Teams

As a result of the AFL–NFL merger in 1970, ten AFL clubs joined the NFL. For purposes of our analysis, we consider these teams NFL expansion franchises placed in the league's American Football Conference (AFC). To determine their success in the NFL, we evaluate their performance, attendance, and estimated market values.

The majority of the former AFL teams have been competitive in the AFC since the early 1970s. Although they played in Super Bowls, the least competitive teams include the Cincinnati Bengals, New York Jets, and San Diego Chargers. We constructed Table 4.6 to analyze how the mean winning percentage and home attendance of the "new" NFL teams changed between 1987 and 1996. The table lists each team's winning percentage and attendance for two five-year periods beginning in 1987. That year a twenty-four-day players' strike reduced the 224-game schedule to 210 games. Five years earlier a fifty-seven-day strike reduced the season to 126 games.[29]

In the late 1980s, the Buffalo Bills at .681 and the Houston Oilers at .607 had the highest, and the New England Patriots at .369 and the San Diego Chargers at .381 had the lowest, winning percentages of the former AFL teams (see Table 4.6). In the 1991 Super Bowl, the Bills lost to the New York Giants, 20–19. The next year the Bills fell to the Washington Redskins, 37–24. The Oilers, meanwhile, ranked third in the AFC from 1987 to 1989 and in 1991. The Oilers also competed in AFC wild card games from 1987 to 1991. The Patriots ranked between third and fourteenth, and the Chargers between sixth and twelfth, in the AFC from 1987 to 1991. Neither the Patriots nor the Chargers made the AFC playoffs during these five seasons.

Overall, the mean winning percentage of the ten teams was .501 from 1987 to 1991, fluctuating from a low of .463 in 1987 to a high of .525 in 1989 and 1990. Comparing the years 1970 to 1974 with 1987 to 1991, the Houston Oilers increased by 157 percent and the Miami Dolphins fell by 35 percent in mean winning percentage.

Table 4.6
Selected AFC Teams, Performance and Attendance, 1987 to 1996

	Performance		Attendance	
Franchise	1987–1991	1992–1996	1987–1991	1992–1996
Buffalo	.681	.625	586	615
Cincinnati	.453	.325	430	391
Denver	.590	.562	565	586
Houston	.607	.487	401	365
Kansas City	.478	.650	466	607
Miami	.531	.587	459	542
New England	.369	.425	362	415
New York	.411	.275	445	475
Oakland	.516	.512	461	419
San Diego	.381	.587	374	457

Note: We calculated Performance and Attendance as in Table 4.4.

Source: Quirk and Fort, *Pay Dirt*, 409–434; Media and Public Relations departments of the teams.

The team performance of the Bills, Chiefs, and Jets fell from 1975 to 1979 then rose between 1987 and 1991. The team performance of the Broncos, Patriots, Raiders, and Chargers increased during the years 1975 to 1979, then decreased between 1987 to 1991. During 1988 to 1992, the Broncos, Bengals, and Bills played in Super Bowls. The Broncos lost to the Giants, 39–20, in the1987 Super Bowl, to the Redskins, 42–10, in the 1988 Super Bowl, and to the FortyNiners, 55–10, in the 1990 Super Bowl. The Bengals lost to the FortyNiners, 20–16, in the 1989 Super Bowl, and the Bills were defeated by the Giants, 20–19, in the 1991 Super Bowl.

After the 1991 season the Chiefs, Dolphins, Patriots, and Chargers played better. From 1992 to 1996, the mean winning percentage of the Chargers increased by 54 percent to .587, and the Chiefs by 35 percent to .650. The Chargers lost to the FortyNiners, 49–26, in the 1995 Super Bowl, and two years later the Patriots lost to the Green Bay Packers in the 1997 Super Bowl. The average winning percentage of the Jets fell by 33 percent to .275, the Bengals by 28 percent to .325, and the Oilers by 19 percent to .487 during 1992 to 1996. Also, in these years the Jets and Bengals ranked no higher than eighth in the AFC.

Collectively, the ten AFC teams listed in Table 4.6 won slightly under 51 percent of their games between 1992 and 1996, even though the mean winning percentage of six teams had declined relative to the years 1987 to 1991. The mean winning percentage of the teams were .484 for 1970 to 1974, .512 for 1975 to 1979, .501 for 1987 to 1991, and .503 for 1992 to 1996. So during the 1970s the AFC teams as a group improved in performance. To be sure, from the late 1980s to the mid-1990s, the performance of the teams leveled out. Yet four of the teams continued to play better during this period. Moreover, the most improved clubs in winning percentage were the Chargers at 54 percent, the Chiefs at 36 percent, the Patriots at 15 percent, and the Dolphins at 11 percent. A significant downward trend in team performance occurred for the Bengals, Oilers, and Jets.

The gap in attendance between the league and the ten AFC teams had nearly closed by 1991. Evidently, improved play by the Bills, Bengals, Oilers, and Chiefs helped attract more fans to their stadiums between 1987 and 1991. That is, established AFC teams such as the Browns, Colts, Steelers, and Seahawks lost playoff games to the Bengals, Broncos, and Oilers. Yet no AFC team listed in Table 4.6 won the Super Bowl between 1981 and 1991. Taken together, the mean annual attendance of the ten AFC teams increased by 113,000 per season, or 30 percent, and the league by 87,000 per season, or 21 percent, during 1987 to 1991, which marked an improvement from the 1970s. Apparently economic growth and prosperity across the nation increased the demand for professional football and consequently attendance rose.

After 1991, average attendance continued rising for the league and for the Bills, Broncos, Chiefs, Dolphins, Patriots, Jets, and Chargers. On the other hand, the Bengals, Oilers, and Raiders drew fewer fans to their stadiums between 1992 and 1996 than from 1987 to 1991. Impressive increases in attendance occurred for the Chiefs between 1993 and 1996 because over 600,000 fans attended home games in Arrowhead Stadium during those years. Otherwise the Bills remain the only former AFL team to top 600,000 per season, a feat the team accomplished each year between 1988 and 1993, and again in 1996.

From 1987 to 1996, the Bills at 600,000 and the Broncos at 585,000 had the highest average seasonal attendance and the Oilers at 383,000 and the Patriots at 388,000 had the lowest. The remaining six AFC franchises drew between 410,000 per season in Cincinnati and 536,000 per season in Kansas City between 1987 and 1996. Meanwhile, during these years the league averaged 484,000 per season and the AFC expansion franchises, 466,000 per season. Improved team performances and hometown support reduced the differences in average attendance between the expansion teams and the league from 15 to 5 percent during the 1970s and between 1987 and 1996. By the mid-1990s, AFC teams such as the Bills, Broncos, Chiefs, and Dolphins had surpassed many of the elite NFC teams in drawing power due to winning more games and competing for division titles and conference championships.

The numbers in Tables 4.5 and 4.6 raise a question. Have the market values of the ten AFC teams changed in recent years? Table 4.7 depicts the growth in the market value of these franchises from 1993 to 1997 along with the teams expansion fees in the year when they joined the AFL. Table 4.7 reveals that from 1993 to 1997 the Dolphins and Raiders appreciated in value between 43 and 51 percent. In 1997, the Dolphins ranked second in the NFL behind the Cowboys at $242 million and second in stadium revenues at $20 million per year. One year later the Cowboys had appreciated to $413 million and the Dolphins to $340 million.

AFC teams that have appreciated between 30 and 40 percent in value include the Bengals, Chiefs, Patriots, Jets, and Chargers. Due to improved play

Table 4.7

Selected AFC Franchises, Expansion Fees, and Change in Franchise Values, 1993 to 1997

Franchise	Expansion Fee (Year)		Change in Franchise Value		
			1993	1997	%Change
Buffalo	25	(1959)	164	200	22
Cincinnati	7	(1967)	142	188	32
Denver	25	(1959)	147	182	24
Houston	25	(1959)	157	193	23
Kansas City	25	(1959)	153	204	33
Miami	7	(1965)	161	242	50
New England	25	(1959)	142	197	39
New York	25	(1959)	142	186	31
Oakland	25	(1959)	146	210	44
San Diego	25	(1959)	142	191	35

Note: Expansion Fees are in thousands of dollars. Change in Franchise Value are in millions of dollars.

Source: Quirk and Fort, *Pay Dirt,* 409–434; Scott Fowler, "List Puts Panthers Among Most Valuable Pro Teams," 1A, 18A; *Information Please Sports Almanac,* 1993–1996.

and greater attendance, the Patriots more than doubled in value at 123 percent, or by $109 million, from 1988 to 1997. Since the mid-1960s, the market values of the Jets and Chargers have risen more than 1,800 percent as the teams' cash flow, operating income, and profits increased from gate receipts, television and radio revenues, merchandise sales, and stadium earnings. Three AFC teams appreciated between 20 and 30 percent from 1993 to 1997. The teams that experienced these gains were the Bills, Broncos (160 percent since 1984), and Oilers (now Titans).

On average, the teams in Table 4.7 appreciated by $50 million, or 33 percent, between 1993 and 1997. The mean increase for all NFL teams was $52 million, or 34 percent, in those years. So since 1970, when ten AFL teams each paid $2 million in compensation to join the NFL, instead of the league expansion franchise fee of $8 million, the market values of the clubs have risen between $180 million and $240 million.[30]

In recent years the financial status of the Miami and Cincinnati franchises has improved. From 1993 to 1997 the Dolphins rose in value by 50 percent—$81 million—ranking third among all professional sports teams in the United States.[31] Likewise, from 1993 to 1997 the Bengals increased in market value by 32 percent—$46 million—ranking twenty-eighth out of all professional sports franchises, and twentieth among NFL clubs. The planned construction of a state-of-the-art stadium in Cincinnati should raise additional revenues and grow the market value of the Bengals in the 1999 season and beyond.

PROFESSIONAL BASKETBALL

National Basketball Association

The NBA expanded by twenty-one teams between 1962 and 1996. Six teams joined the league in the 1960s, eight teams in the 1970s, five teams in the 1980s, and two teams in the 1990s. Eleven expansion teams played in the NBA from 1987 to 1996. The Charlotte Hornets and Miami Heat began play in 1989, the Minnesota Timberwolves and Orlando Magic in 1990, and the Toronto Raptors and Vancouver Grizzlies in 1996. When the tables were constructed, sufficient data were available to analyze expansion teams only through the 1996 season. So we exclude the performance and attendance of the Raptors and Grizzlies from our analysis because of their brief history in the NBA. Still, we examined the ownership histories of both the Raptors and Grizzlies.

Before exploring the performance and attendance of the teams, we describe the ownership of the franchises. Identifying the individuals or groups that own a franchise provides insight to evaluate the structure, operation, and the financial risk and return of a team from an investment and managerial perspective.[32]

After the NBA first expanded in 1966, the ownership of the Chicago Bulls changed hands in 1972 for a price of $5.1 million and in 1983 for an unknown price. In 1985, a syndicate headed by Jerry Reinsdorf bought 56 percent of the Bulls for $9.2 million. With wealth estimated at $80 million from real estate investments, Reinsdorf owns approximately 10 percent of the Bulls and 10 percent of the Chicago White Sox. Since 1994 the Bulls have played in the United

Center, which the team owners built for $175 million with a $15 million subsidy from Illinois taxpayers.[33]

Sam Schulman and Gene Klein owned the Seattle SuperSonics from 1967 to 1973. Schulman bought his partner's interest in the team in 1972 for an unknown price, and then sold the club to Ackerly Communications for $21 million in 1984. With a net worth of $25 million, Barry Ackerly owns nearly 60 percent of the team. *Sports Illustrated* ranked Ackerly eightieth in wealth among professional sports proprietors in 1993. The SuperSonics estimated value of $169 million placed the team fifty-fifth among sports franchises in the United States and Canada in 1998.[34]

For an expansion fee of $2 million levied by the NBA in 1968, a syndicate purchased the Milwaukee Bucks. The syndicate sold the team for an unknown price in 1977. The new owner sold the Bucks again in 1985 for $16.5 million to Herb Kohl, a politically ambitious Wisconsiner. Elected to the U.S. Senate in 1988, Kohl's real estate and other holdings make him worth $275 million. In 1998 the value of the Bucks climbed to $94 million and the club ranked twenty-ninth among NBA franchises.[35]

The Phoenix Suns joined the NBA in 1968. Nineteen years later, the original syndicate owners headed by Richard Block, sold the Suns for $44.5 million to another syndicate led by Jerry Colangelo. With $25 million in wealth, Colangelo owns or controls 36 percent of the Suns, 36 percent of the license of the Phoenix Mercury in the WBNA, 25 percent of the Arizona Rattlers arena football team, and 1 percent of the Arizona Diamondbacks. The value of the Suns ranked thirty-seventh at $235 million among professional sports franchises in 1998.[36]

A syndicate headed by Nick Mileti paid an entry fee of $3.7 million to bring the Cleveland Cavaliers into the NBA in 1970. After Ted Stepien acquired the team in 1980, Gordon and George Gund purchased the Cavaliers for an unknown price in 1983. The Gunds, who inherited their wealth from their father's investments in real estate, cattle, and coffee, had a net worth of $1.6 billion in 1998. They own the Richfield Coliseum and George has a majority interest in the San Jose Sharks of the NHL. The Cavaliers ranked thirteenth in value at $161 million among NBA franchises and the Sharks ranked fifteenth at $108 million among NHL franchises in 1998.[37]

A syndicate paid $3.7 million in 1970 for the Portland Trail Blazers to enter the NBA. The team's ownership changed in 1972, 1973, 1975, and again in 1988 when Larry Weinberg sold the team for $70 million to Paul Allen. A cofounder of Microsoft Corporation along with Bill Gates, Allen is the wealthiest sports team owner with an estimated net worth of $22 billion in 1998. Since 1996 the Trail Blazers have played in the $262 million Rose Garden in Portland that seats twenty-one thousand fans.[38]

Joining the NBA in 1976 for a fee of $3.2 million plus $1.6 in compensation to ABA teams excluded from the NBA, the Denver Nuggets changed owners in 1982, 1985, and 1989. Comsat Denver, Inc., purchased 62 percent of the team in 1989 and acquired the remaining 38 percent in 1992. Six years later, the Nuggets' estimated value reached $110 million, ranking the team twenty-seventh among NBA franchises. The Nuggets will vacate the two-decades-old

McNichols Sports Arena in 1999 and begin play in the new $132 million Pepsi Center in Denver, which seats nineteen thousand. In September 1998, club owners hired director of player personnel Mike D'Antoni as head coach, replacing Bill Hanzlik. D'Antoni posted a 178–70 record for seven seasons in the Italian Professional Basketball League and led his team to the playoffs each year. He played for the Kansas City Kings between 1973 and 1975 and then joined the St. Louis Spirits of the ABA in late 1975. After hiring D'Antoni, general manager Dan Issel stated: "Mike is a tremendous individual with impressive coaching acumen. He is an excellent communicator and will be integral in revitalizing the Nuggets' franchise."[39]

The Indiana Pacers entered the NBA in 1976 for a fee of $3.2 million plus $1.6 million in compensation. Three years later the team's owners sold the Pacers to a syndicate headed by Sam Nassi for an unknown price. Melvin and Herbert Simon purchased the team for an unknown price in 1983. With a net worth of $660 million in 1998, Melvin Simon heads Simon Associates, the largest developer of shopping centers in the United States. Based in Indianapolis, Simon Associates is currently constructing a new $175 million arena in downtown Indianapolis that should keep the team in Indianapolis for at least another ten years.[40]

After joining the NBA in 1976 for a fee of $3.2 million plus a $4 million payment to the New York Knicks for invading their market, the New Jersey Nets were sold for unknown prices to syndicates in 1978 and 1985. Alan Aufzien, who bought a share of the team in 1978, owns 28 percent of the Nets along with David Gerstein and five other minority owners. Aufzien and Gerstein have personal assets worth roughly $15 million and are ranked eighty-seventh and eighty-ninth among the top one hundred sports franchise owners. At a value of $157 million, the Nets ranked in the top half for NBA teams in 1998. Lewis Katz and Finn Wentworth are the principal owners of the club as of 1999.[41]

Red McCombs, a member of a syndicate that purchased the San Antonio Spurs in 1973 for an unknown price, acquired majority control of the team for $47 million in 1988. Nine years later Bob Coleman led an investor group, which included several San Antonio corporations, to purchase the Spurs. As chief executive officer and proprietor of Texace Corporation, in 1993 Coleman's wealth was estimated to be $20 million, and in 1998 the market value of the Spurs reached $122 million. As reported in *Forbes*, in 1999 the principal owner of the club is Peter Holt.[42]

A syndicate headed by Donald Carter has owned the Dallas Mavericks since 1980 when the team joined the NBA for a fee of $12 million. In 1993 Carter owned 95 percent of the Mavericks and 100 percent of the Dallas Sidekicks, an indoor soccer team. Carter's estimated net worth is $225 million. In 1998, the Mavericks ranked seventy-eighth at $119 million among all professional sports teams. As of 1999, *Forbes* lists Ross Perot, Jr., as the team's principal owner.[43]

The owners of the Charlotte Hornets and Miami Heat, George Shinn and Ted Arison, each paid $32.5 million to enter the NBA in 1988. Shinn's estimated net worth nears $100 million, an amount partially earned in 1989 from the sale of a chain of business schools called Rutledge College. In 1997, Shinn sold the Charlotte Knights, a minor league affiliate of the Florida Marlins (in 1999 the Chicago White Sox), to Don Beaver who intended to buy the Minnesota Twins and move the team to Fort Mill, South Carolina, for two seasons and then relocate to Charlotte or the Triad Region of North Carolina as a permanent site. Arison owns 65 percent of the Heat and is a multibillionaire who started Carnival Cruise Lines in 1972. The Heat play in the 15,800-seat, $56 million Miami Arena that was built in 1988 and seats the fewest fans in the NBA. As a result, the franchise started construction of a new arena that will seat twenty thousand fans.[44]

The Minnesota Timberwolves and Orlando Magic joined the NBA in 1989 for an entry fee of $32.5 million per franchise. Marv Wolfenson and Harvey Ratner, who owned the Timberwolves and the team's arena, the Target Center, had a combined net worth of $50 million in 1993. In 1996, Glen Taylor, whose net worth is estimated to be roughly $1 billion, bought the club for $88.5 million. The Timberwolves ranked seventy-seventh at $119 million among all professional sports franchises in 1998.[45]

Richard DeVos, the owner of the Magic, is a billionaire, a cofounder of the Amway Corporation, and a former finance chairman of the Republican Party. In 1998, the Magic ranked sixty-ninth at $134 million among all professional sports franchises.[46]

Following an expansion committee's recommendation in 1993, the NBA awarded the Toronto Raptors a franchise that began play in 1995 and became the twenty-eighth team in the league.[47] The Raptors' original proprietor group consisted of John Bitove, Allan Slaight, and several minority owners, which included former Detroit Pistons' star player Isiah Thomas. Eventually Thomas became the general manager and vice president of the club and the architect of the Raptors roster. During the 1995 NBA expansion draft the team chose veteran players B. J. Armstrong of the Chicago Bulls and Jerome Kersey of the Portland Trail Blazers. In the regular NBA draft held at the Toronto SkyDome, the Raptors selected Damon Stoudamire from the University of Arizona and Jimmy King, one of the vaunted "Fab Five" from the University of Michigan. In the 1996 season, even though Stoudamire scored nineteen points per game and won the Most Valuable Player award during the Rookie Game at All-Star Weekend, the team's winning percentage was only .256. Stoudamire also won Rookie of the Month honors twice and became the NBA Rookie of the Year.[48] The Raptors play in the Toronto SkyDome, a 20,125-seat arena built in 1989 and financed by Canadian taxpayers. But in less than ten years the SkyDome became obsolete. In February 1999, the Raptors will begin play in the Air Canada Center, a $180 million 25,000-seat arena owned by a consortium of thirty businesses. The arena contains forty lounges and fifty-five luxury suites. The suites are available for group rentals and offer an unobstructed view of the court. Along with forty courtside lounges, the suites will appeal to groups willing to pay more dollars for tickets and spend more money in the arena's pub, restaurant, retail team store, and interactive "Raptorfest" area and computer center. In February 1998, Allan Slaight sold the Raptors to Steve Stavro for an unknown price. Stavro is the chairman and chief executive officer of Maple Leaf Gardens Ltd., which purchased the Maple Leafs in 1991. The Bank of

Nova Scotia, which owned 10 percent of the Raptors, also sold its interest in the team.[49]

The NBA approved the Vancouver Grizzlies as the twenty-ninth league franchise in April 1994. The team's original owners, the Vancouver Basketball Partnership, consisted of Arthur Griffiths' Company, Northwest Sports Enterprises, which had been the majority owner of the NHL's Vancouver Canucks. In August 1994, the Vancouver Basketball Partnership officially became the Vancouver Grizzlies. The team plays in the General Motors Place, a $160 million 20,000-seat arena built in 1995 by private investors. In March 1995, Griffiths sold his majority interest in the Grizzlies, Canucks, and the arena to billionaire John McCaw, Jr. A minority shareholder of McCaw Cellular until 1994, by early 1995 McCaw had acquired 60 percent of the team and the arena.[50]

To analyze expansion in professional basketball, Table 4.8 shows the mean winning percentage and home attendance of eleven pre-1990 expansion teams that played in the NBA from 1987 to 1996. We excluded the Toronto Raptors and Vancouver Grizzlies from the table due to their brief histories in the league. But data for the Charlotte Hornets, Miami Heat, Minnesota Timberwolves, and Orlando Magic appear from when each team joined the league to 1996.

Between 1987 and 1991, the Portland Trail Blazers at .641 and the Chicago Bulls at .617 had the highest, and the New Jersey Nets at .273 and the Indiana

Table 4.8
Pre-1990 NBA Expansion Teams, Performance and Attendance, 1987 to 1996

Team (Year)	1987–1991 Seasons		1992–1996 Seasons	
	Performance	Attendance	Performance	Attendance
Chicago (1961)	.617	727	.726	834
Seattle (1966)	.517	477	.694	632
Milwaukee (1968)	.568	587	.336	649
Phoenix (1968)	.556	522	.661	742
Cleveland (1970)	.499	599	.595	748
Portland (1970)	.641	524	.592	592
Denver (1976)	483	505	.434	637
Indiana (1976)	.463	498	.573	583
New Jersey (1976)	.273	486	.458	623
San Antonio (1976)	.465	477	.663	790
Dallas (1980)	.538	692	.263	618
Charlotte (1988)	–	–	.505	973
Miami (1988)	–	–	.463	609
Minnesota (1989)	–	–	.246	688
Orlando (1989)	–	–	.558	646

Note: (Year) is the franchise's expansion year. Performance is the mean five-year winning percentage of the teams. Attendance is the mean five-year home game attendance of the teams in thousands.

Source: Wire memo from NBA Public Relations staff (September 1997), 1; *Media, Information, and Public Relations Guides* of the NBA teams; *The World Almanac and Book of Facts,* 1987–1998.

Pacers at .463 the lowest, mean winning percentage of NBA expansion teams. The Trail Blazers won more than 70 percent of their games in the 1990–91 and 1991–92 seasons after losing to the Los Angeles Lakers in the first three games of a best-of-five series in the 1989 playoffs of the Pacific Division. The Bulls' dominance began in 1991 when the team won the league championship beating the Houston Rockets in five games. The Nets had their highest performance at .317 in 1989 and 1991, and the Pacers had a winning percentage of .512 in 1990. Neither the Nets nor Pacers made the NBA playoffs from 1987 to 1991. Of the four expansion teams with less than five seasons the Hornets won 26 percent, the Heat won 23 percent, the Timberwolves won 31 percent, and the Magic won 29 percent of their games from 1987 to 1991.

The mean winning percentages of the Bulls, Cavaliers, Pacers, Nets, Suns, Spurs, and SuperSonics increased from 1987–1991 to 1992–1996. The mean winning percentage of the Nets increased by 67 percent, the Spurs by 42 percent, the SuperSonics by 34 percent, and the Pacers by 23 percent. The Pacers won the divisional crown in 1995, the Spurs won theirs in 1995 and 1996, and the SuperSonics won their divisional championship in 1994 and 1996.

The play of the Dallas Mavericks, Denver Nuggets, Milwaukee Bucks, and Portland Trail Blazers declined after 1991. The mean winning percentage of the Mavericks fell by 51 percent, or from .538 to .263, and the Bucks by 40 percent, or from .568 to .336, due to inconsistent team play, player trades, and inadequate coaching.

Unlike the Timberwolves, the performances of the Hornets, Heat, and Magic soared after 1991. Key players such as 1992 Rookie of the Year Larry Johnson of the Hornets, and shooting guards Tim Hardaway of the Heat and Anfernee Hardaway of the Magic, led their teams to winning seasons. For example, the Hornets' performance ranged from .232 to .378 during 1989 to 1992. The Hornets beat the Boston Celtics in the first round of the Atlantic Division playoffs then lost to the New York Knicks in five games in the Eastern Conference semifinals in 1993. Two years later the Hornets lost to the Bulls in four games in the first round of the playoffs. Meanwhile, the Heat won over 51 percent of their games in 1994 and 1996, and the Magic won back-to-back division titles in 1995 and 1996. In 1997, the teams continued to excel as winning percentages topped .740 for the Heat, .650 for the Hornets, and .540 for the Magic. The Timberwolves steadily improved from 1992 to 1997 as their winning percentage more than doubled from .183 to .488.

From 1987 to 1996, the Bulls at .671 and the Trail Blazers at .616 had the highest, and the Nets at .365 and the Mavericks at .400 had the lowest, mean winning percentages of the NBA expansion teams. The Hornets mean winning percentage was .384 and the Heat .347 from 1989 to 1997. In these seven seasons, the Timberwolves were .278 and the Magic .428, and in 1996 and 1997 the Raptors were .311 and the Grizzlies .117.

Grouped together the mean winning percentage of the former NBA expansion teams exceeded the league only in 1988 and from 1993 to 1996. During 1987 to 1996, the expansion teams won 48 percent of their games with a high of 54 percent in 1995 and a low of 45 percent in 1989. As an aside, if we exclude the performance of the newest teams such as the Hornets, Heat, Timberwolves, and Magic in 1989 to 1991, and the Raptors and Grizzlies in 1996, then the mean winning percentage of the expansion teams increases to 51 percent for the period, which is above the league average. Therefore, after three or four seasons the NBA expansion teams had become competitive with many of the established teams. By 1997 the Heat and Hornets followed the Bulls and SuperSonics in performance among all NBA expansion teams.

Between 1987 and 1991, the Bulls at 727,000 and the Mavericks at 692,000 had the highest, and the Spurs and SuperSonics at 477,000 had the lowest, mean attendance of NBA expansion teams. The Bulls, with superstars Michael Jordan and Scottie Pippen, and rebound leader Dennis Rodman increased their attendance from 650,000 in 1987 to 757,000 in 1991 while the Mavericks played to capacity crowds between 1987 and 1991. The Hornets between 1989 to 1991, the Timberwolves between 1990 to 1991, the Heat between 1989 to 1991, and the Magic between 1991 to 1992, also filled their arenas (see Table 4.8).

The Hornets and Bulls led the former expansion teams in average attendance from 1992 to 1996. The Pacers and Trail Blazers were the only two expansion teams with less than 600,000 in average attendance between 1992 and 1996. The largest growth in mean attendance from 1987–1991 to 1992–1996 was 65 percent by the Spurs, 42 percent by the Suns, and 32 percent by the SuperSonics. All-pros such as David Robinson of the Spurs, Charles Barkley of the Suns, and Shawn Kemp of the SuperSonics scored and rebounded with the best players in the league, which boosted the home attendance of their teams. Meanwhile, the Mavericks fell in average attendance by 10 percent from 692,000 in 1992 to 618,000 in 1996. Even with 1995 Rookie of the Year Jason Kidd, the Mavericks won fewer than 40 percent of their games in 1995 and 1996.

During 1987 to 1996, the Pacers with 540,000 and the Nets and SuperSonics with 554,000 drew the lowest average attendance of the expansion teams. On the other hand, the Bulls with 780,000 and the Cavaliers with 673,000 had the highest average attendance in the league in those years. Again, the average attendance of the latest expansion teams exceeded expectations. The Hornets, for example, averaged 972,000 from 1989 to 1996, and the Timberwolves 756,000 from 1990 to 1996. What is more, in 1996 the Raptors drew 950,000 and the Grizzlies 704,000 to their arenas despite inferior team performances.

Collectively, the fifteen former expansion teams had a higher mean attendance than the league in 1990, 1991, and from 1993 to 1996. While the attendance of the league increased by 19 percent from 1987 to 1991, and by 9 percent from 1992 to 1996, the attendance of the expansion teams grouped increased on average by 28 percent and 16 percent respectively in those years. This occurred because of the outstanding play of visiting teams such as the Bulls, Cavaliers, and Spurs, and the attraction of new teams in Charlotte, Miami, Minnesota, Orlando, Toronto, and Vancouver. The weak play of established teams such as the Hawks, Warriors, Nets, Clippers, SeventySixers, and Kings kept league attendance to a moderate growth rate.

Summarizing Table 4.8, during 1987 to 1996 the home attendance of the Bulls, Cavaliers, Nets, Pacers, Suns, Spurs, and SuperSonics rose as each team's performance improved. The opposite occurred for the Nuggets, Bucks, and Trail

Blazers. As their performance declined, home attendance increased. Perhaps fans attended games in Denver, Milwaukee, and Portland to watch the visiting elite teams and their star players such as Michael Jordan of the Bulls, Reggie Miller of the Pacers, Shaquille O'Neal of the Lakers, Hakeem Olajuwon of the Rockets, Grant Hill of the Pistons, Patrick Ewing of the Knicks, and Karl Malone of the Jazz.

Since expansion, the performances of the Hornets, Heat, and Magic have improved, but home attendance has remained constant. To the 1997–98 season, the Hornets played to capacity crowds at the 24,000-seat Charlotte Coliseum while the Heat performed before sellout crowds in Miami's small arena.

The attendance and performance of the Mavericks and Timberwolves have declined in recent seasons. The annual seasonal attendance of the Mavericks fell from 695,000 in 1989–90 to 541,000 in 1997–98, and the Timberwolves' from 1,072,000 in 1989–90 to 738,000 in 1997–98. Consequently, with lower gate receipts and higher operating costs, the profit margins of both teams have fallen.

If their substandard performance continues, the attendance and gate receipts of the Raptors and Grizzlies should decline because these teams are located in cities that lack a long tradition of supporting basketball. Currently, neither Toronto nor Vancouver hosts an NFL team and in 1997 they ranked seventeenth and twenty-sixth respectively in *The Sporting News* as the best sports cities.[51]

Tables 2.9, 2.10, 4.7, and 4.8 contain some historical demographic, team-specific, and financial data about NBA expansion teams. Along with player salaries, in recent years team revenues from gate receipts, television and radio broadcasting, luxury suites, permanent seat licenses, club seats, merchandise sales, parking fees, advertising, and concessions have escalated. To determine the impact of these revenues on the market value of the teams between 1993 and 1997, we constructed Table 4.9. The table reveals that the Phoenix Suns, Orlando Magic, and New Jersey Nets had the largest, and the Charlotte Hornets, Dallas Mavericks, and Minneapolis Timberwolves had the smallest, increases in market value from 1993 to 1997. While the average value of a league team increased 29 percent, from $114 million to $148 million, the average value of a pre-1990 expansion team increased 55 percent, from $94 million to $145 million during this period. Nine of the expansion teams in Table 4.9 changed owners in the 1980s. Based on sales prices according to Quirk and Fort, the percentage increase in the market value of each team from the date of sale to 1997 rose 1,304 percent for the Bulls since 1985; 522 percent for the SuperSonics since 1984; 524 percent for the Milwaukee Bucks since 1985; 356 percent for the Phoenix Suns since 1987; 2,400 percent for the Cavaliers since 1980; 155 percent for the Trail Blazers since 1988; 114 percent for the Nuggets since 1989; 231 percent for the Spurs since 1988; and 83 percent for the Magic since 1989.[52] These NBA teams significantly appreciated in value for five reasons. First, professional basketball has become increasingly popular in the United States because of its promotion by the press and frequent broadcasts on cable and network television. Second, the playing styles of retired superstars such as Larry Bird and Magic Johnson and the leagues greatest player Michael Jordan are emulated by the nation's youth beginning in elementary and secondary schools.

Table 4.9
**Selected NBA Expansion Franchises, Expansion Fees and Change in Franchise
Values, 1993 to 1997**

Franchise	Expansion Fee (Year)	Change in Franchise Value		
		1993	1997	%Change
Chicago	1.20 (1966)	149	214	44
Seattle	1.75 (1967)	96	137	43
Milwaukee	2.00 (1968)	77	103	34
Phoenix	2.00 (1968)	108	220	103
Cleveland	3.70 (1970)	118	175	72
Portland	3.70 (1970)	122	179	47
Denver	4.80 (1976)	69	116	68
Indiana	4.80 (1976)	67	114	70
New Jersey	4.80 (1976)	79	137	73
San Antonio	4.80 (1976)	100	156	56
Dallas	20.00 (1980)	79	104	32
Charlotte	32.50 (1988)	104	136	31
Miami	32.50 (1988)	76	118	55
Minnesota	32.50 (1989)	92	123	34
Orlando	32.50 (1989)	84	156	86

Note: Expansion Fees and Change in Franchise Value are in millions of dollars.

Source: James Quirk and Rodney Fort, *Pay Dirt,* 446–463; *Information Please Sports Almanac,* 1993–1997; Scott Fowler, "List Puts Panthers Among Most Valuable Pro Teams," 1A, 18A.

Third, the NBA has successfully exploited the opportunity to commercialize teams and players in retail markets with logos, clothing, shoes, posters, and other merchandise. Fourth, the escalation of cash flows to the teams and the expansion of clubs into untapped markets have increased the rate of return and profits of the franchises. Fifth, new and renovated arenas financed by taxpayers, and higher ticket prices have accelerated the revenue stream and value of the teams.

SUMMARY

For the post-1950 MLB expansion teams, between 1987 and 1996 the Houston Astros, Montreal Expos, and Seattle Mariners played better and increased attendance, while the Anaheim Angels, Kansas City Royals, New York Mets, and San Diego Padres played worse and experienced a decrease in attendance. During this period, changes in winning percentage and attendance correlated positively for the MLB expansion teams. Because of their performance, from 1993 to 1997 the estimated market value of the Mets fell by 2 percent, the Royals by 7 percent, and increased less than 5 percent for the Angels, Expos, and Padres. The value of the Astros and Mariners rose by 34 percent as their performance and attendance improved. Meanwhile, since 1993 the value of the Colorado Rockies and Florida Marlins increased over 50 percent, enlarging the owners' profits. Simply put, the small and large market expansion teams in MLB have appreciated unequally in the 1990s.

Turning to the NFL, from 1987 to 1996 the Atlanta Falcons, Dallas Cowboys, Kansas City Chiefs, Miami Dolphins, Minnesota Vikings, New England Patriots, Tampa Bay Buccaneers, and San Diego Chargers played better and drew more fans, compared to the Cincinnati Bengals, Houston Oilers, New Orleans Saints, Oakland Raiders, and Seattle Seahawks who played worse and drew fewer fans to their stadiums. Furthermore, the performance of the Bills, Broncos, and Jets declined as their attendance rose. Since 1993 all NFL expansion teams and the former AFL teams appreciated in market value, reflecting the growth in demand to attend professional football games and to watch games on television. Similar to the Marlins and Rockies in MLB, the newest NFL expansion teams, the Carolina Panthers and Jacksonville Jaguars, realized large increases in market value from 1995 to 1998. Overall, since 1987 the proprietors of the NFL expansion teams have increased the value of their teams, and the league made economically prudent and lucrative business decisions by granting these cities franchises to play in the NFL.

Team-specific and economic outcomes happened along similar lines in the NBA. Between 1987 and 1996, the Chicago Bulls, Cleveland Cavaliers, Indiana Pacers, New Jersey Nets, Phoenix Suns, San Antonio Spurs, and Seattle SuperSonics won more games and increased attendance, while the Dallas Mavericks won fewer games and experienced a decrease in attendance. The winning percentages of the Nuggets, Bucks, and Trail Blazers fell, but their home attendance rose. So except for the Mavericks, in recent seasons the attendance for all NBA expansion teams increased regardless of whether the team played better. Similar to expansion clubs in the NFL, all former NBA expansion teams appreciated in market value from 1993 to 1998. Therefore, the value of small- and large-market NBA teams increased as the league grew from twenty-three to twenty-nine franchises between 1987 and 1998. Moreover, in the 1997–98 season, the Bulls, SuperSonics, and Suns performed the best, while the Nuggets, Grizzlies, and Mavericks had the worst performances for the expansion clubs.[53] The three expansion teams with the highest and lowest home attendance in the 1997–98 season were, respectively, the Bulls, Hornets, and Trailblazers, and the Nuggets, Mavericks, and Grizzlies.[54]

The market value of NBA and other professional sports franchises changes annually due to the organization's operating income and profit, the performance and attendance of the team, the construction of a new (or renovation of an old) arena, and other factors like the national economy and consumer confidence. During the 1993–94 season, the value of the twenty-seven NBA franchises increased on average by $14 million, or 14 percent. In 1997, the total market value of the twenty-nine NBA franchises topped $4 billion. That is, the mean estimated value per franchise stood at $140 million, which represents a 24 percent increase in worth since 1994 for each team in the league.

Table 4.10 gives the financial risks and the changes in market value for the three highest and lowest valued NBA expansion franchises calculated from 1993 to 1997. During this period, Phoenix, Chicago, Portland, and Indiana increased in market value at a greater rate than the NBA average of 41 percent. Of the 113 franchises surveyed, Phoenix ranked ninth, Chicago eleventh, Portland

Table 4.10
Selected NBA Franchises, Risk and Change in Franchise Value, 1993 to 1997

		Change in Franchise Value	
Franchise	Risk	$	%
Phoenix	Moderate	108	103
Chicago	Low	149	44
Portland	Low	122	47
Milwaukee	Moderate	77	34
Dallas	High	79	32
Indiana	Moderate	67	70

Note: Risk measures the ability of the team to generate sufficient income to compete with other NBA teams over the next three to five years as reported in *Financial World*. The Change in Franchise Value is measured in millions of dollars ($) and in percentages (%).

Source: Atre, et al., "Sports, Stocks, and Bonds," 57, 62–64; *Information Please Sports Almanac,* 573; Fowler, "List Puts Panthers Among Most Valuable Pro Teams," 1A, 18A.

thirty-eighth, Indiana seventy-fifth, Dallas eighty-third, and Milwaukee eighty-sixth.[55] The gate receipts, media revenues, and venue earnings of Milwaukee, Dallas, and Indiana fell below the league average. We rate these franchises as moderate- to high-risk investments unless they manage to generate new arena receipts, or the league shares more revenues, or the teams dramatically improve their performances in the next few seasons. Other NBA expansion teams omitted from Table 4.10 that remain high-risk investments include the Spurs, Timberwolves, Nets, and the Clippers.

Prompted by the commercial success of the NBA, entrepreneurs have devised plans for tapping the lucrative basketball market. In August 1998, for example, Michael Freedman and Rodney Gregory announced a men's International Basketball League (IBL). The IBL will began play in November 1999 with charter teams in Albuquerque, Baltimore, Cincinnati, Jacksonville, Las Vegas, Richmond, San Diego and Tampa. Over the next five years the league plans to place an additional twelve franchises in cities throughout the world. The players will work for the league, sign one-year contracts, and remain with a team for the entire season. At least one non-U.S. player must play on each team.[56]

The success of the IBL will depend largely on how well it cultivates enthusiasm and interest for league games. To be sure, many cities beyond Canada and the United States have the requisite "demographics" that make them suitable candidates for hosting an NBA franchise let alone one of the IBL. Nonetheless, the new league should take nothing for granted, and it would be wise to model itself after the NBA and adopt many of the older association policies, which have contributed to both the NBA's popularity and profitability in the highly competitive world of professional sports. Simply put, the IBL should hinder neither league expansion nor team relocation. If the new league follows such a course, it stands to better position its teams to earn profits and realize success on basketball courts throughout the world.

NOTES

1. We obtained franchise values from three sources. See the *Information Please Sports Almanac* (New York and Boston: Houghton Mifflin Company, 1996), 573; Scott Fowler, "List Puts Panthers Among Most Valuable Pro Teams," *Charlotte Observer* (25 May 1997), 1A, 18A; Michael Ozanian, "Selective Accounting," *Forbes* (14 December 1998), 124–134.

2. The ownership histories of the franchises in the three sports we extracted from James Quirk and Rodney Fort, *Pay Dirt: The Business of Professional Sports* (Princeton, N.J.: Princeton University Press, 1992), 378–478.

3. See Foon Rhee, "Twins Sale on Agenda as Owners Talk Shop," *Charlotte Observer* (11 January 1998), 1A, 18A; "Sticker Shock. Best Seats at Astros' New Park Will Be Pricey," at <http://www.cnnsi.com> cited 24 July 1998.

4. Shea Stadium ranked twenty-eighth among MLB ballparks for the number of foul balls on the field or in the stands in 1997. For a complete ranking of ballparks see Mike McCarthy, "Fair or Foul," *Wall Street Journal* (12 June 1998), W7. For information about the Mets' new baseball only ballpark, see "Plans Progressing on Mets Stadium," at <http://www.cnnsi.com> cited 27 October 1998.

5. Rhee, "Twins Sale on Agenda as Owners Talk Shop," 18A. Between 1993 and 1998 the Expos were the most efficient team in baseball. The team spent $93.4 million on players and produced three winning seasons and reached the post-season playoffs twice in those years. The San Diego Padres, Houston Astros, Atlanta Braves, and Cleveland Indians placed second to fifth respectively in efficiency. The least efficient team was the Oakland Athletics followed by the Minnesota Twins and Pittsburgh Pirates. See two Editorials, "Montreal Knows How to Spend," *USA Today* (9 June 1998), 5C; "Setback for Expos," *Charlotte Observer* (18 September 1998), 4B. For the relocation of the Expos see Foon Rhee, "Expos in Charlotte? Team Not on Market Yet," *Charlotte Observer* (17 September 1998), 2B.

6. Quirk and Fort, *Pay Dirt*, 398–399; Rhee, "Twins Sale on Agenda as Owners Talk Shop," 18A.

7. Elizabeth Comte, "Sports Expansion Box Score," *The Sporting News* (12 March 1990), 12.

8. Tushar Atre, Kristine Auns, Kurt Badenhausen, Kevin McAuliffe, Christopher Nikolov, and Michael K. Ozanian, "Sports, Stocks, and Bonds," *Financial World* (20 May 1996), 58.

9. Attendance appeared in a 1997 memo from the American League and was obtained from the teams in the league.

10. We calculated these percentages using seasonal attendance provided by the league.

11. The seasonal attendance of the Rockies and Marlins we obtained from the league and teams.

12. For the deal to sell the Marlins see "Smiley's Group in Position to Buy the Marlins," at the Worldwide Web site <http://www.sportingnews.com> cited 19 November 1997; "Huizenga Negotiating to Sell Marlins," at <http://www.austin360.com> cited 7 November 1997; Greg Stoda, "Sheffield Won't Help Florida Foot the Bill," *Charlotte Observer* (8 May 1998), 4B; "Marlins Plan More Salary Slashing," *Charlotte Observer* (7 May 1998), 4B; "Huizenga Says He May Keep Marlins Next Season," at the Web site <http://www.cnnsi.com> cited 21 August 1998; "I Have a Handshake Deal. Commodities Trader Says He's Buying Marlins for $150 million," at <http://www.cnnsi.com> cited 11 September 1998.

13. For the values of professional sports franchises, see Scott Fowler, "List Puts Panthers Among Most Valuable Pro Teams," 1A, 18A; Michael Ozanian, "Selective

Accounting," 124–134; "What Major League Franchises Are Worth," *Information Please Sports Almanac* (New York and Boston: Houghton Mifflin Company, 1993), 573; Atre, et al., "Sports, Stocks, and Bonds," 63–64.

14. We obtained attendance from the league and teams.

15. Atre, et al., "Sports, Stocks, and Bonds," 62–64.

16. Ibid.

17. Ibid, 56.

18. *The 1996 Carolina Panthers Official Media Guide,* 7.

19. See John Helyar, "Free Agency Proves to be the Cat's Meow for Jags and Panthers," *Wall Street Journal* (10 January 1997), A1, A5; Quick and Fort, *Pay Dirt,* 440, 444.

20. See John Helyar, "Free Agency Proves to Be the Cat's Meow for Jags and Panthers," A1, A5.

21. For more details on the organizational changes of the Panthers, see Charles Chandler, "Who's Panthers Boss? It's Capers," *Charlotte Observer* (16 January 1998), 1B; Charles Chandler, "Jags' Front Office Stable; Panthers' in Transition," *Charlotte Observer* (8 August 1998), 1B, 5B.

22. Fowler, "List Puts Panthers Among Most Valuable Pro Teams," 1A, 18A; Michael Ozanian, "Selective Accounting," 132.

23. For the AFL and NFL final standings from 1960 to 1995, see *The Oakland Raiders: The Team of the Decades* 1996, 176–184.

24. The attendance of the NFL teams came from each team's annual *Media Guides* and total attendance of the AFL and NFL was obtained from league staff.

25. The values of professional football franchises were reported by Scott Fowler, "List Puts Panthers Among Most Valuable Pro Teams," 1A, 18A; Tushar Atre, et al., "Sports, Stocks, and Bonds," 58; Michael Ozanian, "Selective Accounting," 132.

26. Atre, et al., "Sports, Stocks, and Bonds," 58.

27. See Quirk and Fort, *Pay Dirt,* 409–434..

28. Fowler, "List Puts Panthers Among Most Valuable Pro Teams," 1A, 18A; Ozanian, "Selective Accounting," 132.

29. An NFL Public Relations Memo dated 15 October 1996 gives the total and average NFL paid attendance from 1934 to 1995 for regular season and post season games.

30. For the NFL-AFL agreement, see Quirk and Fort, *Pay Dirt,* 333–361.

31. See Fowler, "List Puts Panthers Among Most Valuable Pro Teams," 1A, 18A; Ozanian, "Selective Accounting," 124–134.

32. We used five sources extensively to develop the history of the teams. These include Quirk and Fort, *Pay Dirt,* 446–459; John Steinbreder, "The Owners," *Sports Illustrated* (13 September 1993), 64–87; Fowler, "List Puts Panthers Among Most Valuable Pro Teams," 1A, 18A; Atre, et al., "Sports, Stocks, and Bonds," 53–65; Ozanian, "Selective Accounting," 124–134.

33. Information and statistics on the Bulls appears at <http://www.nba.com> cited 8 April 1998.

34. Fowler, "List Puts Panthers Among Most Valuable Pro Teams," 1A, 18A; Ozanian, "Selective Accounting," 130.

35. See Quirk and Fort, *Pay Dirt,* 454; Steinbreder, "The Owners," 70; Fowler, "Sports, Stocks, and Bonds," 1A, 18A; Ozanian, "Selective Accounting," 130.

36. Jerry Colangelo owned a team in the Continental Soccer League (CISL). In December 1997 the CISL and the National Soccer Alliance, the first women's professional soccer league, folded. Beginning with seven teams in the summer of 1993, the CISL had added eight teams by 1995. In 1996 four teams left the CISL while a rival league, Major League Soccer, was expanding in size. See Jim Utter, "CISL'S Dwindling Members

Dwindle to 0," *Charlotte Observer* (28 December 1997), 2G. See also Scott Fowler, "List Puts Panthers Among Most Valuable Pro Teams," 1A, 18A; Michael Ozanian, "Selective Accounting," 130.

37. Fowler, "List Puts Panthers Among Most Valuable Pro Teams," 1A, 18A; Ozanian, "Selective Accounting," 130, 134.

38. Steinbreder, "The Owners," 65; Quirk and Fort, *Pay Dirt*, 456.

39. Quirk and Fort, *Pay Dirt*, 450; Fowler, "List Puts Panthers Among Most Valuable Pro Teams," 1A, 18A; Mark Montieth, "MSA Has No Suites, No Space, and Very Likely No Future," *Indianapolis Star* (18 August 1996), 8; "Nuggets Name D'Antoni Head Coach," at <http://www.nba.com> cited 28 September 1998; Ozanian, "Selective Accounting," 130.

40. See Kathleen Johnston, "Pacers Lease Contains Financial Guarantees," *Indianapolis Star* (5 November 1997), 16; Quirk and Fort, *Pay Dirt*, 452; Steinbreder, "The Owners," 70.

41. Fowler, "List Puts Panthers Among Most Valuable Pro Teams," 1A, 18A; Quirk and Fort, *Pay Dirt*, 454–455; Steinbreder, "The Owners," 86; Ozanian, "Selective Accounting," 130.

42. Quirk and Fort, *Pay Dirt*, 457; Fowler, "List Puts Panthers Among Most Valuable Pro Teams," 1A, 18A; Steinbreder, "The Owners," 85; Ozanian, "Selective Accounting," 130.

43. Fowler, "List Puts Panthers Among Valuable Pro Teams," 1A, 18A; Quirk and Fort, *Pay Dirt*, 450; Steinbreder, "The Owners," 72; Ozanian, "Selective Accounting," 130.

44. Montieth, "MSA Has No Suites, No Space, and Very Likely No Future," 8; Fowler, "List Puts Panthers Among Most Valuable Pro Teams," 1A, 18A; Quirk and Fort, *Pay Dirt*, 448, 454; Steinbreder, "The Owners," 78.

45. Fowler, "List Puts Panthers Among Most Valuable Pro Teams," 1A, 18A; Quirk and Fort, *Pay Dirt*, 454–455; Steinbreder, "The Owners," 82; Ozanian, "Selective Accounting," 130.

46. Fowler, "List Puts Panthers Among Most Valuable Pro Teams," 1A, 18A; Steinbreder, "The Owners," 66; Ozanian, "Selective Accounting," 130.

47. The history of the Raptors appears on the Web at <http://www.nba.com> cited 8 April 1998.

48. In February 1998, NBA all-star guard Damon Stoudamire was traded to the Portland Trail Blazers for Kenny Anderson, Gary Trent, and Alvin Williams. In exchange for Stoudamire the Raptors received cash, two first-round draft picks, and the three players. Also, Raptors coach Darrell Walker resigned. See Chris Sheridan, "Raptors Trade Stoudamire in 6-Player Deal; Coach Quits," *Charlotte Observer* (14 February 1998), 2B.

49. See the "Toronto Raptors History" at <http://www.nba.com> cited 8 April 1998; "Slaight Sells Raptors, New Arena to Leafs' Stavro" at <http://bball.yahoo.com> cited 17 February 1998; "If You Can't Beat 'Em, Buy 'Em" at <http://www.cnnsi.com> cited 12 February 1998.

50. For the history of the Grizzlies see the Web site <http://www.nba.com> cited 31 January 1998.

51. See Bob Hille, "Tops by a Mile," *Sporting News* (30 June 1997), 23.

52. Owner Nick Mileti sold his 20 percent interest in the Cleveland Cavaliers to Louis Mitchell for $1.4 million in 1980. Thus, the Cavaliers were valued at $7 million in 1980 and $175 million in 1997. The sales price of a team appears in Quirk and Fort, *Pay Dirt*, 446–463, and the value of a team appears in Scott Fowler, "List Puts Panthers Among Most Valuable Pro Teams," 1A, 18A; Michael Ozanian, "Selective Accounting," 130.

53. Final season standing provided by the Charlotte Hornets media staff.

54. Attendance per team was acquired from the public relations staff of the NBA.

55. Fowler, "List Puts Panthers Among Most Valuable Pro Teams," 1A, 18A; Ozanian, "Selective Accounting," 124–134.

56. For details about the IBL, see Scott Soshnick, "New League to Begin in 1999," *Charlotte Observer* (12 August 1998), 2B.

Chapter 5

Professional Teams Ranked by Sport

In the business of sports, successful teams create and sustain an illusion so potent and so deeply ingrained in the minds of many fans that after a certain point the attachment of fans becomes somewhat involuntary. Franchises keep this illusion of importance alive for long periods of time by outclassing their opponents in games and by other means. Said differently, teams compete in sundry ways to fill their stadiums. In the contest to put fans in stadium seats, the team's performance and the ballpark's appeal both deserve a share of the credit. That partially explains why in recent years cities have been quick to finance and build new, expensive sports complexes.[1]

According to boosters, such facilities attract capacity crowds to home games and consequently help stimulate the local economy. For example, in Baltimore and Cleveland civic leaders claim that their new baseball stadiums have helped eradicate shaky national reputations while contributing to a revival of their downtown business districts. Likewise in Denver, Coors Field opened during an economic expansion and thus helped anchor a prospering entertainment district that only a decade earlier had encompassed the city's skid row. In Phoenix, an expansion club playing in a brand new MLB ballpark has drawn hordes of fans from the outlying suburbs. While team owners have reaped windfalls in on the new ballparks, the cities with the new facilities have realized small, if any, returns on their investments. Conceding that point, such municipalities insist that other, less tangible motives prompted them to build the new sports parks. Denver hoped to shed its image as a cowtown. Baltimore and Cleveland wanted to add luster to their tarnished civic reputations. And, Phoenix wanted to enter the ranks of major league cities. So new multimillion dollar sports facilities enable cities to cast an image, shape a perception, or create an illusion by which they compare themselves to their rivals.[2]

New stadiums alone prove inadequate for ranking professional sports teams. We discussed demographic, team-specific, and economic factors affecting the relocation and expansion of professional sports teams and leagues in Chapters One through Four. We used these factors to analyze the decisions made by team owners and leagues to approve or deny relocation and expansion. In each chapter we assembled historical data that we presented in tables to clarify and support the analysis.

This chapter combines by sport the expansion teams and the teams that relocated into two groups. We then rank and analyze the teams in the groups based on team performance, home attendance, and estimated market value using data collected since 1990. The analysis reveals which of the relocated and expansion teams performed the best and worst in their respective sport during the 1990s. In addition, we identify the teams that have the highest potential to improve. We exclude from the analysis those sports teams (neither relocated nor expansion) that suffer demographic, team-specific, and economic hardships. Some clubs, for example, require a new or renovated venue as a source for money.[3] Other teams need a different mix of coaches and players, or a new management structure and owners to win and earn economic profits.[4] Because of this, we focus exclusively on the teams featured in the previous chapters.

After obtaining each relocated and expansion team's mean winning percentage, home attendance, and estimated market value, we ranked the teams and compared them to one another. In doing so, we assigned one point to the team with the highest average winning percentage, home attendance, and estimated market value (the other teams also received points for each criterion and were ranked accordingly). We rated the teams with the lowest total points superior and those with higher points average or inferior based on their total.

Given the sequencing of sports in earlier chapters, we first analyzed MLB teams followed by those in the NFL and NBA. In the text and with the tables we elaborate and justify the scores and ranks of teams. Each criterion—team performance, home attendance, and estimated market value—was assigned a one-third weight.

PROFESSIONAL BASEBALL

Table 5.1 ranks three NL and five AL teams that relocated prior to 1990. The superior teams scored three to nine total points, average teams scored ten to sixteen points, and inferior teams scored above sixteen points. Between 1990 and 1997 the Baltimore Orioles, Atlanta Braves, and Los Angeles Dodgers ranked first, second, and third respectively among the MLB teams that relocated before 1990. The performance and value of the Orioles rose in the 1990s because of the play and leadership of shortstop Cal Ripken, outfielder Brady Anderson, and pitcher Mike Mussina. Owner Peter Angelos, who acquired the team in 1993 for $173 million, increased the players' payroll to nearly $79 million, the highest in MLB in 1998. Moreover, when the $210 million 48,000-seat Camden Yards opened in 1992, the Orioles' attendance increased from 2.5 to 3.5 million per season and first in the AL. With an average ticket price of $18

Table 5.1
Performance, Attendance, Value, Sum, and Rank of Relocated MLB Franchises

Franchise	Performance	Attendance	Value	Sum	Rank
Baltimore (AL)	.520 (2)	3.1 (1)	207 (1)	(4)	Superior
Atlanta (NL)	.583 (1)	2.6 (3)	199 (2)	(6)	Superior
Los Angeles (NL)	.518 (3)	2.9 (2)	178 (3)	(8)	Superior
San Francisco (NL)	.498 (4)	1.6 (6)	128 (5)	(15)	Average
Oakland (AL)	.495 (5)	1.8 (5)	115 (6)	(16)	Average
Texas (AL)	.466 (8)	2.4 (4)	174 (4)	(16)	Average
Milwaukee (AL)	.481 (6)	1.5 (8)	95 (7)	(21)	Inferior
Minnesota (AL)	.474 (7)	1.7 (7)	77 (8)	(22)	Inferior

Note: Performance is the mean winning percentage of the team from 1990 to 1997. Attendance is the team's mean home game attendance in millions during the 1990s. Value is the estimated market value of the team in millions of dollars in 1997. Compared to this set of teams, Sum is the total points awarded to a team for Performance, Attendance, and Value. Rank is a composite assessment of the Performance, Attendance, and the Value of each team based on total points scored.

Source: *The World Almanac and Book of Fact* (Mahwah, N.J.: World Almanac Books, 1990–1998); Scott Fowler, "List Puts Panthers Among Most Valuable Pro Teams," *Charlotte Observer* (25 May 1997), 1A, 18A; American League of Professional Baseball Clubs (August 1997), 1–3; *Media* and *Information Guides* of the teams.

in 1998, the club earned additional revenues even when they placed behind the New York Yankees, Boston Red Sox and Toronto Blue Jays in their division.[5]

By winning nearly 60 percent of their games, and attracting over 2.5 million fans per season to their home games, the Braves' estimated value reached $299 million in 1998.[6] Pitchers Greg Maddox, Tom Glavine, and John Smoltz coupled with sluggers Andres Galarraga, Javier Lopez, and Chipper Jones should keep the team competitive for many years. Given the marginal appeal of the Atlanta Falcons of the NFL and the Atlanta Hawks of the NBA to fans, the Braves must remain contenders in their division for the club to continue its success in Atlanta.[7]

For the criteria analyzed, the Dodgers finished second in average attendance at 2.8 million per season and third behind the Orioles and Braves in team performance at .518 and in market value at $178 million. With the ownership change from the O'Malley family to the Fox Group headed by Rupert Murdoch, the team will probably remain in Los Angeles, make strategic player trades, change its managerial staff, and renovate Dodger Stadium.[8] To illustrate the point, the owners traded all-star catcher Mike Piazza for three Florida Marlin players, and fired manager Bill Russell and executive vice president Fred Claire in June 1998, given the third-place position of the team in the NL's Western Division. The team finished the 1998 season 83–79, fifteen games behind the San Diego Padres. A few owners expressed concern about the sale of the Dodgers. Ted Turner adamantly opposed Murdoch's purchase of the team. Turner stated, "Like the late Fuhrer, he [Murdoch] controls . . . and is crazed for money and power. I fear him and don't trust him."[9] Perhaps Turner is right. In April 1998 Murdoch's News Corporation received options to buy a minority stake in the Los Angeles Lakers and the Los Angeles Kings. News Corporation already has minority ownership of Madison Square Garden, the New York Knicks, and the New York Rangers. In addition to personnel changes, in August 1998 the club considered renovations. According to Dodger executive Bob Graziano, a renovation of three-decades-old, 56,000-seat Dodger Stadium would exceed $118 million. With the construction of a new $200 million facility containing luxury boxes, retail stores, and restaurants, the owner may replace Dodger Stadium after the 1999 season.[10]

The San Francisco Giants, Oakland Athletics, and Texas Rangers ranked fourth to sixth respectively as average teams. The estimated market value of the Giants and Athletics exceeded $115 million in 1997 and neither team finished lower than sixth place by our criteria. In contrast, the Milwaukee Brewers and Minnesota Twins of the AL ranked as inferior teams because they won less than half of their games between 1990 and 1997, averaged under 1.8 million fans per season at their ballparks, and decreased in market value from 1993 to 1997.[11]

Although ranked as an average team and slightly below the Giants, the Athletics will probably remain in the Bay Area. Oakland's population is smaller than San Francisco's and the Giants will soon play in a new ballpark. Unless the owner of the Athletics, Walter A. Haas, Jr., can obtain money from private investors or local taxpayers, the Athletics should relocate to a city where residents are willing to subsidize the renovation of an old, or construction of a new, ballpark containing club seats, luxury suites, and other amenities. In October 1998 the club triggered a clause in their stadium lease. Public officials were given four months to sell the franchise to a buyer who promised to keep the team in Oakland. If no sale occurs, after February 1999 the Athletics are authorized to sell or move the team from the stadium it shares with the Raiders. Owners Steve Schott and Ken Hofmann, who acquired the club for $85 million in 1995, valued it at $150 million, which includes $20 million in deferred player compensation. The owners have considered San Jose as a future home site for the team.[12]

Likewise, we expect the Twins to remove themselves from Minnesota if taxpayers refuse to finance construction of a modern ballpark. In early 1998 Minnesota's governor Arne Carlson wrote a letter to baseball's commissioner Bud Selig requesting the league to delay the decision regarding the relocation of the Twins.[13] Current MLB rules require that eleven of the fourteen AL owners, and nine of the sixteen NL owners must approve the exodus of the Twins from Minnesota.

Several communities in North Carolina have courted the Twins. During 1997, state legislators in Raleigh introduced and debated several proposals to fund the construction of a new stadium. A marketing campaign was initiated in February 1998 by an advocacy group, "Vote Yes for Major League Baseball," to persuade voters in Forsyth and Guilford Counties to support a tax on prepared foods and on tickets in a spring referendum. In May 1998 voters rejected the tax increases. Three months later the Twins signed a new two-year lease with the Minneapolis Metropolitan Sports Facilities Commission to play in the Metrodome. The club will remain in Minnesota through 2000 and perhaps until 2003 given its three one-year options to extend the lease. Beginning in 1999, the club will receive $1 million annually from a 10 percent admissions tax. Carl Pohlad, the team's owner, is committed to finding a local buyer and keeping the franchise in Minnesota whether a new stadium is built.[14]

The Braves ranked first, Dodgers third, and Giants fourth in performance; the Dodgers second, Braves third, and Giants sixth in attendance; and the Braves second, Dodgers third, and Giants fifth in estimated market value (see Table 5.1). Accordingly, since 1950 NL teams have relocated only after careful deliberations. In other words, they made prudent business decisions in the best interests of the owners and the league.

Table 5.2 summarizes the success of the former expansion teams in the NL and AL from 1990 to 1997. Six NL and four AL teams appear in the table. The criteria for the Colorado Rockies and Florida Marlins is included from their inaugural season in 1993 to 1997. Since organized ball added ten expansion teams, we adjusted the total points as follows: three to eleven points ranked a team as superior, twelve to twenty points as average, and above twenty points as inferior.

The Rockies ranked first in average attendance at 3.8 million per season, first in estimated market value at $184 million, and fifth in performance at .484. The Blue Jays ranked second in performance at .506, second in attendance at 3.5 million per season, and third in market value at $155 million. With a new stadium under construction in Seattle, the Mariners should improve their rank because of a higher market value and greater expected attendance at home games. Led by the MVP Ken Griffey, Jr., sluggers Alex Rodriguez, Edgar Martinez, and David Segui, and manager Lou Piniella, and buoyed by a 35 percent increase in team revenues in 1997, the Mariners are poised to improve in their division and contend for the league title before 2000. After a disappointing finish in 1998, it is apparent the Mariners need better starters, relief pitching, and defense to win more games.

Table 5.2
Performance, Attendance, Value, Sum, and Rank of MLB Expansion Franchises

Franchise	Performance	Attendance	Value	Sum	Rank
Colorado (NL)	.484 (5)	3.8 (1)	184 (1)	(7)	Superior
Toronto (AL)	.506 (2)	3.5 (2)	155 (3)	(7)	Superior
Seattle (AL)	.493 (4)	1.8 (5)	171 (2)	(11)	Superior
New York (NL)	.480 (7)	1.8 (6)	144 (4)	(17)	Average
Florida (NL)	.463 (10)	2.1 (3)	123 (5)	(18)	Average
Houston (NL)	.501 (3)	1.6 (9)	114 (6)	(18)	Average
Anaheim (AL)	.478 (8)	1.9 (4)	93 (7)	(19)	Average
Montreal (NL)	.525 (1)	1.4 (10)	77 (10)	(21)	Inferior
Kansas City (AL)	.482 (6)	1.7 (7)	88 (9)	(22)	Inferior
San Diego (NL)	.472 (9)	1.5 (8)	86 (8)	(25)	Inferior

Note: Performance is the mean winning percentage of the team from 1990 to 1997. Attendance is the average home attendance of the team in millions during the 1990s. Value is the estimated worth of a franchise in 1997 in millions of dollars. Compared to this set of teams, Sum is the total points of the Performance, Attendance, and Value of a franchise. Rank is a composite assessment of the Performance, Attendance, and Value based on the total points scored. The data for the Colorado Rockies and Florida Marlins are for 1993 to 1997.

Source: The sources consulted are listed in Table 5.1.

Three NL teams and one AL team scored average ranks in Table 5.2. Between 1990 and 1997 the Anaheim Angels and New York Mets won less than half their games but placed in the top six in average attendance and in the top seven in market value among the former expansion teams. Below the Mets fell owner Drayton McLane, Jr.'s, Houston Astros, who played before sparse crowds in the Astrodome despite winning over 50 percent of their games during the period.

Regarding the inferior expansion teams in MLB, the Kansas City Royals placed sixth or lower, and the San Diego Padres no higher than eighth, in each of the criteria in Table 5.2. The Montreal Expos placed tenth in market value at $77 million and tenth in average attendance at 1.4 million per season even though the team had a .525 mean winning percentage. In fact, between 1990 and 1997 only the Atlanta Braves had a higher winning percentage than the Expos. Given the recent history of the teams and their status as of 1998, we expect the following changes to occur. After 1999 the winning percentage, attendance, and market value of the Florida Marlins will continue its downward trend. Former owner Wayne Huizenga traded many of the high-salaried World Champion Marlins to reduce operating costs, to pay team expenses, and to finance the $100 million debt on Pro Player Stadium. Indeed, all-star shortstop Edgar Renteria was the only starter remaining from the 1997 line-up. In 1998 the Marlins increased ticket prices by 13 percent, to roughly $11, making them the tenth most expensive tickets in the NL.[15] Because the team finished 54–108 and fifty-two games behind the division leader in 1998, its value should diminish.

To increase gate receipts the other MLB teams with average or inferior rankings increased average ticket prices in 1998 as follows: the Angels 20 percent, the Astros 24 percent, the Royals 15 percent, the Expos 44 percent, the Mets 24 percent, and the Padres 7 percent.[16] With the tenth highest priced tickets in the AL, and a declining fan base since the late 1980s, the Angels have renovated their ballpark, Edison International Field, to attract younger, upscale fans. After acquiring operating control of the team from owner Gene Autry in May 1996, Walt Disney Company planned to create a cable channel for the Angels and to increase marketing efforts to attract local Hispanics to home games. In addition, Disney streamlined team operations by reducing the administrative staff.[17]

Like the Angels, the Royals saw their attendance peak in the late 1980s. In 1998, the Royals' tickets ranged in price from $6 to $15, making them the eleventh highest in the AL.[18] By playing in the Central Division of the AL against powerhouse clubs such as the Cleveland Indians, the Royals seem destined to play consistently below .500 and thereby decrease in market value. Not surprisingly, the Royals ranked ninth among the expansion teams listed in Table 5.2.

To become superior the Mets must win more games. They played above .500 from 1987 to 1990 and again in 1997. With a record 65,000 opening day tickets sold in 1998, and after winning eighty-eight games and missing a wild card playoff berth by four games in 1997, the Mets realized higher gate receipts and added market value. As a result of such success the Mets placed higher among the expansion teams. In 1998 the club finished 88–74 and in second place, eighteen games behind the Braves in the Eastern Division. Manager

Bobby Valentine, sluggers John Olerud and Mike Piazza, and pitchers Al Leiter, Rick Reed, and Bobby Jones have improved the Mets and increased the club's expectations for the future.

The San Diego Padres ranked tenth among the expansion teams in Table 5.2. The club's low average ticket prices helped boost attendance in 1998. Surprisingly, that year the Padres placed first in the NL's Western Division at 98–64 and fourth in winning percentage in MLB behind the Yankees, Braves, and Astros. Sluggers Tony Gwynn and Greg Vaughn and pitchers Kevin Brown, Andy Ashby, and Sterling Hitchcock led the team to the NL title. The Padres lost to the Yankees in a four-game sweep in 1998's World Series. Despite the Padres recent success, in the long run without a new ballpark, a change in ownership, or a realignment of teams and divisions in the NL, the franchise has little hope of rising above inferior ranking while located in San Diego. After the departure of pitching ace Kevin Brown, slugger Greg Vaughn, outfielder Steve Finley, and infielder Ken Caminiti in 1998, the Padres embarked on a three-year rebuilding program aimed at putting a young, exciting team into their $411 million 42,000-seat stadium, which will open in 2002.

The rankings in Tables 5.1 and 5.2 update the differences in the success of the MLB teams that relocated, and the new teams that joined organized ball since 1950. Comparing the teams in the tables collectively, the seven relocated teams won 50 percent, and the ten expansion teams 48 percent of their games between 1990 and 1997. Furthermore as a group, the attendance of the relocated teams declined by an average of two million per season during the period, but the teams reached a greater average market value of $123 to $137 million in 1997. Minor differences in performance and attendance, coupled with a 10 percent difference in market value, notwithstanding, 25 percent of the relocated teams and 30 percent of the expansion teams achieved inferior ranking by our criteria.

MLB expansion teams in Montreal, Kansas City, and San Diego have appreciated little in the 1990s due to either poor play, outdated ballparks, apathetic hometown fans, or possibly because of their small markets and other local demographic factors. In 1994, for example, the metropolitan population of Kansas City had 1.7 million people and San Diego 2.6 million. So in the long run, Kansas City and San Diego seem too small to sustain a superior team in MLB. Yet with a renovated ballpark and lease agreement, the Padres appear committed to San Diego for several years. Likewise, with bids from Miles Prentice, the owner of a Class AA baseball team, and from Lamar Hunt and a Topeka, Kansas, utilities firm, the sale of the Royals seems eminent. However, in August 1998 Hunt withdrew his bid for the team. Hunt's offer of $52 million was $23 million below the minimum price set by the club's board of directors. In the meantime Prentice announced that Buck O'Neil, a star player with the Kansas City Monarchs of the old Negro Leagues, and golf professional Tom Watson had joined his ownership group. O'Neil and Watson decided to invest, hoping to keep the franchise in Kansas City. Royals' president Mike Herman stated that "if we don't get 50 percent ownership in Kansas City, we might end up losing the team." According to the team's corporate charter, a 50 percent local ownership requirement must be met to approve the sale.[19] In November 1998 Prentice received unanimous approval from the club's board of directors to acquire the Royals for $75 million. According to the terms of the sale, the new proprietor must first try to sell the club to Kansas City interests if he should want to unload it. To increase profits in 1999, the club will reduce payroll, raise ticket prices, and renovate twenty-five-year-old Kauffman Stadium.

PROFESSIONAL FOOTBALL

We measured and analyzed the ranks of four relocated NFL teams. From 1990 to 1994, the Raiders won 58 percent of their games but attendance slumped to 449,000 per season in the Los Angeles Coliseum. After moving from Los Angeles to Oakland in 1995, the winning percentage and attendance of the Raiders declined. In Oakland, the team's average winning percentage dropped to 39 percent and attendance fell to 410,000 between 1995 and 1996. In contrast, the average winning percentage of the Rams increased from 28 to 37 percent, and its average attendance rose from 394,000 to 499,000 per season after relocating to St. Louis and playing in the Trans World Dome. In Oakland, an adversarial relationship between team owner Al Davis and the city and Alameda County over the stadium lease may prompt the Raiders to relocate to Los Angeles or elsewhere. Even with a market value of $235 million in 1998 (the twenty-sixth highest among NFL teams), the Raiders remain an inferior team based on the criteria in Table 5.3. Meanwhile, despite a 7–9 record in 1995, 6–10 in 1996, and 5–11 record in 1997, and finishing last in the NFC's Western Division, St. Louis fans enthusiastically support the Rams. Still the club, with an estimated market value of $322 million in 1998, represents an average team that ranks with the Denver Broncos, Minnesota Vikings, and New Orleans Saints.

Between 1990 and 1996 the Indianapolis Colts and Phoenix (now Arizona) Cardinals were inferior teams. The Colts had a mean winning percentage of .420 and averaged 424,000 per season in home attendance in those years, and ranked thirtieth in the NFL with an estimated market value of $227 million in 1998. The Cardinals had a mean winning percentage of .336, averaged 371,000 per season in home attendance, and in 1998 had an estimated market value of $231 million.[20] After two years of negotiations, the Colts and the city of Indianapolis signed a ten-year lease on the RCA Dome. Under its terms the Colts will receive an additional $8.9 million in annual revenues from the stadium, a commitment from the city to spend $18 million for stadium renovations, and the option to cancel the lease in 2007. More revenues from team operations permitted the Colts to sign prominent college players, such as their first-round draft pick in 1997, Peyton Manning, an all-American quarterback who graduated from the University of Tennessee.[21]

The Cardinals finished 4–12 in the cellar of their division in 1997 and earned a wild card berth in 1998. Unless all-pro players Larry Centers, Eric Swann, and Aeneas Williams, quarterback Jake Plummer, and coach Vince Tobin motivate the team to improve, the Cardinals should remain an inferior NFL team throughout the late 1990s and early 2000s. Since 1932 the Bidwell family has owned the Cardinals. The family hired and fired three different head coaches in the 1980s and 1990s. Perhaps a change in ownership would provide the leadership and stability that the team needs to succeed in the NFL.

Table 5.3 reveals the criteria and ranks of the fifteen former expansion teams that played in the NFL from 1990 to 1996. Five clubs played in the NFC, and ten in the AFC. We excluded the Carolina Panthers of the NFC and Jacksonville Jaguars of the AFC from the table since they began play in 1995. But we included teams from the old AFL and, for our purposes, considered them as expansion clubs. To determine total points and ranks, the team with the highest mean winning percentage between 1990 and 1996 received one point as did the team with the highest mean home attendance and the one with the highest 1997 estimated market value. Other teams received points based on their placement within each criterion. We assigned teams receiving a total of three to fourteen points a superior ranking, fifteen to twenty-six points an average ranking, and above twenty-six points an inferior ranking.

Accordingly, between 1990 and 1996 four former expansion teams ranked superior, three teams ranked average, and eight teams ranked inferior. Superior teams were the Buffalo Bills, Dallas Cowboys, Kansas City Chiefs, and Miami Dolphins. The Cowboys ranked first in average winning percentage at .687 and

Table 5.3
Performance, Attendance, Value, Sum, and Rank of Selected NFL Franchises

Franchise	Performance	Attendance	Value	Sum	Rank
Dallas (NFC)	.687 (1)	505 (5)	320 (1)	(7)	Superior
Buffalo (AFC)	.678 (2)	618 (1)	200 (4)	(7)	Superior
Kansas City (AFC)	.652 (3)	599 (2)	204 (3)	(8)	Superior
Miami (AFC)	.598 (4)	528 (4)	242 (2)	(10)	Superior
New Orleans (NFC)	.509 (8)	476 (7)	199 (5)	(20)	Average
Denver (AFC)	.553 (5)	582 (3)	182 (14)	(22)	Average
Minnesota (NFC)	.544 (6)	450 (8)	187 (11)	(25)	Average
San Diego (AFC)	.508 (9)	438 (9)	190 (9)	(27)	Inferior
Houston (AFC)	.527 (7)	393 (14)	193 (7)	(28)	Inferior
Atlanta (NFC)	.411 (11)	432 (10)	191 (8)	(30)	Inferior
New England (AFC)	.366 (12)	384 (15)	197 (6)	(33)	Inferior
New York (AFC)	.321 (15)	477 (6)	185 (13)	(34)	Inferior
Seattle (AFC)	.413 (10)	421 (11)	171 (15)	(36)	Inferior
Cincinnati (AFC)	.339 (14)	407 (13)	188 (10)	(37)	Inferior
Tampa Bay (NFC)	.341 (13)	417 (12)	186 (12)	(37)	Inferior

Note: Performance is the team's mean winning percentage, and Attendance is the mean home game attendance of a team (in hundreds of thousands) during 1990 to 1996. Value is the estimated market value of a team in millions in 1997. Compared to this selection of teams, Sum is the teams' total points for Performance, Attendance, and Value. Rank is a composite assessment of each franchise based on the total points assigned. The Oilers played in Houston between 1990 and 1996, in Memphis in 1997, and in Nashville in 1998.

Source: *The World Almanac and Book of Facts*, 1991–1998; *Media* and *Public Relations Guides* of the NFL teams; Scott Fowler, "List Puts Panthers Among Most Valuable Pro Teams," *Charlotte Observer* (25 May 1997), 1A, 18A.

in market value at $320 million. The Bills had the highest average attendance at 618,000 per season. Led by veteran quarterback Jim Kelly, the Bills appeared in and lost four consecutive Super Bowls between 1990 and 1993 and the Cowboys, led by Troy Aikman, won Super Bowls in 1992, 1993, and 1995. After the retirement of Kelly in 1996, however, the Bills finished fourth in their division at 6–10, and the following year their opponents outscored them by 112 points. Between 1990 and 1996 the attendance of the Cowboys at Texas Stadium increased by 9 percent, or five thousand per game. Despite injuries, the suspension of key players for violating team and league rules, and a drop in winning percentage in the 1996 and 1997 seasons, the Cowboys remain a superior team.

In performance, attendance, and estimated market value the Chiefs ranked third at .652, second at 599,000 per season, and third at $204 million, and the Dolphins ranked fourth at .598, fourth at 528,000 per season, and second at $242 million among the NFL's expansion teams between 1990 and 1996. Although neither team appeared in Super Bowls, the Chiefs and Dolphins each played in an AFC Championship game in the early 1990s. In 1997 the Chiefs won the AFC Western Division title and the Dolphins finished behind the New England Patriots in the Eastern Division and earned a wild card berth. So the future of the Chiefs in Kansas City and the Dolphins in Miami seems secure. Since 1993 the attendance of the Chiefs has exceeded 600,000 per season at Arrowhead Stadium, which was built in 1972 to seat 79,451 fans. The stadium contains eighty luxury suites, thirty-three luxury field boxes, and 10,199 club seats.[22] Meanwhile, even when quarterback Dan Marino stops calling the signals, head coach Jimmy Johnson and owner Wayne Huizenga should keep the Dolphins a superior team as it moves into the new millennium.

In Table 5.3 the Denver Broncos, New Orleans Saints, and Minnesota Vikings rank as average expansion teams for the years 1990 to 1996. The Broncos finished third behind the Bills and Chiefs in average attendance at 582,000 per season, and ahead of the Seahawks in market value at $182 million. Although the Broncos upset the Green Bay Packers in the 1998 Super Bowl, John Elway has reached near the end of his playing days. His retirement, and a 25 percent increase in 1999 ticket prices, could threaten the twenty-nine consecutive season ticket sellouts at Mile High Stadium.

In performance, attendance, and market value, the Saints ranked eighth at .509, seventh at 476,000 per season, and fifth at $199 million, and the Vikings ranked sixth at .544, eighth at 450,000 per season, and eleventh at $187 million. In 1996 and 1997, the Saints won nine and lost twenty-three games and scored two hundred points less than their opponents. The club peaked in the early 1990s when they made the playoffs as a wild card team but lost 27–20 to the Falcons in 1991 and 36–20 to the Philadelphia Eagles in 1992. With their current mix of players, and head coach Mike Ditka, the Saints should remain an average team when the century turns.

The sale of the Vikings in 1998 to Red McCombs ensures that the team will stay in the Twin Cities. Coach Denny Green's threat to sue the club's partnership disrupted team relations in 1997. Yet the Vikings spent $93 million in 1997 and 1998 to sign free agents John Randle and Robert Smith, and rookie wide receiver Randy Moss to multiple-year contracts. The Vikings won eighteen regular season games during 1996 and 1997 as well as a wild card berth. In 1998, the club finished 15–1 but was upset by the Atlanta Falcons playing for the NFC title. With McCombs as the owner, the internal conflicts seem settled and the Vikings, led by quarterback Randall Cunningham, should improve its ranking as an average NFL team.

The Falcons, Bengals, Oilers, Patriots, Jets, Chargers, Seahawks, and Buccaneers all ranked as inferior expansion teams from 1990 to 1996. Given the criteria in Table 5.3, the Seahawks ranked higher in performance than the Bengals, Buccaneers, Falcons, and Jets. The Buccaneers and Jets ranked high in attendance while the Oilers and Patriots ranked low. And the Bengals, Falcons, Oilers, and Patriots ranked high in estimated market value and the Seahawks ranked low. The Chargers ranked ninth in each criteria and the Buccaneers ranked twelfth in attendance and market value.

For the inferior teams to become average clubs over the next three to five years each franchise should concentrate on improving its weaknesses. With that in mind, some recent improvements have occurred for these teams. In 1996 and 1997, for instance, the Bengals won fifteen games and the Buccaneers sixteen games, which increased each team's mean winning percentage. Hamilton County, Ohio voters approved a sales tax in 1996 to finance a new $400 million, 67,000-seat stadium. Foreseeing no major obstacles, the Bengals will begin play in their new facility in 2000. Cincinnati's Paul Brown Stadium will contain 7,600 club seats and 104 private suites. Hamilton County donated a dozen acres of land, contributed $10 million for redesigning roads surrounding the stadium, and budgeted $7 million to construct a floodgate to protect the stadium from nearby streams and rivers. With these developments, the Bengals have an opportunity to rise above its current inferior ranking.[23]

With coach Tony Dungy, quarterback Trent Dilfer, and running back Eric Rhett, the Buccaneers finished 10–6 in 1997 and earned a berth in the playoffs as a wild card team. In 1998 the Buccaneers were selected the third best team in the NFL during the pre-season then proceeded to make the selectors look foolish by placing third in their division for the season. So perhaps the club will not achieve a higher ranking in the future.

Coach Bill Parcells deserves much credit for the Jets' second place finish at 9–7 in the AFC's Eastern Division in 1997 and for challenging but losing to the Denver Broncos for the AFC title in 1999 (a great improvement from 1–15 in 1996 and 3–13 in 1995). His determination, enthusiasm, leadership, and previous coaching success in Super Bowls should make the Jets more competitive and a contender for the division title in and after 2000. If so, the Jets should shed their inferior ranking.

The Titans (formerly Oilers) will play in a 67,000-seat $280 million domed stadium in downtown Nashville in 1999. Regardless of poor attendance at the Liberty Bowl in Memphis in 1997, and despite the team's 8–8 season record in 1997 and 1998, the Titans sold over 43,000 permanent seat licenses, at a cost of $250 to $1,500 per seat for 1999. The revenue from the seat licenses and the gate receipts from attendance in Nashville should enable the team to attract free agents and sign first-rate players in the college draft. Therefore, the market value of the Titans in Nashville should rise above $322 million after 1999.

Since Robert Kraft became owner in 1994, the Patriots have tied for or won divisional titles in 1994, 1996, 1997, and 1998. Between 1994 and 1996, the home attendance of the Patriots exceeded 450,000 per year. In February 1998, Massachusetts state officials and the club jointly proposed to build a $200 million stadium in Foxboro, committing the team to stay in Massachusetts another quarter century.[24] The stadium plan included three components: an income tax on players of the visiting team; state expenditures of $52 million for infrastructure and improved road access; and the purchase of 336 acres of land for $20 million by the state, which the team would lease. But the strategy of Kraft has changed. After playing in five different stadiums since 1960, and failing to agree with Massachusetts on a new facility in Foxboro, in November 1998 Kraft announced the Patriots will relocate to Hartford, Connecticut. By 2001, the club expects to move its equipment to that city and provide $50 million to construct a hotel at a $1 billion redevelopment project called Adriaen's Landing, $20 million for an NFL retail and entertainment pavilion, and $5 million for a downtown fitness center. Connecticut's taxpayers will finance a $350 million 68,000-seat open-air stadium for the team and upgrade the infrastructure and parking area surrounding the stadium. Patriot tickets are expected to average $50 per seat in Hartford, and fans may purchase luxury boxes or premium club seats. Simply put, the Patriots' organization has made smart investments to increase the team's future value and rank as an NFL franchise.[25]

Likewise, the market value of the Seattle Seahawks should rise in 1999. The team won fifteen games and attendance exceeded 400,000 per year in 1996 and 1997. With the immense wealth of owner Paul Allen and a new high-tech open-air $425 million stadium to play in, the value of the Seahawks should rise in the near future. Since joining the NFL in 1976 the team appeared in playoff games in 1983, 1984, 1987, and 1988 led by quarterback Dave Krieg and Pro Bowl players such as Bryan Millard, Curt Warner, and Steve Largent. Yet neither recent players nor coaches Chuck Knox, Dennis Erickson, and Tom Flores have managed to improve the team's rank above inferior in the 1990s. If the new stadium fails to generate sufficient revenues, billionaire Allen should hire better coaches and players to make the team competitive after 2001. Because of his wealth and determination to win, in 1999 Allen hired Green Bay Packer head coach Mike Holmgren to be general manager and head coach of the Seahawks.

If improvements in performance and coaching continues, and the teams' ownership remains intact, the Buccaneers, Jets, and Patriots should remain average teams through 2005. Although the Bengals, Chargers, Falcons, Titans, and Seahawks will likely continue playing at their present sites, these teams probably will remain inferior clubs. Yet despite inferior rankings, due to league revenues of $17.6 billion from a new eight-year television contract, even the weaker NFL teams should break even financially or earn profits during the term of the contract.

PROFESSIONAL BASKETBALL

Nine NBA teams relocated to their current sites before 1990. In the Eastern Conference, the Philadelphia SeventySixers played in the Atlantic Division, and the Atlanta Hawks and Detroit Pistons in the Central Division. In the Western Conference, the Houston Rockets and Utah Jazz played in the Midwest Division, and the Golden State Warriors, Los Angeles Clippers, Los Angeles Lakers, and Sacramento Kings in the Pacific Division. In Table 5.4 each NBA team that relocated before 1990 is ranked as either superior, average, or inferior. With nine teams ranked, we established a point system whereby a superior team received three to ten points, an average team received eleven to eighteen points, and an inferior team received more than eighteen points. As in MLB and the NFL, a club's performance, home attendance, and estimated market value were weighted equally. Three teams ranked as superior, average, and inferior during 1990 to 1997.

Of the superior teams, the Jazz ranked the highest followed by the Pistons and Lakers. The Jazz won over 64 percent of their games played per year except in 1993, and the team's attendance exceeded 806,000 per season from 1992 to 1997. In 1995, point guard John Stockton became the all-time assists leader in the NBA by surpassing former Laker star Magic Johnson's total of 9,921assists. Two years later, Jazz forward Karl Malone became the fifth player in NBA history to score 25,000 points and make 10,000 rebounds. Also, in 1997 Stockton and Malone extended their streaks of consecutive games played to 609 and 467 games, respectively. With their most productive seasons behind them, when Malone and Stockton retire the Jazz may have difficulty replacing such talent. In August 1998 agent Dwight Manley announced that Malone would accept nothing less than a $20 million salary when he becomes a free agent following the shortened 1998–99 season. At $6 million per season, Malone appears to be underpaid so the Jazz must negotiate or lose their most prominent player. Should

Table 5.4
Performance, Attendance, Value, Sum, and Rank of Relocated NBA Franchises

Franchise	Performance	Attendance	Value	Sum	Rank
Utah	.675 (1)	738 (2)	163 (3)	(6)	Superior
Detroit	.526 (5)	824 (1)	202 (2)	(8)	Superior
Los Angeles Lakers	.598 (3)	653 (4)	211 (1)	(8)	Superior
Houston	.609 (2)	626 (5)	154 (4)	(11)	Average
Sacramento	.368 (9)	705 (3)	131 (5)	(17)	Average
Golden State	.475 (6)	616 (6)	130 (6)	(18)	Average
Atlanta	.557 (4)	530 (8)	111 (8)	(20)	Inferior
Philadelphia	.376 (8)	553 (7)	113 (7)	(22)	Inferior
Los Angeles Clippers	.389 (7)	470 (9)	95 (9)	(25)	Inferior

Note: Performance, Attendance, Value, Sum, and Rank were determined as in Table 5.3.

Source: *The World Almanac and Book of Facts*, 1991–1998; *Media* and *Public Relations Guides* of the teams; Scott Fowler, "List Puts Panthers Among Most Valuable Pro Teams," *Charlotte Observer* (25 May 1997), 1A, 18A.

Malone or Stockton sign with another team, the franchise must find other talented players to retain its status as a superior team.[26]

The Pistons placed first in average attendance at 824,000 per season to earn a rank of superior. In 1998 the Pistons fired head coach Doug Collins because the team won less than half their games. So its superior ranking appears tenuous at best. The Lakers placed first in market value at $211 million to achieve the same ranking and competed with the Trail Blazers and SuperSonics for the Pacific Division title.

The Golden State Warriors, Houston Rockets, and Sacramento Kings represent average teams for the 1990s. Excluding 1992, the Rockets made the playoffs each year between 1990 and 1997, averaged 647,000 fans at home between 1986 and 1991, and drew 650,000 fans to home games between 1995 and 1997. In Table 5.4 the Kings ranked third in average attendance at 705,000 per season, and fifth in market value at $131 million. The Warriors ranked sixth in all three categories: in market value at $130 million, in performance at .475, and in attendance at 616,000 per season from 1990 to 1997. Warrior players Chris Mullin, Tim Hardaway, and Latrell Sprewell received all-pro recognition or played in the annual all-star game in various seasons between 1990 and 1997. In addition, the Warriors placed five players on the NBA's all-rookie team: Billy Owens in 1992, Chris Webber in 1994, Donyell Marshall and Clifford Rozier in 1995, and Joe Smith in 1996. Between 1990 and 1997 the team has played to capacity crowds in the Oakland Coliseum Arena and made the NBA playoffs in 1991, 1992, and 1994. In 1998 the Kings finished fifth and the Warriors sixth in the Pacific Division and failed to make the playoffs. One year earlier the market value of the teams differed by only $1 million, that is, $131 million for the Kings and $130 million for the Warriors. Judged by these variables, both teams seem destined to remain average clubs.

The inferior-ranked relocated NBA teams included the Hawks, Clippers, and SeventySixers. Although the Hawks won nearly 56 percent of their games from 1990 to 1997, the team placed eighth in mean attendance at 530,000 per season and rated eighth in market value at $111 million in 1997. For this and other reasons the future of the Hawks in Atlanta appears dubious. The club ranked twenty-seventh in the NBA in attendance in 1996 and 1997. According to *Financial World*, the team ranked last in the league in operating income in 1995. In *Forbes,* the team had an operating loss of $9 million in 1997.[27] Despite the media hype and programming expertise of the Time Warner Corporation, and because of the popularity of local NCAA basketball teams such as Georgia Tech and Georgia State University, Atlanta fans remain indifferent toward professional hoops, which keeps the Hawks from becoming an average or superior ranked NBA team.

Between 1990 and 1997 the Clippers won less than 40 percent of their games and placed ninth in average attendance at 470,000 per season, and ranked ninth in market value at $95 million in 1997. During the same years the SeventySixers won fewer games than the Clippers but drew 553,000 per season in attendance and reached a market value of $113 million in 1997. From 1991 to 1996 the winning percentage of the SeventySixers fell from .524 to .220 and home attendance fell from 634,000 to 489,000. Trading starters such as Charles

Barkley, Jeff Hornacek, Shawn Bradley, and Jerry Stackhouse destabilized the team. In the 1997–98 season, after trading veteran Clarence Weatherspoon, the SeventySixers finished at .378 and twenty-four games behind the Miami Heat, the division leader. Even with all-star forward Derrick Coleman, and the team's first-round pick in the 1996 NBA draft, Allen Iverson, the SeventySixers ranked inferior in 1998. It would take something along the lines of a miracle to turn the franchise around.[28]

Collectively the nine relocated NBA teams in Table 5.4 won 51 percent of their games and attracted 635,000 fans per season between 1990 and 1997. What is more, in 1997 the estimated average market value of the teams had reached $145 million, or $3 million below the league average.

Table 5.5 lists the fifteen expansion teams that played in the NBA from 1990 to 1997, but excludes the Toronto Raptors and the Vancouver Grizzlies, given their brief histories. We ranked each team from first to fifteenth for each criterion—team performance, home attendance, and estimated market value for 1997. We established a relative point system in which a superior expansion team received a total of three to fourteen points, an average team fifteen to twenty-nine points, and an inferior team above twenty-nine points. The points awarded indicate that two teams ranked superior, seven teams ranked average, and six teams ranked inferior. The Bulls and Suns received superior ratings for the period. The Bulls won 73 percent of their games and ranked second to the Hornets in average attendance at 832,000 per season and second to the Suns in market value at $214 million in 1997. Upon winning their sixth championship in 1998,

Table 5.5
Performance, Attendance, Value, Sum, and Rank of Selected NBA Franchises

Franchise	Performance	Attendance	Value	Sum	Rank
Chicago	.736 (1)	832 (2)	214 (2)	(5)	Superior
Phoenix	.640 (3)	707 (6)	220 (1)	(10)	Superior
San Antonio	.614 (5)	738 (4)	155 (6)	(15)	Average
Cleveland	.550 (6)	719 (5)	175 (4)	(15)	Average
Charlotte	.466 (9)	976 (1)	136 (9)	(19)	Average
Portland	.631 (4)	608 (13)	179 (3)	(20)	Average
Seattle	.647 (2)	609 (12)	139 (7)	(21)	Average
Orlando	.492 (8)	648 (9)	156 (5)	(22)	Average
New Jersey	.437 (11)	658 (7)	137 (8)	(26)	Average
Minnesota	.292 (15)	749 (3)	123 (10)	(28)	Inferior
Miami	.446 (10)	611 (11)	118 (11)	(32)	Inferior
Indiana	.544 (7)	569 (15)	114 (13)	(35)	Inferior
Milwaukee	.400 (12)	652 (8)	103 (15)	(35)	Inferior
Dallas	.315 (14)	635 (10)	104 (14)	(38)	Inferior
Denver	.399 (13)	575 (14)	116 (12)	(39)	Inferior

Note: Performance, Attendance, Value, Sum, and Rank were determined as in Table 5.3.

Source: *The World Almanac and Book of Facts*, 1991–1998; *Media* and *Public Relations Guides* of the teams; Fowler, "List Puts Panthers Among Most Valuable Pro Teams," 1A, 18A.

the Bulls ranked among the all-time best NBA teams. The Suns placed third in performance at .640 after the Bulls and SuperSonics and sixth in attendance at 707,000 per season. From 1993 to 1997, the Suns played to capacity crowds at the America West Arena, despite mediocre seasons in 1994, 1996, and 1997. In rank order, the seven average teams were the Spurs and Cavaliers who tied for third, followed by the Hornets, Trail Blazers, SuperSonics, Magic, and Nets. For the criteria in Table 5.5, each team demonstrated strength and weakness as follows: the Spurs, in home attendance and market value; the Cavaliers, in market value and team performance; the Hornets, in home attendance and market value; the Trail Blazers, in market value and home attendance; the SuperSonics, in team performance and attendance; the Magic, in market value and home attendance; and the Nets, in home attendance and team performance. In other words, team performance proved an advantage for the SuperSonics and a disadvantage for the Cavaliers and Nets; attendance proved an advantage for the Hornets, Nets, and Spurs, and a disadvantage for the SuperSonics, Trail Blazers, and Magic; market value proved an advantage for the Cavaliers, Trail Blazers, and Magic, and a disadvantage for the Spurs and Hornets. The above raises a question. Which teams will earn superior or inferior rankings between 1999 and 2003? With 1997–1998 Rookie of the Year Tim Duncan, and veteran all-pro center David Robinson, the Spurs should win more games and increase in value. If so, the team will eventually surpass the Timberwolves in average attendance and attain a higher rank.

All-pro forward Shawn Kemp and team assist leader Brevin Knight should help the Cavaliers achieve a superior rating by 2000. If former University of Utah all-american Keith Horn develops and becomes a team leader, and center Jason Williams stays healthy, the Nets should increase their winning percentage. From 1993 to 1997 the Nets' home attendance has exceeded 620,000 per season. Eventually these and other improvements should boost the team's competitiveness and rank. Without a new mix of players the Magic, SuperSonics, and Trail Blazers will probably remain average teams in the near future.

The Dallas Mavericks, Denver Nuggets, Indiana Pacers, Miami Heat, Milwaukee Bucks, and Minnesota Timberwolves (despite high average attendance) ranked as inferior teams between 1990 and 1997. During this time the Mavericks ranked tenth in average attendance at 635,000 per season, fourteenth in performance at .315, and in 1997 fourteenth in market value at $104 million. In January 1998, voters in Dallas narrowly approved tax increases on automobile rentals and hotel rooms to raise $125 million to finance a $232 million, 21,000-seat downtown arena for the Mavericks and the Dallas Stars hockey team. Ross Perot, Jr., and Stars' owner multimillionaire Tom Hicks will pay $105 million of the debt on the arena, which will contain one hundred luxury boxes and sales outlets. Still, even the new arena has little potential of elevating the Mavericks above inferior status in the NBA.[29]

With the new $160 million, 20,100-seat Pepsi Center scheduled to open in Denver in 1999, the home attendance and market value of the Nuggets should increase. In early March 1998, the team's record was 5–56 including 1–31 for away games and mired in a fifteen-game losing streak. They finished the season

11–71, matching the second-worst record in league history. Little wonder the Nuggets scored the lowest ranking of the NBA teams during 1990 to 1997.[30]

In Table 5.5 the Pacers ranked fifteenth in average attendance at 569,000 per season and thirteenth in market value at $114 million. The Pacers began play in a new $175 million, 18,500-seat arena in downtown Indianapolis in 1999. Consequently, the home attendance and market value of the team should soar. The new arena, named the Conseco Fieldhouse, connects the team with Indiana high school and college basketball traditions by containing metal seat signs printed with an old-style font, vintage advertising signs, a scoreboard with an old-fashioned nondigitial clock, and a section with pullout wooden bleachers. The Fieldhouse will contain sixty-five suites, 102 concession stands, and host entertainment activities such as free-throw competitions to provide additional revenues. With superb coaching by Larry Bird, and outstanding play by Reggie Miller and Rik Smits, the Pacers lost to the Bulls in a hard-fought NBA Eastern Conference championship in 1998 after taking Michael Jordan and the defending champions to a seventh game.[31]

With Alonzo Mourning, Tim Hardaway, and Dan Majerle, the Miami Heat won 51 percent of their games in 1995–96, 74 percent in 1996–97, and 70 percent in 1997–98. Yet with the smallest arena in the NBA, the Heat's market value failed to keep pace with its rivals throughout the 1990s. However, by playing in the new $200 million, 20,000-seat American Airlines Arena in 1999, the Heat's attendance, gate receipts, operating income (total revenues less operating expenses), and market value should swell and raise the team's rank to average by 2000.

The Bucks have drawn 652,000 fans per season since 1990. Yet the team ranked twelfth in average winning percentage at .400 between 1990 and 1997, and fifteenth in market value at $103 million in 1997. Even with former Purdue University all-american and marque forward Glenn Robinson and guard Ray Allen, the Bucks struggled to fill the 18,633 seats at the Bradley Center between 1997 and 1998. The team will likely remain inferior through the turn of the century despite choosing centers Dirk Nowitzki, a German player (subsequently traded to the Dallas Mavericks), and Pat Garrity, a twenty-point-per-game scorer from the University of Notre Dame, in the first round of the 1998 NBA draft.

The Timberwolves placed tenth in market value at $123 million in 1997 and were fifteenth in performance at .292 between 1990 and 1997. With home attendance declining from one million to 600,000 per season from 1990 to 1997, and with a winning percentage below .250 from 1992 to 1996, the Timberwolves remained inferior throughout the 1990s. In 1998 the team played above .530 and earned a playoff berth only to lose to the SuperSonics. The future of the franchise depends on the development of all-star Kevin Garnett, point guard Bobby Jackson, the club's 1998 first-round draft choice Radoslav Nesterovic, a center who played in Italy, and on the coaching skills of Flip Saunders. Given Garnett's $125 million contract, however, it is unlikely the owners will pay the other star players enough to retain them. In January 1999, for example, forward Tom Gugliotti signed a $58 million five-year contract with the Phoenix Suns. This should hinder the future performance of the Timberwolves.

In sum, in the NBA the mean winning percentages of the nine relocated teams and the fifteen expansion teams were equal at 50 percent from 1990 to 1997. And, the teams had an average market value at $145 million in 1997. In attendance, however, the expansion teams averaged 685,000 per season and the relocated teams 635,000 per season for the period. While the fifteenth-ranked Pacers averaged just 569,000 per season, established relocated teams such as the SeventySixers drew 553,000, the Hawks 530,000, and the Clippers 470,000 per season. Thus, despite proportionately fewer superior teams and relatively more average and inferior teams, the mean attendance of the NBA's expansion teams was 8 percent greater than the relocated teams between 1990 and 1997.

Table 5.6 shows the percentage of relocated and expansion teams, by sport, that ranked superior, average, and inferior between 1990 and 1997. The table excludes the Carolina Panthers and Jacksonville Jaguars of the NFL, and the Toronto Raptors and Vancouver Grizzlies of the NBA because they began play after 1990. After grouping by sport, Table 5.6 reveals that on average 25 percent of the relocated and expansion teams ranked superior, 34 percent ranked average, and 41 percent ranked inferior in the 1990s. This suggests that because of demographic, team-specific, and economic factors, a greater proportion of superior teams existed in baseball, average teams in basketball, and inferior teams in football.

Due to increased gate receipts and lucrative television contracts, NBA revenues increased from $1 billion in 1993 to $1.7 billion in 1998. This allowed the average player's salary to more than double. Consequently, the league's operating income fell from a positive $195 million to a $44 million loss in those years. To better control escalating player costs, commissioner David Stern seeks to limit the rise in payroll costs by eliminating loopholes in the salary cap. Teams violating the cap would incur a luxury tax. Players and their union cite inefficient league and team management as the critical problem in the 1998 lockout. With a new $2.65 billion broadcasting contract, league revenues will increase and players want a percentage share of that money above the 51.8 percent proposed by Stern. In January 1999 the lockout was settled and the players and owners agreed to a percentage share of league revenues, the maximum salary for rookies, a salary cap exception, minimum salaries, performance bonuses, penalties for player misconduct, and an end to opt-out clauses.[32]

Table 5.6
Relocated and Expansion Teams Ranked by Sport, 1990 to 1997

Sport	Superior	Rank Average	Inferior
MLB	33%	39%	28%
NFL	21%	21%	58%
NBA	21%	42%	37%

Source: See Tables 5.1–5.5.

SUMMARY

Of the eighteen MLB teams we ranked, nine played in each league in the 1990s (see Tables 5.1–5.2). Six relocated clubs in the NL and AL scored either superior or average ranking. The winning percentage, home attendance, and estimated market value of the AL's Milwaukee Brewers and Minnesota Twins placed them inferior during this period. We ranked six NL and four AL expansion teams. Thirty percent of them scored either superior or inferior. The NL's Florida Marlins, Houston Astros, and New York Mets, and the AL's Anaheim Angels had average rankings between 1990 and 1997. Thus since 1990, the majority of the relocated and new baseball teams either played competitively in their division, compared favorable to the league in attendance, or increased in value as the sport became more popular and appealing to fans who viewed games on television and at ballparks in cities hosting major league teams. Because of new parks or extended leases, in the short run the inferior-ranked Brewers will probably remain in Milwaukee, the Twins in Minnesota, and the Padres in San Diego. Nonetheless, without a new or renovated venue, or a change in ownership, players, and coaches, we expect the Expos eventually to leave Montreal and the Royals to vacate Kansas City. With local (Kansas City) owners and an increase in player salaries, however, in 1999 the Royals should improve, thereby reducing the likelihood of a move.

In the NFL we ranked four relocated and fifteen expansion clubs (see Table 5.3). Except for the Dallas Cowboys, Buffalo Bills, Kansas City Chiefs, and Miami Dolphins, the teams ranked either average or inferior. In 1998 the Cincinnati Bengals, Oakland Raiders, Indianapolis Colts, and San Diego Chargers represented inferior teams. Collectively they seem destined to relocate to non-NFL cities such as Houston or San Antonio. Between 1999 and 2007 every league team should be profitable. That is, expanded network television coverage and new stadiums built in Baltimore, Cincinnati, Cleveland, Denver, Detroit, Hartford, Nashville, Seattle, St. Louis, Tampa Bay, and Washington will lure fans to games, generate more interest in the sport, and earn profits for the teams. If no clubs relocate by 2000, we expect the NFL to place an expansion franchise in Los Angeles.

We ranked five NBA relocated and expansion teams as superior, ten as average, and nine as inferior (see Tables 5.4–5.5). Based on their mean winning percentage, attendance, and estimated market value the Chicago Bulls, Utah Jazz, Detroit Pistons, Los Angeles Lakers, and Phoenix Suns earned a superior ranking in the 1990s. The most inferior teams were the Dallas Mavericks, Denver Nuggets, Indiana Pacers, Los Angeles Clippers, Milwaukee Bucks, and Philadelphia SeventySixers. With new arenas in Indianapolis and Miami, and better team performances, the Pacers and Heat should draw more enthusiastic fans and by 2002 improve their rank to average. The Clippers, Mavericks, and Nuggets also will play in new arenas. But, unless they become playoff contenders, these clubs have little chance of becoming average in the next five years. In essence, without new ownership and a change in management or coaches, the Bucks, Clippers, Mavericks, Nuggets, and SeventySixers will retain inferior rankings after 2000.

NOTES

1. Leonard Koppett, *Sports Illusions, Sports Reality: A Reporter's View of Sports, Journalism, and Society,* 2nd ed. (Urbana and Chicago: University of Illinois Press, 1994), 13, 14.

2. Luke Cyphers, "New Parks Show Path," *Charlotte Observer* (21 April 1998), 4B.

3. The Milwaukee Brewers and Pittsburgh Pirates, for example, play in small cities where local radio and television markets are less lucrative revenue sources. New ballparks with luxury boxes and club seats are needed to increase the team's operating revenues and profits. According to baseball officials such as commissioner Bud Selig, the Twins cannot exist in Minnesota without a new ballpark. Even large city teams such as the Detroit Tigers are building new stadiums. See "Loan Closed Tuesday to Finance New Tiger Ballpark," at <http://www.baseball.yahoo.com> cited 26 August 1998; "Report: Sumitomo to Bankroll Tigers' Stadium," at <http://www.cnnsi.com> cited 17 March 1998.

4. New owners purchased the Minnesota Vikings and the Florida Marlins, and eight NFL coaches were fired after the 1998 season. Consequently, changes in the management structure and operations of the teams should improve the performance and economic value of the teams. See "Cubas Waits. Smiley Will Decide This Week on Marlins Purchase," at the Web site <http://www.cnnsi.com> cited 21 July 1998; "Huizenga Says He May Keep Marlins Next Season," at <http://www.cnnsi.com> cited 21 August 1998; "I Have a Handshake Deal. Commodities Trader Says He's Buying Marlins for $150 million," at the Web site <http://www.cnnsi.com> cited 11 September 1998; "Sold! Vikings Accept Red McCombs Bid for Ownership," at <http://www.cnnsi.com> cited 6 July 1998; Observer News Services, "McCombs Buys Vikings," *Charlotte Observer* (3 July 1998), 5B.

5. In 1996 the revenues from Camden Yards exceeded $21 million, the fifth highest in MLB. Even so, the Orioles began the 1998 season with an $8 million budget deficit due to high payroll costs and a $10 million payment for revenue-sharing. In 1997 the team earned $9 million, that is, $5 million from expansion fees and $4 million from playing in the post season. Thus in 1998 the Orioles increased ticket prices by 15 percent, an average exceeding $18 per ticket, the second highest in MLB. See Mel Antonen, "Baseball Fans Pick Up Tab," *USA Today* (22 January 1998), 3C; "Hands-On Approach. Politician Wants Controls on Orioles' Ticket Prices," at <http://www.cnnsi.com> cited 24 February 1998.

6. In 1998 TBS televised ninety Braves' games, thirty-five fewer than the previous year. TBS merged with Time Warner to become a basic cable network on 1 January 1998. Other networks broadcasting Braves' games include Fox Sports South, the Braves Southeast Network, ESPN, and Fox. See Paul Newberry, "Braves Coverage Diversifies," *Charlotte Observer* (22 March 1998), 14H.

7. In March 1998 the American Basketball League announced that the Atlanta Glory would relocate to another site for the 1998–99 season. The Glory's revenues consistently fell below expectations and the team's financial performance was the worst in the league. The Glory finished 15–29 and averaged 3,898 in attendance per game for the season. See the Observer News Services, "Purdue Coach Steps Down," *Charlotte Observer* (20 March 1998), 10B; Marjo Rankin Bliss, "Final Four a Fertile Recruiting Ground for the Sting," *Charlotte Observer* (22 March 1998), 2H.

8. Stefan Fatsis, "Los Angeles Dodgers Put Up for Sale, Marking the End of Family Ownership," *Wall Street Journal* (7 January 1997), B8; Editorial, "Deal for Dodgers Is Agreed Upon at $350 million," *Charlotte Observer* (5 September 1997), 4B. The MLB owners approved the sale of the Dodgers 27–2 on 19 March 1998. Thus, for $311 mil-

lion the Fox network acquired one of the marque sports franchises in North America. See Sports Today, "Lasorda: Dodgers Sale to Murdoch Good," *Charlotte Observer* (20 March 1998), 2B; "Baseball Owners Approve Sale of Dodgers to Fox Group," at the Web site <http://www.baseball.yahoo.com> cited 15 March 1998; "Management Shifts Signal Dodgers Sale Will Be OK'd," at <http://www.usatoday.com> cited 18 March 1998.

9. See, for example, "Turner Apparently Has Murdoch in His Sights," at the Web site <http://www.usatoday.com> cited 18 March 1998.

10. John Lippman, "Murdoch Tries to Turn a Triple Play by Adding Lakers, Kings to His Dodgers," *Wall Street Journal* (20 April 1998), B9; "A New Ballpark in L.A.? Fox Contemplates Replacing Dodger Stadium," at the Web site <http://www.cnnsi.com> cited 26 August 1998.

11. The Brewers' switch to the Central Division of the National League in 1998 and the completion of Miller Park in 2000 will improve the team's ability to compete. In 1998 season ticket sales for Brewers' games reached an all-time high and Milwaukee fans overwhelmingly favored the team's transfer of leagues. At nearly $10 per seat, the Brewer's ticket prices are the fourth lowest in the NL after the Cincinnati Reds at $8.37, Pittsburgh Pirates at $9.67, and Montreal Expos at $9.81 per seat. See Frederick C. Klein, "For the Brewers of Milwaukee; a Brave Change," *Wall Street Journal* (13 March 1998), B10.

12. In early 1998, the Athletics evaluated Las Vegas to determine whether the city could support a major league baseball team. But owners Steve Schott and Ken Hofmann preferred San Jose as a future home for the team. See, "Lasorda: Dodgers Sale to Murdoch Good," *Sports Today*, 2B. In 1998, the Athletics kept their tickets priced at $10.50 per seat. The lowest ticket prices in the AL are $10.33 for the Minnesota Twins and $10.40 for the Detroit Tigers.

13. See Bill Wareham, "Minnesota: Give Us a Year," *Charlotte Observer* (20 February 1998), 3B.

14. For more information about this campaign see Editorial, "Group Starts Drive to Pass Triad Ballpark Tax Plan," *Charlotte Observer* (16 February 1998), 3C. The campaign faced voter opposition, and in March 1998, the Subway and Wendy's restaurants in Greensboro, North Carolina, stopped supporting the prepared food tax that would help finance the stadium in the Triad. See Editorial, "Twins Stadium Setback," *Charlotte Observer* (13 March 1998), 11B. The details of the lease agreement are described by Ron Lesko, "Twins Sign New Lease; Will Stay Another 2 Years," *Charlotte Observer* (15 August 1998), 4B. In addition see "Hotel Tax Urged to Fund N.C. Ballpark," at <http://www.cnnsi.com> cited 10 February 1998; "Voters Reject Triad Referendum for Baseball Stadium," at <http://www.cnnsi.com> cited 6 May 1998.

15. For the ticket prices of all NL and AL teams, see Antonen, "Baseball Fans Pick Up Tab," 3C.

16. Ibid.

17. For the strategy of Walt Disney Company see Stefan Fatsis, "Money-Losing Angels Seem Immune to Disney Magic," *Wall Street Journal* (22 September 1997), B1.

18. Antonen, "Baseball Fans Pick Up the Tab," 3C.

19. See *The World Almanac and Book of Facts* (Mahwah, N.J.: World Almanac Books, 1990–1998), and the *Information Please Sports Almanac* (New York and Boston: Houghton Mifflin Company, 1990–1996). Both sources report demographic data on cities, states, and regions. See also "Royals Leaning Toward Prentice Bid. Team Says Ownership Group Needs More Local Involvement," at <http://www.cnnsi.com> cited 21 August 1998; "Hunt Withdraws Bid to Buy Royals. N.Y. Lawyer Appears to Have Inside Track on K.C. Team," at the Web site <http://www.cnnsi.com> cited 26 August 1998;

"Tom Watson Joins Bid to Buy Royals," at <http://baseball.yahoo.com> cited 29 August 1998.

20. We obtained winning percentages from various issues of *The World Almanac and Book of Facts*. Attendance was reported by the teams in their *Media Guides*. Estimated market values appeared in Scott Fowler, "List Puts Panthers Among Most Valuable Pro Teams," *Charlotte Observer* (25 May 1997), 1A, 18A; Michael Ozanian, "Selective Accounting," *Forbes* (14 December 1998), 124–134.

21. For more details on the lease agreement, see Sean Horgan, "Mayor, Colts Sign Lease Agreement," at the Web site <http://www.starnews.com> cited 21 January 1998.

22. Attendance and data for Arrowhead Stadium were provided by the Media Relations staff of the Chiefs.

23. The article on the Bengals stadium was "Bengals' New Stadium Receives Approval," at the Web site <http://www.football.com> cited 3 February 1998. In addition see "Get 'Em Quick. High-End Tickets Selling Fast for New Bengals Stadium," at <http://www.cnnsi.com> cited 21 July 1998.

24. See "Latest Stadium Plan for Pats Includes Athletes' Tax," at the Web site <http://www.cnnsi.com> cited 25 February 1998.

25. For highlights of the deal between Connecticut governor John Rowland and Robert Kraft, see Jean McMillan, "Patriots' Departure Disappointing to Fans," *Charlotte Observer* (20 November 1998), 10B; "2001: A Stadium Odyssey," at the Web site <http://www.cnnsi.com> cited 19 November 1998.

26. See "Mailman May Not Stick in Salt Lake City. Agent Wants to Make Mountain Out of Malone's Money," at the Web site <http://www.cnnsi.com> cited 21 August 1998; "Malone Chides Jazz Owner Miller. The Mailman Says He Is Underpaid and Underappreiated," at <http://www.cnnsi.com> cited 17 March 1998.

27. See Tushar Atre, Kristine Auns, Kurt Badenhausen, Kevin McAuliffe, Christopher Nikolov, and Michael K. Ozanian, "Sports, Stocks, and Bonds," *Financial World* (20 May 1996), 57; Michael Ozanian, "Selective Accounting," 130.

28. In the first round of the 1998 NBA draft, the SeventySixers picked eighth and chose Larry Hughes, a St. Louis University guard and Conference USA's scoring leader in 1997–98. For a complete list of players selected in the draft see Leonard Laye, "Youth Movement," *Charlotte Observer* (25 June 1998), 1B.

29. Two editorials detailed a description of the vote. See "Dallas Voters Approve Rise in Taxes to Fund Arena," *Wall Street Journal* (19 January 1998), B10A; "Dallas Voters Approve Tax Hike for New Arena," *Charlotte Observer* (18 January 1998), 4A.

30. To be sure, by selecting forward Raef LaFrentz from the University of Kansas, and Tyronn Lue, a guard from the University of Nebraska, the Nuggets should improve. But General Manager Dan Issel must hire a coach to lead the team. See Laye, "Youth Movement," 1B.

31. For the marketing strategy of the Pacers see John Helyar, "An Unpalatial Arena Designated to Please Just Plain Folks," *Wall Street Journal* (10 October 1997), B1.

32. See Anthony Bianco, "David Stern: This Time, It's Personal," *Business Week* (13 July 1998), 114–118.

Chapter 6 _____

Alternative Leagues and Sports Facilities

Baltimore confronted serious economic problems in 1980. A quarter of its population lived below the federal poverty line. In the previous decade its population had declined 13 percent and it lost fifty thousand jobs. Between 1980 and 1983 another twenty thousand Baltimore jobs vanished. In the midst of these hard times, the owner of the NFL Colts, Bob Irsay, began playing Baltimore against Indianapolis to secure the best deal for his club. Baltimore refused to build a new stadium for the Colts, claiming that Memorial Stadium was sufficient if not "one of the best in sports." So one night in March 1983, Irsay had his team's property loaded into moving vans and sent the vehicles west to Indianapolis, where the Colts would play in the new Hoosier Dome.[1]

The loss of the Colts struck a responsive chord with Baltimore's civic leaders. They then accepted the notion "that cities had to meet the demands of the leagues and franchises." Meanwhile, following Irsay's lead, the owner of the Orioles, Edward Bennett Williams, hinted that he might transfer the team to Washington if Baltimore refused to build a new ballpark. As Charles C. Euchner put it: "Williams was in the driver's seat."[2]

By the late 1980s Baltimore residents demonstrated little enthusiasm for building a new stadium. Even so, William Schaefer, the city's former mayor who had opposed Irsay's demand for a new facility, had changed his position on the issue. Now governor of Maryland, Schaefer acted quickly. He did not want to be held accountable for losing another major league franchise in Baltimore. He pressed for and promoted the stadium as an economic development package to revitalize downtown Baltimore. A large public works project would involve big contracts and create jobs. At the same time, the project would help restore the luster of the city, which had dulled considerably after the departure of the Colts. With all this in mind, the Maryland Stadium Authority was established "to operate above the tangled politics of Baltimore City." As Euchner described it: "The authority was an instrument of the state but also separate from the state. Its fund-raising capacity lay in the sale of tax-exempt bonds and the operation of lotteries. These devices avoided the direct coercion of taxes but were provided the state's fiscal backing. In short, the device of the authority could so blur the distinctions between public and private that a meaningful public discourse could not develop."[3]

The authority had its way. It selected Camden Yards as the site of the planned stadium, a place adjacent to the Inner Harbor and with direct connections to the suburban and Washington markets by expressways, interstate highways, and a number of major downtown arteries. In the spring of 1992, Oriole Park at Camden Yards neared its completion. By then much of the skepticism concerning the project had faded. The Stadium Authority had selected an architectural design that echoed baseball's traditional neighborhood parks. With its irregular field shape, fewer seats, use of a historic warehouse as a backdrop for the right field fence, Camden Yards seemed lived-in before it ever opened. Not surprisingly, complaints about cost overruns, favoritism, and political pressure tactics seemed to matter little "amidst the national and local media celebrations of the new facility." Yet as Euchner pointed out, "The public may have financed the show, but it never managed to land a significant speaking part."[4]

Euchner's keen insight in municipal political battles over sports teams says much about the current state of sports franchises and the leagues. In this chapter, we provide a brief synopsis of Women's Professional Basketball. Pursuing that objective, we evaluate the current state of the WNBA and suggest several measures the league should consider to improve its chance for success in the highly competitive business of professional sports. Clearly, the history of MLB, the NFL, and the NBA offers valuable lessons that the women's league should learn. Finally, we discuss at length the status of sports venues indicating which franchises are building or upgrading their ballparks, stadiums, or arenas.

WOMEN'S PROFESSIONAL BASKETBALL

One of the earliest women's professional sports organizations was the Women's Professional Basketball League (WPBL), which began play in December 1978. The eight-team WPBL lasted three seasons. In 1991, the Liberty Basketball Association (LBA) was formed. It folded after one exhibition game. One year later the Women's World Basketball Association (WWBA) was established in the Midwest and comprised six teams. Due to financial and managerial reasons, the WWBA terminated operations in 1992. To the early 1990s, then, various attempts to offer women's professional basketball to the American public have failed miserably.[5]

Hoping to capitalize on the goodwill generated by the U.S. women's basketball team victory in the 1996 Summer Olympics in Atlanta, the American Basketball League (ABL) began play in October 1996. Based in Palo Alto, California, the ABL fielded eight teams situated in Portland, San Jose, Seattle, Atlanta, Denver, Richmond, Columbus, Ohio, and Hartford, Connecticut. Structured like the NBA, the ABL had adopted a forty-game season that would end in January 1997, capped by a playoff tournament among the league leaders boosting demand and attendance. An average ticket price of $10 made ABL games affordable while the target fan base for the ABL was women, aged twenty-five to forty-four who earned $45,000 or more per year.[6]

In the 1996–97 season the ABL averaged attendance of 3,536 per game, supported by the sale of eight thousand season tickets. Player salaries averaged $70 thousand to $80 thousand with a minimum of $40 thousand and a maximum of $125 thousand. Nonetheless, due to weak attendance, limited television coverage, and operating with a minuscule $1.5 million marketing budget, the ABL finished the 1996–97 season with a loss of $10 million.[7]

To remain viable, the ABL made some strategic changes for the 1997–98 season. These included relocating the Richmond Rage to Philadelphia; expanding the league to nine teams and the schedule to forty-four games; doubling the marketing budget to $3 million; increasing the average player's salary to $80 thousand, with a maximum salary of $150 thousand; boosting season ticket sales to between thirteen and fourteen thousand; adding more sponsors; and negotiating for additional network and cable broadcasting coverage.

Did the new strategies succeed? The mean attendance of the ABL increased by 23 percent between 1997 and 1998. The New England Blizzard playing at Civic Centers in Hartford, Connecticut, and Springfield, Massachusetts, had the highest per game attendance at 8,857, and the Long Beach StingRays had the lowest at 2,117. For road games the Seattle Reign placed first with 5,063 per game, and the Portland Power placed last with 3,362 per game. Due to poor season ticket sales and weak corporate sponsorship, the StingRays terminated operations in August 1998. According to Gary Cavelli, the ABL's chief operating officer and co-founder, "This decision to close the doors in Long Beach is part of our ongoing effort to streamline operations, reduce expenses and improve profitability." To that end, the ABL reduced the salaries of office employees by 10 percent and also requested that coaches volunteer for salary cuts. The savings would be spent on advertising and marketing by the league. With a two-year television agreement to broadcast games one and three of the league's championship series by CBS, and after relocating the Atlanta franchise to Chicago (renamed the Condors) and launching a new franchise in Nashville (the Noise), the ABL began its third season in November 1998. After replacing the franchises in Atlanta and Long Beach due to poor attendance, 1998 season ticket sales increased by 30 percent for the nine-team league. Despite playing fourteen of its games on Fox Sports Net and two on CBS, the ABL's $5 million advertising budget was only one-third of the Women's National Basketball Association (WNBA). Cavelli, therefore, expected the league to break even in 1999 and to expand in either Baltimore, Dallas, Kansas City, New Jersey, New York, or St. Louis.[8]

Benefiting from global marketing capabilities, arena leases, and the sponsorships and infrastructure of the NBA, the WNBA began its inaugural season on 21 June 1997. The eight WNBA teams represented New York, Phoenix, Los Angeles, Houston, Cleveland, Sacramento, Salt Lake City, and Charlotte—all cities with NBA teams. The 1997–98 season consisted of twenty-eight games in ten weeks, and a playoff between the top four teams in the Eastern and Western Conferences.[9]

The WNBA established the following operating plans and strategies for the 1997–98 season: (a) a four thousand per game attendance at an average ticket price of $15; (b) nurturing a fan base consisting primarily of women between the ages of eighteen to thirty-four who are physically active and may play basketball themselves, and children of both sexes between the ages of seven and seventeen, who may bring their parents to games; (c) getting endorsements from national sponsors such as Bud Light, General Motors, Nike, and Sears; (d) contracting for national television coverage with NBC, ESPN, and Lifetime; (e) paying players on a sliding scale from $10 thousand to $15 thousand per season; and (f) budgeting at least $10 million for marketing and promotion. Additionally, the NBA agreed to pay all WNBA expenses including advertising, operations, and the salaries of players, league officials, and referees. The NBA in return receives revenues from the WNBA's national television contracts, sponsorships, and licensing agreements.[10]

The WNBA reached some goals and exceeded others in their first season. Per game attendance, for example, averaged nine thousand, which more than doubled the expected turnout of four thousand fans per game. Also, nationwide exposure and ratings from network and cable broadcasting met the league's expectations by reaching three million households per week.[11]

A demographic profile of the areas of the eight original and two expansion (Detroit and Washington) WNBA teams, and the nine original ABL teams, is provided in Table 6.1 These data are useful to analyze how the two leagues differed in the spacing and selection of sites to place teams. The WNBA teams represent areas with higher populations, similar population growth rates, and lower per capita income levels than the areas hosted by ABL teams. On average, an WNBA area had 6.4 million people in 1994, with personal income of $22,800 per capita, and a 6 percent growth rate in population between 1990 and 1994. The averages for an ABL area were 4 million, $24,600, and 7 percent, respectively. As noted, all WNBA teams play in NBA cities.[12] For the most part, ABL teams were dispersed across the nation. After the 1996–97 season, Richmond of the ABL relocated to Philadelphia.

In the 1998–99 season, Detroit and Washington entered the WNBA as the ninth and tenth franchises. By August 1998, Minnesota and Orlando had received sufficient season ticket deposits from fans to meet the WNBA's minimum requirement to field an expansion team in the following year's season. Minnesota will play in the Western, and Orlando in the Eastern Conference. If arena space becomes available, Atlanta and Toronto may become the thirteenth and fourteenth franchises to play in the 1999–2000 WNBA season.[13]

Some populated U.S. cities like Boston, Dallas, and Miami lack a women's professional basketball team. It seems most likely that the WNBA will gradually expand and place teams in those and other NBA cities based on arena availability and schedules, and on local, regional, and national broadcasting markets.

Could the ABL and WNBA survive in the long run? With fewer sponsors and less television coverage, and with relatively higher player costs, the ABL was at a competitive disadvantage to the WNBA. Although ABL season ticket

Table 6.1
WNBA and ABL Teams, Areas, and Demographic Data for Selected Years

Area	Population	Income	%Growth
WNBA			
Charlotte	1.3	20,894	8.5
Cleveland	2.9	22,921	1.4
Detroit	5.2	24,458	1.3
Houston	4.1	22,651	9.9
Los Angeles	15.3	29,021	5.3
New York	19.8	21,696	1.3
Phoenix	2.5	20,999	10.5
Sacramento	1.6	21,810	7.2
Salt Lake City	1.1	18,623	9.5
Washington	7.1	25,257	4.8
ABL			
Atlanta	3.3	23,633	12.6
Denver	2.2	24,379	10.6
Columbus	1.4	22,058	5.8
Long Beach	15.3	29,021	5.3
New England	1.1	26,147	−0.5
Richmond	.9	23,262	5.9
Portland	1.9	22,172	10.5
San Jose	6.5	26,919	4.2
Seattle	3.2	23,949	8.6

Note: Population is the total MSA population in millions in 1994. Income is the per capita personal income of the MSA in hundreds of thousands of dollars. The %Growth is the percentage growth of the MSA population between 1990 and 1994.

Source: *The World Almanac and Book of Facts* (Mahwah, N.J.: World Almanac Books, 1990–1995); U.S. Department of Commerce, Bureau of the Census, *Statistical Abstracts of the United States* (Washington, D.C., 1990–1995).

sales increased over 60 percent in the 1997–98 season, the ABL's total attendance was less than 50 percent of the WNBA's. In ninety-nine games, the WNBA's 1998 attendance exceeded one million, and attendance per game increased to 10,200 from 9,400 in 1997.[14]

Due to the lack of national television rights, small crowds, and head-to-head competition with college basketball, in December 1998 the ABL suspended operations and filed for bankruptcy. Boston Herald sports writer Steve Bulpett said: "It was the ABL's failure to pick up a decent share of NBA refugee fans that essentially spelled its demise. The last numbers I saw had the league averaging 3,979 a game—more than 350 fewer per game than last year's count."[15] We predict former ABL cities such as Denver, Philadelphia, Portland, and Seattle will eventually join the WNBA. Along with teams in Atlanta, Toronto, and possibly Chicago, the WNBA can field twelve or more teams divided among four divisions in two conferences. If that happens, the league will provide an optimal mix of teams located in metropolitan areas that can support each franchise. Over time, say in the first decade of the next century, the WNBA may expand to Boston, Dallas, Miami, and to other NBA cities. If the attendance of the league continues to grow, and more games are televised, we foresee one league with six to ten teams in each of two divisions to exist after 2000. League franchises will locate in cities of NBA teams. Moreover, games would be scheduled between March and June, and clubs will add corporate sponsors and earn profits as women improve their skills as professional athletes and become role models and sports heroes to our youth.

SPORTS VENUES

In the last hundred years baseball parks have evolved in three distinct eras. Between 1900 and 1960, in the classic era, the importance of gate receipts mandated the construction of large, open-air natural grass single-purpose ballparks such as Forbes Field in Pittsburgh, Ebbets Field in Brooklyn, and Crosley Field in Cincinnati. Of these parks, four still host teams in 1999—Tiger Stadium in Detroit, Fenway Park in Boston, Wrigley Field in Chicago, and Yankee Stadium in New York. From 1960 to 1990 a new era of the super-stadium characterized by multipurpose ballparks built on suburban lots that feature symmetrical fields, artificial turf, and concrete frames. Fulton County Stadium in Atlanta, Dodger Stadium in Los Angeles, and Veterans Stadium in Philadelphia illustrate this kind of facility. In the 1990s, new parks designed to "recapture the charm and intimacy of the classic ballpark era" were erected in many major-league cities. For example, Comiskey Park in Chicago, Jacobs Field in Cleveland, and Coors Field in Denver have natural grass fields and an "architecture that tends to blend naturally into their environment with space opened to the sky, sun and city."[16]

To maximize profits a team owner exploits all potential sources of revenue including taxpayer subsidies to finance the construction of a new, or the renovation of an old, ballpark, stadium, or arena (BSA). Franchise owners began aggressively seeking taxpayer subsidies for their venues in the 1980s. Throughout the 1990s at least twelve MLB, thirteen NFL, and four NBA owners threatened to relocate their teams due to inadequate venues.[17] Also, during this period various team owners evaluated the construction of sixty-three professional sports facilities. As a result, between 1998 and 2000 sixteen new BSAs will be opened in thirteen cities across the nation.[18]

Despite the lack of economic benefits from investing in BSAs, team owners justify their expenditures to local and state authorities for the following four reasons. First, sports fans demand and deserve the comforts and conveniences that modern facilities provide when attending games. Second, ballclubs do not share all revenues from BSAs with other league teams and therefore owners use such money to acquire skilled players and coaches in the competitive marketplace. Third, profitable sites are available in other cities where taxpayers appear willing to subsidize the construction of a new BSA. Fourth, the downtown area of a city is revitalized when a sports BSA locates there. Given these reasons, proprietors request, promote, lobby, and demand taxpayer subsidies from city, county, state, and perhaps regional governments.[19]

Between 1990 and 1998 nine MLB teams opened their seasons in new ballparks. These included the Chicago White Sox in 1991, Baltimore Orioles in 1992, Cleveland Indians and Texas Rangers in 1994, Colorado Rockies and

Florida Marlins in 1995, and the Atlanta Braves, Arizona Diamondbacks, and Tampa Bay Devil Rays in 1998. The ballparks of the two latest baseball expansion teams seem particularly noteworthy. Bank One Ballpark in Phoenix, owned by the Maricopa County Stadium District, seats 49,000 and includes sixty-nine luxury suites and six party suites. Of the stadium's cost, 68 percent—$238 million—is funded by a county sales tax, and 32 percent—$111 million—by the proprietors of the team.[20] The $138 million 46,000-seat Florida Suncoast Dome, now Tropicana Field, was built in St. Petersburg in 1990 to lure the White Sox from Chicago or as a home site for an expansion team. After Tampa Bay received a MLB franchise the city of St. Petersburg renovated the dome in 1998 for $70 million and installed an interactive game room, a post office, sports and cigar bars, a hair salon, and ninety reclining chairs—priced equally at $195 per ticket—behind home plate equipped with television sets to watch replays and monitor team statistics.[21]

Other MLB owners recently upgraded their facilities, too. Rather than build a new ballpark for the Angels, for example, the city of Anaheim and Walt Disney Company began a $118 million renovation of 33,800-seat Edison International Field in 1997 to generate more stadium income for the team. In Kansas City, a planned three-year improvement to twenty-five-year-old Kauffman Stadium began in 1998.[22]

Between 1999 and 2002 the Boston Red Sox, Cincinnati Reds, Detroit Tigers, Houston Astros, Milwaukee Brewers, New York Mets, Pittsburgh Pirates, San Diego Padres, San Francisco Giants, Seattle Mariners, and possibly the Los Angeles Dodgers and New York Yankees are scheduled to play in new ballparks. The Minnesota Twins, Montreal Expos, and the Oakland Athletics are threatening to move after their leases expire unless new facilities with abundant luxury boxes and club seats are constructed to accommodate their fans.

What do studies show about the effects of new MLB ballparks on team attendance? After gathering data on MLB ballparks in nine cities, journalists Allen Barra and Allen St. John have argued that "A new ballpark increases attendance, but not by itself. Teams in new ballparks sell more tickets—for a while. But if the win-loss record slips below .500, the ballpark stops looking very new."[23] Economists Roger G. Noll and Andrew Zimbalist contend that "the local economic impact of sports teams and facilities is far smaller than proponents allege; in some cases it is negative. These findings are valid regardless of whether the benefits are measured for the local neighborhood, for the city, or for the entire metropolitan area in which a facility is located."[24]

Between 1990 and 1998, the Baltimore Ravens, Carolina Panthers, St. Louis Rams, Tampa Bay Buccaneers, and Washington Redskins all erected new stadiums. Furthermore, new stadiums should open in 1999 for the expansion Cleveland Browns, in 2000 for the Cincinnati Bengals, Seattle Seahawks, and Tennessee Titans, in 2001 for the Pittsburgh Steelers and New England Patriots, in 2002 for the San Francisco FortyNiners, in 2004 for the Detroit Lions, and by 2005 for the Chicago Bears and Denver Broncos. Regarding the 1998 Super Bowl champions, Colorado's secretary of state recently approved a petition to place the Broncos' new stadium initiative (Referendum 4A) on the fall ballot. Approved by a 14 percent margin in November 1998, voters in the six-county

Denver area decided to extend a sales tax to finance 75 percent of the 76,125-seat stadium's $360 million construction cost, with team owner Pat Bowlen contributing $90 million. After a local board terminated the Broncos' lease at Mile High Stadium in September 1998, the city must sell the stadium and McNichols Sports Arena to the Metropolitan Football Stadium District. By 2000, stadium renovations and renegotiated leases seem likely to occur for the Arizona Cardinals, Dallas Cowboys, Green Bay Packers, and Oakland Raiders.[25]

All NFL teams played in stadiums with luxury suites in the late 1990s. The number of suites varied from twenty at Riverfront Stadium in Cincinnati to 370 at Texas Stadium in Dallas. The average price per suite ranged from $27 thousand per season at Riverfront Stadium and Arrowhead Stadium in Kansas City to $109 thousand at the Meadowlands in New Jersey.[26] In sum, the revenue sources to construct and maintain NFL stadiums include interest income from bonds, various taxes, luxury suites, permanent seat licenses, club seats, retail shops, and private money. Yet, contrary to the views and preferences of team owners, Mark S. Rosentraub argues against taxing the public and advocates user fees, ticket surcharges, and concession fees to finance sports facilities.[27]

In the NBA four arenas went up in the 1960s and 1970s, eight in the 1980s, and seventeen between 1990 and 1998. In 1999, six new facilities are scheduled to open: the Air Canada Center for the Raptors in Toronto, the American Airlines Arena for the Heat in Miami, the CNN Center for the Hawks in Atlanta, the Conseco Fieldhouse for the Pacers in Indianapolis, the Pepsi Center for the Nuggets in Denver, and the Staples Center for the Lakers and Clippers in Los Angeles. Located on a twenty-eight acre site, the $350 million 21,000-seat Staples Center will contain 160 luxury boxes generating $40 million in annual revenues, and lay-down basketball floors on top of hockey ice will allow for two games in one day. Philip Anschultz and Ed Roski, Jr., co-owners of the Kings, put up the money for the arena. Whether the facility will revive downtown Los Angeles is debatable. Proponents claim that the Staples Center has already spurred more investment than past projects such as the Los Angeles Convention Center. Others contend, however, that the arena's net benefits are exaggerated and downtown Los Angeles needs a residential area.[28]

The Dallas Arena will open as the home court of the Mavericks and the NHL's Dallas Stars in 2000.[29] Some of these arenas will contain retail shops and premium seats such as luxury boxes, corporate suites, club seats, party lounges, and skyboxes. In 1997 the number of suites at NBA arenas varied from zero at the Reunion Arena in Dallas, Market Square Arena in Indianapolis, and the Great Western Forum and Sports Arena in Los Angeles, to 216 at the United Center in Chicago.[30] Thus, the new NBA arenas should generate more unshared revenues for the teams to spend on players, coaches, and staff or to retain as profits.

Because of inadequate arenas, between 1990 and 1999 the owners of the Mavericks, Spurs, and SuperSonics threatened to move their teams from Dallas, San Antonio, and Seattle, respectively. The threats induced action. In January 1998 Dallas voters approved two tax increases and a $125 million bond issue to fund a new $230 million 21,000-seat arena. The new arena will have club seats and luxury boxes and replace the $27 million 18,000-seat Reunion Arena built in 1980. Meanwhile, the Spurs plan to improve the 36,000-seat Alamodome, which was erected in downtown San Antonio in 1993 for $186 million. A $73 million renovation of Seattle's Key Arena was completed in October 1995. Revenues from the arena will pay the renovation cost and support other Seattle Center programs. Besides the SuperSonics, the arena's tenants include the World Hockey League's Seattle Thunderbirds.[31]

Beginning in 1997 the *Charlotte Observer* published talks held between business, political, and community leaders to build a new arena in downtown Charlotte for the Hornets. Civic leaders discussed three arena proposals involving taxpayer contributions of roughly $50 million. In March 1997, the city of Charlotte offered $26 million as its share of the $161 million needed to construct the arena. Fifty-eight percent of municipal money would come from a hotel/motel tax and the remainder from the sale of an old convention center and savings from local capital projects. Eventually George Shinn, the owner of the Hornets, abandoned his quest for a downtown arena, perhaps because of the estimated $109 million he would have had to contribute for the facility. Shinn then offered to pay $29 million to purchase and renovate the Charlotte Coliseum for the team. In June 1997, Bruton Smith, the owner of the Charlotte (now Lowe's) Motor Speedway, bid $40 million for the coliseum and for related arena amenities. Five months later Shinn stated that, without a new lease from the city, the Hornets will discontinue play in the coliseum after the 1999–2000 season. In 1998, various arena proposals continued entering in public discourse. One proposal called for the construction of a $477 million retail/entertainment complex in downtown Charlotte with local taxpayers assuming 25 percent or $120 million of the cost. An arena within the complex would cost $192 million with taxpayers liable for 30 percent or $58 million. Without public subsidies to renovate the Coliseum or build a new arena for the team, it appears that Shinn will relocate the Hornets by 2001. In November 1998, Charlotte's New Arena Committee visited three professional basketball arenas to compare them to the coliseum and to evaluate the feasibility of constructing a new arena for the Hornets. The three-day trip, paid for by Charlotte's City Council, cost $20 thousand for the fifteen committee members. To save transportation expenses, the Hornets's jet flew the group to view the Gund Arena in Cleveland, the First Union Center in Philadelphia, and the MCI Center in Washington. After the tour a majority of the committee favored the construction of a downtown arena for the Hornets. Some committee members prefer to limit the taxpayer's subsidy to upgrading the land, roads, and infrastructure surrounding the facility. According to one member, "You can certainly better appreciate the arguments that the Hornets make that our building simply does not produce the money for our NBA team that these arenas produce for their NBA teams." In a preliminary draft report written for the committee in November 1998, city staff said building a $200 million 20,000-seat uptown arena, adaptable to professional hockey, "would be in the best, long-term interests of [Charlotte]." At the same time, a poll taken by the *Charlotte Observer* indicated that 64 percent oppose spending public money to help build an arena. Team executives, meanwhile, have suggested car rental taxes, and Charlotte mayor Pat McCrory has recommended a hotel-motel tax as sources of revenue for constructing an arena.[32]

NBA attendance declined by 15–20 percent in cities such as Portland and San Francisco in 1998.[33] With gate receipts and arena revenues comprising 30 percent of the income of a basketball team, it behooves NBA franchise owners to prod local politicians and community leaders for subsidies to pay for the construction costs of a new arena. Subsidies primarily benefit NBA proprietors by shifting a portion of the facility's costs to the taxpayer.

Taxpayers paid 90 percent of the construction costs of new BSAs in the 1970s. By 1995, the public's share had dropped to 60 percent.[34] In a study of eleven arenas built since 1990, the accounting firm Coopers and Lybrand determined that taxpayers funded 36 percent of an arena's cost. Taxpayer contributions, for example, funded 9 percent of the United Center in Chicago, 13 percent of the Rose Garden in Portland, 16 percent of the Cores State Center in Philadelphia, and 30 percent of the MCI Center in Washington.[35] Given the public's growing aversion to higher taxes and subsidies, team owners expect to rely more on revenues from seat licenses, retail shops, luxury suites, skyboxes, theme restaurants, club seats, naming rights, and corporate sponsors to fund the cost of their venues. Otherwise, cities seeking sports teams must forgo investments in community projects such as new school buildings, street maintenance, and social and cultural programs to host a professional sports team and provide a major league venue for the team.

Economist Donald A. Coffin has used regression analysis to estimate the demand for attendance at major league baseball games between 1962 and 1992, 1962 and 1975, and 1976 and 1992. His economic model includes five groups of explanatory variables, such as three market, six product quality, two stadium capacity, three specific events, and team variables. Based on their statistical significance, ticket prices and the 1981 baseball strike negatively affected attendance. Furthermore, the presence of a new stadium and an existing expansion team, current and post-season winning percentages, and time trends positively affected attendance. Other variables of less significance were mean family income, population, games behind the division leader, and the stadium's capacity. Coffin further estimated that the costs of constructing a new stadium exceeds the present value of the incremental revenues from the additional attendance and luxury boxes at the facility. Given their inadequate private economic returns, therefore, most new stadium proposals include financial subsidies from taxpayers.[36]

Proposals to protect fans and their communities by restricting the monopolistic practices of sports leagues have been suggested by economists. Roger Noll and Andrew Zimbalist contend that provisions in stadium leases, the invocation of eminent domain, federal tax reform, antitrust policy, and congressional regulation of the sports business are ineffective ways to stop team owners from exploiting their economic power and harming the public. In their view, "the most likely source of reform, though still a long shot, will be grass roots disgruntlement and citizen education." Although Columbus, Ohio, Pittsburgh, and the Triad region in North Carolina recently rejected tax increases to finance sports facilities, public subsidies will continue to grow as a source of revenue for professional sports franchises. As noted by Noll and Zimbalist, "Until the monopoly structure and cultural centrality [of professional sports in a community] are modified, large-scale public subsidies to wealthy team owners and athletes will be a feature of the professional sports landscape."[37]

In *Field of Schemes: How the Great Stadium Swindle Turns Public Money Into Private Profit*, journalists Joanna Cagan and Neil deMause expose and condemn the billions of dollars that franchise owners demand and receive from public monies. Such corporate welfare "serves the rich and powerful at the expense of the average fan, the average taxpayer, the average citizen."[38] With financial support from local and state politicians, and assistance from the media and corporate interests, wealthy owners often threaten to move their teams unless local officials bribe owners with a new stadium or lease. Meanwhile, social investments in public schools, libraries, roads, and housing remain underfunded or ignored. Cagan and deMause cite the struggle by various groups, activists, and fans to keep teams from moving, to preserve neighborhoods adjacent to existing and proposed facilities, and to oppose tax increases, tax abatements, and other subsidies benefiting team owners and leagues.

To curb the power of private interests allied with government officials while reducing stadium construction costs and minimizing the loss of a team to another city, Cagan and deMause have proposed public ownership of professional teams. They maintained that, unless local taxpayers hold club owners accountable, professional teams will continue wielding unchecked power over cities. As a result, this adversely affects the respective community and working-class poor, and undermines the social needs of inner cities devastated by unemployment and the rise of the global marketplace.[39]

However, in the best interest of fans we advocate private, instead of public (government) ownership of teams. Private proprietors operate their clubs to maximize profits. Because of this, owners know best how to manage the franchise. Contrary to Cagan and deMause, we prefer a limited role for government in the industry and thus recommend a gradual phase-out of any public subsidies to teams.

Still, in the end the question of public subsidies to professional franchises may be settled by the fans. Dan McGraw has illuminated why fans have become disgusted with professional sports. For one, increases in the average ticket prices for the NFL, the NBA, and MLB have exceeded the rate of inflation for all consumer goods and services during the 1990s. As ticket prices have climbed, so too have the costs of parking, food, beverages, and souvenirs sold at games. In 1998 it cost an average family of four roughly 30 percent of their household's weekly income to attend either an NBA game at $214 or an NFL game at $228. MLB, which charges lower ticket prices because the league plays more games than the NFL or NBA, costs the typical family of four $114 per game or about 16 percent of its weekly income. In McGraw's article, Professor Zimbalist states that "the middle-income and lower-income fans are being priced out of the game." This factor, coupled with network ratings that have steadily dropped during the past decade while player's salaries have skyrocketed, could spell disaster for the major leagues. Indeed, many major-league teams are losing money, especially those in small markets. As McGraw framed the question: "Are these economic indicators a sign that the sports bubble is going to burst or merely evidence of a cyclical shakeout that occurs in any industry?"[40]

To fix the big league troubles some politicians advocate amending the anti-trust laws. Others have called for increased governmental control. Say, for example, a federal sports agency designed to regulate ticket prices, team relocation, and salaries. Economists Zimbalist and Noll have argued that competition will save the big leagues. To that end, they favor "breaking the sports leagues into separate businesses" that would compete against each other for players, markets, and broadcast rights.[41] Introducing competition in professional sports would negate the monopoly behavior of owners and reduce player costs and league revenues from the media as teams compete for these cash flows.

But according to McGraw, these solutions have little promise. "Competing leagues could drive up costs, and more franchises would water down an already depleted talent level. And [prohibiting] sports leagues to pool broadcast rights might put small-market teams at a further disadvantage, as each club would cut its own deal and the weaker clubs would get left with the scraps."[42]

Instead, McGraw sees merit in a few modest proposals floated by *United Sports Fans of America*. First, modify the NFL's home-market black-out rule, which bans televised broadcasts locally of any games not sold-out. Second, require all NFL franchises to stay put for the duration of the league's new eight-year television contract. Third, if a game fails to sell out, leagues should make cheaper seats available the day of the game. Fourth, the NBA should establish and uphold a code of conduct for its players. Unless the major leagues take action, fans will find other ways to entertain themselves and shift "their allegiance away from big-money sports." Minor-league baseball, for example, is setting attendance records not seen since its heydays of the 1940s. "Low-cost independent hockey leagues" are experiencing a similar surge in fan interest. And after thirteen years, the Arena Football League is averaging in excess of ten-thousand fans per game. This is partially due to "its image as a fan-friendly, low cost alternative to the NFL." McGraw has concluded that fans will ultimately determine the future of big-league sports by refusing either to pay higher prices for tickets and merchandise, or subsidizing the venues of their home teams with tax dollars. That is, unless professional teams and leagues treat fans as customers, they may vote with their feet.[43]

While the Consumer Price Index rose 18.6 percent between 1991 and 1997, the cost of attending games increased by 37.5 percent in MLB, 46.3 percent in the NFL, and 56.3 percent in the NBA. These escalating costs adversely impacted the various leagues and teams in 1998. The World Series, for one, received the all-time lowest national and local television ratings. Second, a majority of baseball clubs saw attendance decline. Third, the regular-season television network ratings for the four major sports fell from 1997 to 1998. Journalist Rick Burton complained, "I have seen America's sports future, and I'm here to tell you the current economic model for the professional leagues no longer works efficiently for all interested parties [television, the gate, owners, and the league]." Burton speculates that in 1999 television ratings will further recede, attendance will decline because of higher ticket prices and fan disenchantment, and owner profits will drop due to escalating player salaries. Unless the leagues promote more equality in playing strengths between large- and small-market teams by permitting owners greater freedom to move to more promising sites, we concur with Burton's scenario of economic distress for the industry.[44]

NOTES

1. Charles C. Euchner, *Playing the Field: Why Sports Teams Move and Cities Fight to Keep Them* (Baltimore: Johns Hopkins University Press, 1993), 104–130.

2. Ibid.

3. Ibid.

4. See also Peter Richmond, *Ballpark: Camden Yards and the Building of an American Dream* (Hamden, Conn.: Fireside Press, 1993).

5. The history of women's basketball was found at various Web sites on the Internet. The history began in 1892 when gymnastics instructor Senda Berenson Abbott adapted James Naismith's basketball rules for women and introduced the game to her students at Smith College.

6. See Ted Reed, "A Pro League of Their Own," *Charlotte Observer* (26 May 1997), 8D.

7. To understand the strategies of the ABL and WNBA, see Roger Thurow, "Woman's Hoops Out-Glitzes Rival," *Wall Street Journal* (19 September 1997), B12.

8. See Marjo Rankin Bliss, "ABL Requests Contract Cutbacks," *Charlotte Observer* (16 August 1998), 2H; "One Year Wonder. ABL Shuts Down Long Beach Franchise After Successful First Season," at the Web site <http://www.cnnsi.com> cited 27 August 1998; "ABL's Top-25 All-Time Attendance Marks," at the Worldwide Web site <http://www.ableague.com> cited 29 August 1998; "American Basketball League Attendance Report (through Tuesday, February 17)," at <http://www.cnnsi.com> cited 27 August 1998.

9. See Erica Schacter, "WNBA Season: Hoops but No Skirts," *Wall Street Journal* (27 August 1997), A10.

10. For a profile of various players and a discussion of the viability of the WNBA, see John Leland, "Up in the Air," *Newsweek* (1 September 1997), 56–62.

11. For an analysis of the WNBA's inaugural season see Ellen Alperstein, "WNBA's Rookie Season Is the Start of Something Big," *Charlotte Observer* (31 August 1997), 1G.

12. Detroit and Washington were awarded the ninth and tenth WNBA franchises, which began play in the 1998–99 season. Detroit was one of the original markets targeted by the WNBA before its inaugural season, but officials with the Palace of Auburn Hills decided to wait and see how the league fared. Washington wanted one of the eight original franchises, but the league wanted to wait until a new uptown arena, which opened in December 1997, was ready.

13. For the future growth of the WNBA see Chris Sheridan, "WNBA Goes to Detroit, Washington," *Charlotte Observer* (1 October 1997), 2B. See also "Join In. Deposits Secure WNBA Team for Minnesota," at <http://www.cnnsi.com> cited 1 September 1998.

14. See Cliff Mehrtens, "WNBA May Expand Next Year," *Charlotte Observer* (24 August 1997), 3H; Erica Schacter, "WNBA Season: Hoops but No Skirts," A10; Ted Reed, "A Pro League of Their Own," 8D; John Leland, "Up in the Air," 56–62; Editorial, "WNBA," *Charlotte Observer* (29 July 1998), 5B.

15. For a preview of the ABL's 1998–99 season and why the league folded in December 1998 see Frederick Klein, "A Women's League Comes Into Its Own," *Wall Street Journal* (15 December 1998), A20. See also Cliff Mehrtens, "ABL Refugees Look

to WNBA," *Charlotte Observer* (23 December 1998), 1B, 8B; Steve Bulpett, "And Then There Was One," *Boston Herald* (23 December 1998), 88.

16. See "A Heritage With a Rich History Baseball: One Hundred Years of Tradition in Montreal," at the Web site <http://www.montrealexpos.com> cited 6 October 1998.

17. See Mark S. Rosentraub, *Major League Losers: The Real Costs of Sports and Who's Paying for It* (New York: Basic Books, 1997), 18.

18. See Tom Farrey, "Too Much of a Good Thing?" *Business Week* (11 May 1998), 70; Carrick Mollenkamp and Jeffrey Ball, "Midsize Cities Scramble to Woo Stadium Sponsors," *Wall Street Journal* (13 May 1998), S1.

19. Webcams, which transmit images every second, minute, or day, permit a viewer to watch the construction of their sports venue online. The creation of a baseball park in Houston, football stadiums in Cleveland and Nashville, basketball arenas in Indianapolis and Miami, a hockey rink in Atlanta, and Pacific Bell Park in San Francisco are being tracked on Webcams. See David Sweet, "Catch That Jackhammer Action! Stadium-Building as Cybersport," *Wall Street Journal* (16 July 1998), B1.

20. Foon Rhee, "Disputed Tax Builds Baseball Taj Mahal," *Charlotte Observer* (15 January 1998), 1A, 18A.

21. See David Sweet, "Take Me Out to the Ball Game, Take Me Out to the Hair Salon," *Wall Street Journal* (12 December 1997), B1; Foon Rhee, "Twins Sale on Agenda as Owners Talk Shop," *Charlotte Observer* (11 January 1998), 1A, 18A.

22. Ibid.

23. Allen Barra and Allen St. John, "Debunking Baseball's Stadium Myth," B9.

24. Frederick C. Klein, "Stadium Deals Rarely Add Up to a Good Thing," *Wall Street Journal* (19 December 1997), B15; Roger G. Noll and Andrew Zimbalist, "Build the Stadium—Create the Jobs!" in Roger G. Noll and Andrew Zimbalist, eds., *Sports, Jobs, and Taxes: The Economic Impact of Sports Teams and Stadiums* (Washington, D.C.: The Brookings Institution, 1997), 1–54.

25. For a recent update on the construction of new NFL stadiums see <http://www.nfl.com> cited 28 September 1998. See also "Broncos Stadium Ballot Initiative Approved," at <http://www.cnnsi.com> cited 1 September 1998; "Cards' Stadium Drive Gets Big Boost. Developer Pledges $185 million to Arizona Complex," at <http://www.cnnsi.com> cited 3 July 1998; "Let the Handshaking Begin. Broncos Stadium Drive Launches $1 Million Campaign," at <http://www.cnnsi.com> cited 8 September 1998; "New Stadiums to Cost Team Owners More. Pirates, Steelers Consider New Funding Approaches," at <http://www.cnnsi.com> cited 10 March 1998; "Pacers Stock Sale Raises $24 Million," at the Web site <http://www.cnnsi.com> cited 17 March 1998; "Problems Plaguing the Bills. Lagging Suite Sales Endanger Team's Future in Buffalo," at <http://www.cnnsi.com> cited 6 July 1998; "Seahawks Get Land for Open-Air Stadium. Proposed Park Would Open in 2002, Seat 72,000," at the Web site <http://www.cnnsi.com> cited 7 July 1998; "Vandy Looks Dandy to Bud Adams," at <http://www.cnnsi.com> cited 25 February 1998; "Oilers Get Buyout from Memphis," at <http://www.sportingnews.com> cited 4 March 1998. In November 1998, NFL Commissioner Paul Tagliabue said the league would assist Chicago and Arizona to acquire new stadiums. The league will analyze the financial proposals and the approval process of stadiums in other NFL cities and then recommend successful tactics to the owners of the Bears and Cardinals. For the strategy of Tagliabue, see "Tagliabue to the Rescue: NFL Says It Will Help Chicago, Arizona Get New Stadiums," at the Worldwide Web site <http://www.cnnsi.com> cited 9 November 1998.

26. See Sean Horgan, "Corporate Community Has Central Role in Colts' Future," *Indianapolis Star* (26 October 1997), E1.

27. Rosentraub, *Major League Losers*, 18.

28. For the expected economic impact of the Staples Center, see Stacy Kravetz, "A New Sports Home Rises. Big Los Angeles Complex Raises Hopes for Downtown Revival," *Wall Street Journal* (23 September 1998), B12.

29. See the Web Site <http://www.nba.com> cited 1 May 1998.

30. Mark Montieth, "MSA Has No Suites, No Space, and Very Likely No Future," *Indianapolis Star* (18 August 1996), 8.

31. See Rosentraub, *Major League Losers*, 18; "Dallas Voters Approve Tax Hike for New Arena," 4A; "Dallas Voters Approve Rise in Taxes to Fund Arena," B10A.

32. Various issues of the *Charlotte Observer* from 1996 to 1998 address the negotiations on the arena. See, for example, Tony Mecia, "City to Pay Hornets for Jet to Visit Arenas," *Charlotte Observer* (29 September 1998), 4C; Tony Mecia, "Arena Committee Completes Tour, Look at Facilities," *Charlotte Observer* (19 November 1998), 1C, 5C.

33. See Stefan Fatsis, "NBA's Problems Mount," *Wall Street Journal* (24 February 1998), W9.

34. See Ames Alexander, "Some Teams Ask More, Some Less," *Charlotte Observer* (8 December 1996), 1A.

35. Ibid.

36. See Donald A. Coffin, "If You Build It, Will They Come? Attendance and New Stadium Construction," in John Fizel, et al., eds., *Baseball Economics: Current Research* (Westport, Conn.: Praeger Publishers, 1996), 33–46.

37. See Noll and Zimbalist, "Sports, Jobs, and Taxes: The Real Connection," in *Sports, Jobs, and Taxes*, 494–508.

38. See Joanna Cagan and Neil deMause, *Field of Schemes: How the Great Stadium Swindle Turns Public Money Into Private Profit* (Monroe, Maine: Common Courage Press, 1998).

39. Ibid., 185–200.

40. Dan McGraw, "Big League Troubles: Pro Sports Has a Problem. Fans Are Disgusted. What If They Stopped Watching?" *U.S. News & World Report* (13 July 1998), 40–46.

41. Ibid.

42. Ibid.

43. Ibid.

44. See Rick Burton, "Apocalypse Soon: Pro Sports Teetering on Edge of an Abyss," *Street & Smith's SportsBusiness Journal* (Charlotte, N.C.: American City Business Journals, Inc., 2–8 November 1998), 30–31.

Conclusion

We conclude this book by stating the significant findings for relocation and expansion of professional teams in baseball, football, and basketball. Our analysis underscores when, where, and why big-league teams relocated, and professional leagues expanded during the past fifty years. We also predict which teams will relocate after 1999.

Chapters One and Three revealed reasons for relocating four NL and six AL baseball teams. We found that five clubs moved in the 1950s, four in the 1960s, and one in the 1970s. Chapter Five used team performance, home attendance, and estimated market value as measures of success. These measures indicate that during the 1990s three relocated MLB teams ranked superior, three teams ranked average, and two teams ranked inferior. As a result, in the long run there is a greater probability that a relocated MLB team will rank either superior or average instead of inferior following a move. Of the three sports analyzed, baseball's team owners realized the most success in deciding to move their teams and choosing profitable sites.

After relocation the mean performance and home attendance of the relocated MLB teams tended to either remain constant or improve at the post-move sites. So not only did MLB owners relocate their teams to areas that proved demographically similar, but their teams achieved comparable performances and attendance at the post-move sites. The metropolitan areas of these sites had smaller populations and fewer professional sports teams than the areas of departure. We discovered that NL teams moved to areas where the average per capita personal income exceeded that of the AL relocated teams.

Between 1987 and 1992 the average performance and home attendance of relocated MLB teams rose, then fell from 1993 to 1996. Despite the decrease in performance and attendance, however, the estimated market value of most relocated teams increased between 1987 and 1996. Given these changes in performance, attendance, and market value from 1987 to 1996, two NL teams and one AL team ranked superior, one NL team and two AL teams ranked average, and two AL teams ranked inferior in the 1990s. In short, even though the relocated AL teams played better than the relocated NL teams on average, AL teams in Milwaukee, Minnesota, Oakland, and Texas realized lower attendance and therefore appreciated at a slower rate in market value than the NL teams.

Since 1950 the relocation of franchises in MLB has succeeded when viewed from the perspective of team owners and the leagues. The Braves, Dodgers, and Orioles should remain superior in Atlanta, Los Angeles, and Baltimore respectively beyond 2000. Throughout their tenures at these cities the team proprietors have wisely invested in players and management, in modernizing and maintaining their ballparks, and in establishing a positive relationship with their fans and with the media who report the progress of the club to the public. The San Francisco Giants and Texas Rangers should continue as average teams at their current sites over the next decade. But with additional revenues from a modern ballpark in San Francisco, and with an expanding fan base in Arlington, Texas, the Giants and Rangers should improve their chances of becoming superior teams by 2005.

The Twins will probably move from Minnesota within the next decade unless taxpayers subsidize a new ballpark that would generate greater revenues and profits for the club's owners. Clearly, the proprietors need additional revenues to acquire free agents and to bid for skilled players in the draft. Upon the opening of Miller Park and the shift from the AL to the NL, the Brewers should earn sufficient revenues to remain in Milwaukee beyond 2000.[1] But unless the NL adopts a more liberal redistribution of revenues from large- to small-market teams, the Brewers will probably remain an inferior team in the next century even though they may occasionally play better and compete for their division title. The club placed fourth in their division in 1998 behind the Astros, Cubs, and Cardinals.

In Chapters One and Three we analyzed the migration of ten professional football teams that included eight NFL teams and two AFL teams. Three of the teams moved in the 1950s, two in the 1960s, three in the 1980s, and two in the 1990s. In Chapter Five two of the relocated teams, the Indianapolis Colts and Phoenix Cardinals, scored inferior rankings from 1990 to 1997 based on their mean performance, home attendance, and 1997 estimated market value. So the moves from Baltimore to Indianapolis in 1984, and St. Louis to Phoenix in 1988, enhanced neither the Colts' nor the Cardinals' status in the NFL during the 1990s.

At the post-move sites 50 percent of the relocated football teams played better and increased their average winning percentages. Prior to relocation each team's home attendance fell below the league average for one or more seasons. Except for the Raiders in Los Angeles and Oakland and the Colts in Baltimore, the relocated teams continued to draw fewer fans to their home games than did the majority of league teams.

The NFL teams relocated to areas with smaller populations and lower per capita income levels than the areas of the pre-move sites. But the growth in population at the post-move sites in Baltimore, Dallas, and St. Louis in the

1950s, in San Diego in the 1960s, in Indianapolis, Los Angeles, and Phoenix in the 1980s, and in Oakland in the 1990s outpaced the league average. Also, the post-move areas generally hosted fewer MLB teams, and other NFL and AFL clubs, than did the pre-move areas.

Between 1987 and 1996 the mean winning percentages of the NFL relocated teams fluctuated while their home attendance and estimated market value gradually rose. Though the play of the Cardinals, Colts, Raiders, and Rams remained inconsistent in this period, the Raiders had the best performance, and the Cardinals the worst among these teams. Despite their dismal performances the estimated market values of the relocated teams increased as league attendance rose, television revenues expanded, and teams tapped innovative sources of revenue such as stadium concessions and advertising, the sale of team merchandise and clothing, retail shops, luxury suites, club seats, personal seat licenses, parking fees, and naming rights to the stadium. These rights authorize a company to advertise its name on tickets, programs, news releases, letter heads, and on distinctive signs in the stadium.[2]

For the relocated NFL teams playing in the 1990s, we ranked the Los Angeles (now St. Louis) Rams as an average team and the Indianapolis Colts, Los Angeles (now Oakland) Raiders and Arizona (formerly Phoenix) Cardinals as inferior teams. Despite changes in players and coaches, the Colts, Raiders, and Cardinals remained noncompetitive in their conferences, had low attendance at home games, and experienced marginal increases in estimated market value relative to the other relocated NFL teams. The Raiders seem the most likely franchise in the group to move after 1999 due to owner Al Davis's dispute with the city of Oakland and Alameda County and the lure of available sites in Houston, Las Vegas, Los Angeles, or Birmingham, Alabama.[3]

Taken together, the NFL teams that relocated after 1950 realized less success than their counterparts in MLB because of their weak fan base or financial and competitive instabilities. The Dallas Texans, for example, folded in 1952, the Colts left Baltimore in 1984, the Cardinals moved from Chicago to St. Louis in 1959 then to Phoenix in 1988, the Raiders abandoned Oakland for Los Angeles in 1981 and then returned to Oakland in 1995, while the Los Angeles Rams concurrently moved to St. Louis. The New England Patriots, meanwhile, will move from Foxboro, Massachusetts, to Hartford, Connecticut, in 2001.

After analyzing relocated teams in MLB and the NFL, one question looms: do any findings apply to the movement of NBA and ABA teams? Fifteen NBA teams and eleven ABA clubs moved between 1950 and 1995. Four moves occurred in the 1950s, ten in the 1960s and 1970s, and two in the 1980s. About 50 percent of the relocated NBA and ABA teams improved their winning percentages and increased their home attendance in the ten seasons following relocation. On average the areas selected by NBA and ABA owners for relocation had larger populations, residents with higher per capita incomes, and a greater percentage of African Americans than the areas the teams left. Beginning in 1959 for NBA teams, and in 1968 for ABA teams, professional basketball migrated to growing areas in California, Florida, Georgia, Texas, and Utah.

Of the big-league basketball teams that moved since 1950, fourteen clubs played in the NBA between 1986 and 1997. For these ten seasons eight of the fourteen relocated teams performed better and ten teams played before larger home crowds. The remaining relocated teams played worse and drew smaller crowds as the seasons progressed.

In the 1990s, three relocated NBA teams ranked superior, average, and inferior, given their mean winning percentages, home attendance, and estimated market value. The Detroit Pistons and Utah Jazz represented the two elite teams of the group and the Los Angeles Clippers and Philadelphia SeventySixers comprised the group's two worst teams. Based on our findings we suggest that the owners of the Clippers and Golden State Warriors move their teams to either Kansas City, Las Vegas, Memphis, Norfolk, Pittsburgh, San Diego, or St. Louis. The Lakers remain the dominant NBA team in Los Angeles and the Sacramento Kings lead the Warriors in home attendance and estimated market value in the Bay Area. By moving to another city the Clippers and Warriors would probably play more competitive ball before more enthusiastic fans. The other NBA teams that ranked inferior in the 1990s, the Hawks and SeventySixers, should stay in Atlanta and Philadelphia respectively beyond 2000 since those markets have sufficient populations and wealth to support inferior teams on a long-term basis.

In the final analysis, NBA teams that moved between 1950 and 1995 collectively achieved more success following relocation than their NFL counterparts, but experienced less success than the relocated MLB teams. By permitting owners to relocate their clubs to optimum sites in growing markets and establishing a strong fan base in those communities, MLB has been the most effective sport in maximizing the value of its franchises since 1950.

In Chapter Two we analyzed a twenty-seven-year history of expansion teams in professional baseball, football, and basketball and identified three demographic characteristics of the areas where the teams played. In Chapter Four we examined the average winning percentage, home attendance, and estimated market value of new teams added during 1977 to 1995. In Chapter Five we ranked all relocated and expansion teams as either superior, average, or inferior. Now we conclude by speculating about the future of expansion teams and the leagues.

Between 1950 and 1995 the NL and AL each added six expansion teams. Eight teams joined MLB in the 1960s, two in the 1970s, and two in the 1990s. Similar to the NFL, MLB did not expand in the 1950s and 1980s. In the 1950s five MLB teams relocated, and in the 1980s five expansion teams entered the NBA.

Generally the metropolitan areas that MLB expanded to had smaller populations, higher per capita incomes, and greater population growth than the areas of the other league teams. From the first season the average performance of baseball's expansion teams improved except for the Los Angeles (now Anaheim) Angels. In 1969 the Pilots folded in Seattle after one season, and since 1993 the Colorado Rockies and Florida Marlins have played better except in 1998. Excluding the Montreal Expos in the NL and the Washington Senators in the AL, the mean attendance of MLB expansion teams increased during their first ten seasons. Even the Rockies and Marlins have maintained above-average attendance throughout their first six years in Denver and Miami, respectively.

The average performance and home attendance of the expansion teams is reflected in their estimated market value. Between 1993 and 1996 the value of the Mets and Royals decreased, and it increased less than 4 percent for the Angels, Expos, Padres, and Blue Jays. The 1994 and 1995 player strikes, lethargic team performances, and weak fan support partially justify the deflated market value of these baseball teams in the mid-1990s.

Even so, MLB has vastly improved its financial health since the mid-1980s. In 1993, according to Roger Noll, "the total benefits of ownership accruing to baseball investors [ranged from] $200–300 million." Doubtless, some teams actually operate in the red. But no teams, regardless of market size, Noll argues, are determined "to be persistent losers in the present structure."[4]

Since 1987 the mean winning percentage and attendance of two NL expansion teams, and one AL expansion team, increased. Meanwhile, two NL and three AL expansion clubs played worse and their average attendance fell. Thus, the average performance and attendance of these teams correlated perfectly positive between 1987 and 1996.

During the 1990s three MLB expansion teams ranked superior, four ranked average, and three ranked inferior (see Table 5.2). The highest ranked expansion teams were the Colorado Rockies and Toronto Blue Jays, and the lowest ranked teams were the Kansas City Royals and San Diego Padres. Even though they play in small markets, the Royals and Padres seek to increase their franchise's economic value by winning more games and by receiving a larger share of league and television revenues. Also, if implemented a future realignment of divisions in the NL and AL should benefit the Expos, Royals, Padres, and Twins. With the entry of the Arizona Diamondbacks and Tampa Bay Devil Rays in 1998, it seems unlikely that MLB will expand until after the current national television contract expires in 2000 and after the league evaluates the relocation of unprofitable teams from small markets such as Kansas City, Montreal, Oakland, Pittsburgh, and San Diego. As Justin Catanoso has argued, "baseball should go where the money is." In other words, small-market teams confronting financial difficulties should "move to a big market." Because Milwaukee, Montreal, Pittsburgh, and San Diego in the NL, and Kansas City and Oakland in the AL, lack significant local broadcasting markets and corporate money and have below average ballpark amenities, these teams earn insufficient income to pay players higher salaries, which subsequently prohibits the team from competing successfully in MLB. New York City, for example, has over one thousand firms with five hundred or more employees and only two hundred luxury suites. That means the "Big Apple" has "one of the lowest ratios of big corporations to high-priced seating in the country." Furthermore, the Mets and Yankees have combined revenues exceeding $225 million, and local broadcast revenues of $85 million annually, which is ten times greater than what the Twins earn. And by adding four new clubs over the last six years, MLB has thus occupied "virtually every viable new market." Catanoso concludes that "baseball needs to consider drastic steps like letting a second franchise locate in Los Angeles or a third in New York."[5]

Since 1950 eight non-AFL teams joined the NFL, and in the 1960s two expansion teams entered the AFL. Six expansions occurred in the 1960s and two in the 1970s and 1990s. Relative to the league, NFL owners generally chose sites in areas with a below average population and per capita income level. With growing populations and above average economic growth, the southern cities of Atlanta, Charlotte, Dallas, Jacksonville, New Orleans, and Tampa Bay qualified for and received new NFL teams between 1950 and 1995.

During their first ten seasons, seven NFL expansion teams improved by increasing their mean winning percentage. The eighth expansion team, the Saints, won merely 25 percent of their games over the first five and ten seasons in New Orleans. Although they played better the mean attendance of the Atlanta Falcons, Seattle Seahawks, and Tampa Bay Buccaneers fell between their first and tenth season. These teams neither competed for titles nor entertained their fans the way the Carolina Panthers, Dallas Cowboys, Jacksonville Jaguars, and Minnesota Vikings did. Yet, by the mid-1990s professional football had soared in popularity across the nation, which increased the estimated market value of the former eight NFL expansion teams. Given the nation's seemingly insatiable demand for professional football, and an eight-year $17.6 billion national television contract, all NFL expansion teams will probably remain at their present sites until 2005.

As AFL expansion teams, the Cincinnati Bengals and Miami Dolphins struggled to compete and experienced low attendance at their home games. After the NFL and AFL merged in 1970 the mean attendance of the Bengals and Dolphins doubled and both teams made the AFC playoffs. Since 1970 the Dolphins have won more division and AFC titles and NFL championships than the Bengals.

Between 1987 and 1996 six of the eight NFL expansion teams played better and drew more fans to their home games. In those years the mean performance of the New Orleans Saints and Seattle Seahawks fell. Meanwhile, the play and home attendance of the Carolina Panthers and Jacksonville Jaguars placed both teams in the upper half of the league. Of the ten AFL teams that joined the NFL in 1970, four teams increased in average performance and seven in attendance between 1987 and 1996. The Bills, Chiefs, Dolphins, and Raiders dominated other conference rivals in performance. Similar to NFC expansion teams, since the late 1980s the estimated market value of the ten former AFL teams also increased due to the public's growing desire to view professional football on television and to attend games.

Table 5.3 ranks fifteen NFL expansion teams. Of these, over 25 percent ranked superior, 20 percent ranked average, and 55 percent ranked inferior. The Bills and Cowboys ranked highest, and the Bengals and Buccaneers lowest, in average team performance, attendance, and estimated market value. By 1998 the performance of the Bills and Cowboys had declined and the Buccaneers made the NFC playoffs in 1997. Earlier we suggested that no NFL expansion team should relocate between 1999 and 2005. A reason for this is that adequate revenues from their stadiums, the league, and the national television contracts will compel all league teams, excluding the New England Patriots, to remain at their current sites. In 1999 the Tennessee Titans will play in Nashville where they anticipate capacity crowds. If their play improves and market value rises while in "Music City," the Titans should become an average team by 2005.

A larger proportion of NFL expansion teams ranked inferior and a smaller proportion of them ranked superior and average than those in MLB. Sixty percent of the former AFL teams, and 40 percent of the NFC expansion teams ranked inferior in the league for the 1990s. The lowest ranked teams included the New York Jets and Cincinnati Bengals for average performance; the New England Patriots and Tennessee Oilers for average attendance; and the Seattle Seahawks and New York Jets for 1997 estimated market value. Since these teams play in the AFC, it indicates the inequality of the two conferences. Following the merger in 1970, if the league had placed several former AFL teams in the NFC, the two conferences would have had better parity in the 1990s. Moreover, a realignment of conference teams after 1998 whereby inferior teams such as the Titans, Chargers, and Seahawks play in the NFC would decrease the inequities between superior, average, and inferior NFL teams.

Regarding the NBA, sixteen expansion teams joined the league in the 1960s, eight in the 1970s, five in the 1980s, and two in the 1990s. Tables 2.9–2.10, 4.8, and 5.5 show the areas' demographics, list team performances, and indicate the estimated market values of the expansion teams in the NBA. According to the tables, the areas of the expansion teams' post-move sites fell below the league average in population and per capita income, but above average in population growth.

During their first ten seasons the majority of the former NBA expansion teams played better before larger home crowds. Apparently as the seasons progressed, the demand to attend games increased for these expansion teams. Between 1987 and 1996 the average winning percentage of expansion teams such as the Dallas Mavericks, Denver Nuggets, Milwaukee Bucks, and Portland Trail Blazers declined, and the home attendance of the Mavericks fell, too. As experienced by the expansion teams in the NFL since the late 1980s, the nation's demand for professional basketball has boomed and the attendance of most NBA expansion teams has also risen. Along with demand and attendance, the estimated market value of the NBA expansion teams, excluding the Mavericks, has increased, especially in the mid-1990s.

The metropolitan areas of eight ABA expansion teams appeared similar in population, per capita income, and population growth to the areas of the NBA expansion teams (see Table 2.11). Without sufficient revenues from attendance and television, however, nearly two-thirds of the initial ABA expansion teams either relocated or terminated operations between 1968 and 1976. The Denver Nuggets, Indiana Pacers, and New Jersey Nets won more than 50 percent of their games, kept their attendance above the league average, and along with the San Antonio Spurs earned the opportunity to join the NBA in 1976 (see Table 2.12).

Fifteen expansion teams played in the NBA in the 1990s. Table 5.5 ranked and evaluated these teams. From these data three significant results arise. First, compared to the three superior, average, and inferior relocated NBA teams, only two expansion teams ranked superior, seven ranked average, and six ranked inferior. Second, a smaller proportion of expansion teams in the NBA ranked superior, and a larger proportion ranked average and inferior relative to those in MLB. Third, a greater proportion of expansion teams in the NBA ranked average, and a smaller proportion ranked inferior relative to those in the NFL. In contrast, the expansion teams in MLB achieved greater success in average performance, attendance, and market value in the 1990s than the expansion teams in the other sports.

We suggest that the future growth and success of these sports leagues depend on team rivalries, the competitiveness of the teams, and the entertainment value of the sports to the public. The sport that offers the opportunity for average and inferior teams in small- and medium-markets to improve performance, that attracts fans from their local and regional areas, and that broadcasts into international markets, will dominate the sports industry in the early twenty-first century.[6]

We also concur with sports researchers Dennis Zimmerman and William A. Cox that leagues should ease restrictions on the relocation of franchises. While they concede that fans and public officials in cities loosing a team would mourn the loss, their counterparts in the newly enfranchised cities "would be jubilant." Although fan satisfaction remains difficult to quantify, Zimmerman and Cox contend that it may increase after the move. Accordingly, owners move their teams to sites with better prospects for earning profits. Thus, the owner anticipates more fans supporting the team at the new location.[7]

Besides relaxing constraints on franchise relocation, MLB should also ease the restrictions on the number of teams and situating new ones in the most lucrative markets that have large populations and "valuable local radio and television rights." As Zimmerman and Cox put it: "Increasing the supply of franchises in large-revenue markets could make the large-revenue clubs economically similar to small-revenue clubs. If competitive balance is sensitive to equality of financial resources, this would be an effective policy."[8]

NOTES

1. In 1998, ticket sales rose 25 percent for the Brewers and the team's travel expenses diminished and television ratings increased due to realignment. See Frederick Klein, "For the Brewers of Milwaukee, a Brave Change," *Wall Street Journal* (13 March 1998), B10; "What Will Switch Do to Brewers?" at <http://www.austin360.com> cited 11 November 1997; Bob Wolf, "N.L. Brewers Can Go Home Again," at the Web site <http://www.sportingnews.com> cited 18 March 1998.

2. Since 1988 forty-two naming rights agreements totaling $1 billion have been signed and another $2 billion in deals are likely by 2002. Professional sports teams in Atlanta, Charlotte, Los Angeles, Nashville, and Raleigh have recently signed agreements or are seeking sponsors through naming rights for their stadiums or arenas. See Stefan Fatsis, "Staples to Attach Its Name to Arena in Los Angeles," *Wall Street Journal* (2 December 1997), B6; H. Bodley, "Selling of Stadium Names Reveals Sorry State," at the Web site <http://www.usatoday.com> cited 24 March 1998; "Ilitch Might Have to Sell Ballpark Name," at <http://www.cnnsi.com> cited 10 March 1998; "Tampa Bay's New Stadium Get a Name," at the Web site <http://www.cnnsi.com> cited 7 July 1998.

3. To appreciate what cities will do to lure a professional sports team, see Jeffrey Ball, "Hail Mary? Birmingham Dreams of a New Stadium," *Wall Street Journal* (14 January 1998), S1.

4. See Roger Noll, "Baseball Economics in the 1990s—A Report to Major League Baseball Players Association," unpublished, pages 22–23. This article and other readings on sports were reprinted in "The Business of Sports—A Case Study: The Economics of Baseball" (*Newsweek,* 1995), 1–32.

5. Justin Catanoso, "Baseball Should Go Where the Money Is," *Business Week* (29 June 1998), 131.

6. In July 1998, TV Azteca and the NBA agreed to air sixty games in 1999 and 2000 to fans across Mexico. Also, a thirty-minute basketball magazine program and a series of grassroots initiatives aimed at increasing basketball participation in Mexico will be available for youth in Mexico. NBA games are broadcast in 196 countries and the players and teams have become more popular throughout the world. See "TV Azteca and the NBA Extend Broadcast Partnership," at <http://www.nba.com> cited 29 August 1998.

7. See Dennis Zimmerman and William A. Cox, "The Baseball Strike and Federal Policy: An Economic Analysis," *Congressional Research Service,* The Library of Congress (13 January 1995), 18–21.

8. Ibid.

Selected Bibliography

PUBLISHED GOVERNMENT DOCUMENTS

U.S. Congress. House Judiciary Committee, *Organized Baseball, Hearings Before Subcommittee on Study of Monopoly Power*, 82nd Cong., 1st sess., 1951, ser. 1, pt. 6 (Washington D.C., 1952), 1616–1619.

————. House Judiciary Committee, *Organized Professional Team Sports, Hearings Before the Antitrust Subcommittee of the House Committee on the Judiciary,* 95th Cong., 1st sess. (Washington D.C., 1958), 353–354.

U.S. Department of Commerce. Bureau of Economic Analysis. *Survey of Current Business.* Washington, D.C., 1950–1997.

————. Bureau of the Census. *Census of Population.* Social and Economic Characteristics. Metropolitan Areas. Washington, D.C., 1950–1990.

————. Bureau of the Census. *Statistical Abstracts of the United States.* Washington, D.C., 1950–1997.

————. Economics and Statistics Administration. *County and City Data Book.* Washington, D.C., Government Printing Office, 1950–1997.

ARTICLES

Ahmed-Taylor, Ty. "Who Is Major Enough for the Major Leagues?" *New York Times* (2 April 1995): 5.

Alexander Ames. "Poll: Few Back Ballpark Taxes." *Charlotte Observer* (7 May 1998): 1A.

————. "Public Opposes Using Tax Money for Arenas." *Charlotte Observer* (25 January 1997): 1A.

————. "Some Teams Ask More, Some Less." *Charlotte Observer* (8 December 1996): 1A.

Alperstein, Ellen. "WNBA's Rookie Season Is the Start of Something Big." *Charlotte Observer* (31 August 1997): 1G.

"Anaheim." *Charlotte Observer* (9 October 1998): 4B.

Antonen, Mel. "Baseball Fans Pick Up Tab." *USA Today* (22 January 1998): 3C.

Associated Press. "Cleveland Indians Plan Stock Offerings, First in Big Leagues." *Charlotte Observer* (28 March 1998): 6C.

———. "NFL Picks Browns Owner." *Daytona Beach News Journal* (9 September 1998): 3B.

Atre, Tushar, Kristine Auns, Kurt Badenhausen, Kevin McAuliffe, Christopher Nikolov, and Michael K. Ozanian. "Sports, Stocks, and Bonds." *Financial World* (20 May 1996): 53–64.

Attner, Paul. "How Professional Sports Governs Expansion Will Mean Success or Failure for 21st Century." *The Sporting News* (18 March 1991): 13–19.

Bai, Matt. "A League of Their Own." *Newsweek* (11 May 1998): 68.

Baker, Stephen. "Baseball's Losers Still Lose." *Business Week* (16 December 1996): 42.

Ball, Jeffrey. "Hail Mary? Birmingham Dreams of a New Stadium." *Wall Street Journal* (14 January 1998): S1.

Barra, Allen, and Allen St. John. "Debunking Baseball's Stadium Myth." *Wall Street Journal* (18 July 1997): B9.

Battenfeld, Joe, and Carolyn Ryan. "Sox Won't Get a Break." *Boston Herald* (25 November 1997): 1.

Becker, Gary. "A Flatter Tax Just Might Keep Fickle Teams at Home." *Business Week* (12 February 1996): 24.

"Benefits of Triad Team May Not Be as Billed." *Charlotte Observer* (1 May 1998): 4B.

Berman, Dennis. "A Home Team of Your Very Own." *Business Week* (22 September 1997): 120.

Bianco, Anthony. "David Stern: This Time, It's Personal." *Business Week* (13 July 1998): 114–118.

———. "The Money Machine. Why George Steinbrenner May Be Tempted to Sell the New York Yankees." *Wall Street Journal* (23 September 1998): 102–108.

Bliss, Marjo Rankin. "ABL Requests Contract Cutbacks." *Charlotte Observer* (16 August 1998): 2H.

———. "Final Four a Fertile Recruiting Ground for the Sting." *Charlotte Observer* (22 March 1998): 2H.

———. "Ice Rewards." *Charlotte Observer* (1 March 1998): 2H.

Bloom, Barry M. "Padres May Bid San Diego So Long." *Charlotte Observer* (1 July 1998): 4B.

Blount, Ericka. "Help Wanted: Need Big Name, Hoop Dream, Experience Optional." *Wall Street Journal* (10 December 1997): B1.

Bluthhardt, Robert F. "Fenway Park and the Golden Age of the Baseball Park." *Journal of Popular Culture* 21 (Summer 1987): 4L.

Bonnell, Richard. "Charlotte Not Elite, But Not Bad." *Charlotte Observer* (5 July 1998): 2H.

———. "Divac's Agent Doesn't Believe Lockout Talks." *Charlotte Observer* (16 November 1997): 5H.

Brenton Welling, Jonathon Tasini, and Don Cook. "Basketball: Business Is Booming." *Business Week* (4 March 1985): 75–76.

Bulpett, Steve. "And Then There Was One." *Boston Herald* (23 December 1998): 88.

Burck, Charles G. "It's Promoters vs. Taxpayers in the Superstadium Game." *Fortune* 87 (March 1973): 106, 180, 182.

Burton, Rick. "Apocalypse Soon: Pro Sports Teetering on Edge of an Abyss." *Street & Smith's SportsBusiness Journal* (2–8 November 1998): 30–31.

"The Business of Sports—A Case Study: The Economics of Baseball." *Newsweek* (New York 1995): 1–32.

Caple, Jim. "Pohlad Joins Bottom Feeders in Extortion Pool." *Charlotte Observer* (21 September 1997): 2C.

Casstevens, David. "Astrodome Outlives Status as a Wonder." *Charlotte Observer* (5 July 1998): 7H.

Catanoso, Justin. "Baseball Should Go Where the Money Is." *Business Week* (29 June 1998): 131.

———. "Loading the Bases in North Carolina?" *Business Week* (7 April 1997): 98–99.

Cayley, Leslie. "To Pay the NFL, ESPN Plans a Blitz of Football Shows." *Wall Street Journal* (17 August 1998): B1.

Chandler, Charles. "Jags' Front Office Stable; Panthers' in Transition." *Charlotte Observer* (8 August 1998): 1B, 5B.

———. "TV Bonanza Means Panthers Won't Hike Ticket Prices." *Charlotte Observer* (14 January 1998): 3B.

———. "Who's Panthers Boss? It's Capers." *Charlotte Observer* (16 January 1998): 1B.

Chass, Murray. "Let's Play Two: Expansion and Creation." *New York Times* (30 October 1994): B23.

———. "Mexico Is Now in Picture for Possible Expansion." *New York Times* (10 June 1994): B17.

Cline, Andrew. "Striking Out. How Pro Sports Beans the Taxpayers." *Carolina Journal* (April/May 1997): 25.

"Coca-Cola, NBA Sign 100-year Deal." *Bloomberg News* (9 June 1998): E8.

Coffin, Donald A. "If You Build It, Will They Come? Attendance and New Stadium Construction." In John Fizel, Elizabeth Gustafson, and Lawrence Hadley, eds., *Baseball Economics: Current Research*. Westport, Conn.: Praeger Publishers, 1996, 33–46.

Comte, Elizabeth. "Sports Expansion Box Score." *The Sporting News* (12 March 1990): 12.

Corliss, Richard. "Build It, and They Might Come." *Time* (24 August 1992): 50–54.

Crasnick, Jerry. "How to Build a Baseball Franchise." *The Sporting News* (30 June 1997): 27.

Crothers, Tim. "The Shakedown." *Sports Illustrated* (19 June 1995): 78–82.

Cyphers, Luke. "New Parks Show Path." *Charlotte Observer* (21 April 1998): 4B.

"Dallas Voters Approve Rise in Taxes to Fund Arena." *Wall Street Journal* (19 January 1998): B10A.

"Dallas Voters Approve Tax Hike for New Arena." *Charlotte Observer* (18 January 1998): 4A.

"Deal for Dodgers Is Agreed Upon at $350 Million." *Charlotte Observer* (5 September 1997): 4B.

DeGeorge, Gail. "Costs Are Out of the Ballpark." *Business Week* (14 July 1997): 32.

DeSantis, Solange, "Blue Jays Pitch Poems to Draw Women, Kids." *Wall Street Journal* (9 April 1998): B1.

"Domed Stadium: Spur to City's Economy." *U.S. News & World Report* (11 October 1965): 10.

Draper, Robert. "Spoils Sports: Houston Professional Sports Teams Threaten to Relocate." *Texas Monthly* (January 1996): 10–116.

Dubow, Joseph. "It's a Wonderful World for NFL's TV." *Charlotte Observer* (14 January 1998): 1B, 3B.

Dwyer, Paula. "Would Trust Busting Be Good For Baseball?" *Business Week* (2 June 1997): 40.

Editorial. *Charlotte Observer* (9 August 1997): 1A, 14A.

Edmond, Alfred, Jr. "So You Want to Buy a Team?" *Black Enterprise* (September 1988): 79–88.

Farrey, Tom. "Too Much of a Good Thing?" *Business Week* (11 May 1998): 70.

Fatsis, Stefan. "At Last! Here's a Way to Measure Just How Pathetic Your Team Is." *Wall Street Journal* (6 March 1998): B1.

———. "Baseball Tickets Are Outta Here." *Wall Street Journal* (3 April 1998): W6.

———. "The 'Coolest Game on Earth' Tries to Match the NHL Hype." *Wall Street Journal* (25 April 1997): B9.

———. "For Pro Football, Giant TV Pacts May Carry a Price." *Wall Street Journal* (15 January 1998): B1, B6.

———. "Los Angeles Dodgers Put Up for Sale, Marking the End of Family Ownership." *Wall Street Journal* (7 January 1997): B8.

———. "Money-Losing Angels Seem Immune to Disney Magic." *Wall Street Journal* (22 September 1997): B1.

———. "NBA Bravely Plans for Post-Jordan Era." *Wall Street Journal* (6 February 1998): B1.

———. "NBA's Problems Mount." *Wall Street Journal* (24 February 1998): W9.

———. "NBA to Join Hard Rock Café in Packed Arena." *Wall Street Journal* (2 February 1998): B1.

———. "New Double Play: Win World Series, Then Sell the Team." *Wall Street Journal* (7 November 1997): B16.

———. "NFL Players May Help Get Fatter TV Deal." *Wall Street Journal* (2 January 1998): 3.

———. "Staples to Attach Its Name to Arena in Los Angeles." *Wall Street Journal* (2 December 1997): B6.

Fitzsimmons, Kara. "Stadium Bonds Are Finding Tough Going These Days." *Wall Street Journal* (22 August 1996): W5.

Forsyth, Randall W. "Ground Out." *Barrons* (13 November 1995): 63.

Fort, Rodney D., and Roger Noll. "Pay and Performance in Baseball: Modeling Regulars, Reserves, and Expansion." *Division of Humanities and Social Science Working Paper 527*, California Institute of Technology, 1984.

Fowler, Scott. "List Puts Panthers Among Most Valuable Pro Teams." *Charlotte Observer* (25 May 1997): 1A, 18A.

Fowler, Scott, and Ron Green, Jr. "Next 2 Days Bad Time for 18 Players." *Charlotte Observer* (23 August 1998): 9H.

The Franchise of Americans Needing Sports. Detroit, Michigan: Vol. 1, Part 2. *Encyclopedia of Associations*, National Organizations of U.S., 1996.

Freeman, Mike. "Bruins Owner Gives Browns 7th Pursuer." *Charlotte Observer* (16 August 1998): 13H.

Galuszka, Peter. "Battle for the Browns." *Business Week* (20 July 1998): 42.

Gattuso, James. "Congress and Rule-Making." *Society* (May/June 1986): 6–10.

Geewax, Marilyn. "What's the True Worth of Arenas." *Charlotte Observer* (22 October 1997): 21A.

Gerlach, Larry. "Not Quite Ready for Prime Time: Baseball History, 1983–1993." *Journal of Sport History* 21 (Summer 1994), 103–137.

Gibson, Richard. "Buy Me Some Couscous and Caberet." *Wall Street Journal* (30 April 1998): B1.

Gietschier, Steve. "What Glitters Isn't Golden." *The Sporting News* (4 November 1996): 47.

Glick, J. "Professional Sports Franchise Movements and the Sherman Act: When and Where Teams Should Be Able to Move." *Santa Clara Law Review* 23 (Winter 1983): 55–94.

Glickman, Clifford. "More City Leaders May Be Going to Bat for Uptown Baseball." *Charlotte Observer* (30 March 1998): 3D.

Gorham, John, Peter Kafka, and Shailaja Neelakanten. "The *Forbes* 400." *Forbes* (12 October 1998): 165–428.

Grady, Sandy. "Packers Owners Take Greed Out of Sports." *USA Today* (22 January 1998): 13A.

Green, Ron. "Charlotte Should Tell Twins Owner to Take a Hike." *Charlotte Observer* (21 July 1998): 1B.

"Group Starts Drive to Pass Triad Ballpark Tax Plan." *Charlotte Observer* (16 February 1998): 3C.

Grover, Ronald. "Pitching 100 MPH in Phoenix." *Business Week* (26 March 1998): 62.

———. "Pro Football in L.A.? Don't Bet the Bentley." *Business Week* (26 October 1998): 72.

Grover, Ronald, Amy Barrett, Richard A. Melcher, and Nicole Harris. "Playing for Keeps." *Business Week* (22 September 1997): 32–33.

Hamilton, Bruce W., and Peter Kahn. "Baltimore's Camden Yards Ballparks." In Roger G. Noll and Andrew Zimbalist, eds., *Sports, Jobs, And Taxes: The Economic Impact of Sports Teams and Stadiums.* Washington, D.C.: Brookings Institution Press, 1997, 245–281.

Hardy, Stephen H. "Entrepreneurs, Organizations, and the Sports Marketplace." *Journal of Sport History 13* (1986): 14–33.

Heath, Thomas. "Pollin: Player Salaries Cause Increases in Ticket Prices." *Washington Post* (27 November 1997): B7.

Helyar, John.. "Cities Face Off to Join the NHL's Game." *Wall Street Journal* (17 January 1997): B9.

———. "Free Agency Proves to be the Cat's Meow for Jags and Panthers." *Wall Street Journal* (10 January 1997): A1, A5.

———. "Luxury Stadiums Draw Fans, Players Too." *Wall Street Journal* (30 August 1996): B5.

———. "More NFL Fans Stay at Home." *Wall Street Journal* (4 October 1996): B4.

———. "An Unpalatial Arena Designated to Please Just Plain Folks." *Wall Street Journal* (10 October 1997): B1

Henderson, Cary S. "Los Angeles and the Dodger War, 1957–1962." *Southern California Quarterly* 62 (Fall 1980): 263.

"He's Back on the Job After Heart Surgery." *Charlotte Observer* (1 December 1997): 2D.

Hille, Bob. "Tops by a Mile." *The Sporting News* (30 June 1997): 23.

———. "TSN's Best Sports Cities." *The Sporting News* (30 June 1997): 14–23.

Ho, Rodney. "Entrepreneurs Aim to Elbow NCAA With New Leagues." *Wall Street Journal* (18 August 1998): B1.

Horgan, Sean. "Corporate Community Has Central Role in Colts' Future." *Indianapolis Star* (26 October 1997): E1–E2.

Horowitz, Ira. "Sports Broadcasting." In Roger G. Noll ed., *Government and the Sports Business.* Washington, D.C.: The Brookings Institution, 1974, 275–323.

"Houses With Holes." *Sports Illustrated* (4 March 1968): 9.

Hyman, Mark. "From Tears to Cheers in Cleveland." *Business Week* (16 November 1998): 108–116.

———. "How to Lose Fans and Get Richer." *Business Week* (26 January 1998): 70.

———. "A League of Their Own." *Business Week* (15 June 1998): 66.

———. "I Led Three Lives." *Business Week* (23 February 1998): 110.

———. "Sports: Prognosis 1998." *Business Week* (12 January 1998): 124.

Hyman, Mark, and Jay Weiner. "The NBA: Why Push May Come to Shove." *Business Week* (25 May 1998): 77.

Insider. *Charlotte Observer* (1 December 1997): 2D.

Jereski, Laura. "Take Me Out to the Ball Game." *Wall Street Journal* (17 December 1997): B12.

Johnson, Arthur T. "Balancing Interests." *Society*. (May/June 1986): 11–16.

———. "Municipal Administration and the Sports Franchise Relocation Issue." *Public Administration Review* 43 (November/December 1983): 519–528.

———. "The Sports Franchise Relocation Issue and Public Policy Responses." In Arthur T. Johnson and James H. Frey, eds., *Government and Sport: The Public Policy Issues*. Totowa, N.J.: Rowman and Allanheld, 1985.

Johnston, Kathleen. "Pacers Lease Contains Financial Guarantees." *Indianapolis Star* (5 November 1997): 16.

Klass, Tim. "Seahawks: New Owner, New Stadium, $10 Tickets." *Charlotte Observer* (1 July 1997): 2B.

Klein, Frederick. "Arizona Manager to Hear (Finally) Cry of 'Play Ball!'," *Wall Street Journal* (6 March 1998): B8.

———. "Baseball Makes a Move, Sort of, to Realignment." *Wall Street Journal* (17 October 1997): B13.

———. "The Big Guys' Burden." *Wall Street Journal* (14 August 1998): W5.

———. "For the Brewers of Milwaukee, a Brave Change." *Wall Street Journal* (13 March 1998): B10.

———. "Hey Padres: If You Win, They Will Build It." *Wall Street Journal* (19 May 1998): A20.

———. "Show Them the Money." *Wall Street Journal* (10 March 1998): A20.

———. "Stadium Deals Rarely Add Up to a Good Thing." *Wall Street Journal* (19 December 1997): B15.

———. "Why L.A. Doesn't Need the NFL." *Wall Street Journal* (4 September 1998): W4.

———. "A Women's League Comes Into Its Own." *Wall Street Journal* (15 December 1998): A20.

Koretz, Gene. "How Much Is a Coach Worth." *Business Week* (27 October 1997): 34.

Kraker, Daniel, and David Morris. "Let Public Own Pro Teams." *Charlotte Observer* (4 December 1997): 22A.

Kravetz, Stacy. "A New Sports Home: Big Los Angeles Complex Raises Hopes for Downtown Revival." *Wall Street Journal* (23 September 1998): B12.

Laye, Leonard. "Stern: Arena Upgrades are Common." *Charlotte Observer* (26 June 1997): 4B.

———. "Youth Movement." *Charlotte Observer* (25 June 1998): 1B.

Lazaroff, D. "The Antitrust Implications of Franchise Relocation Restrictions in Professional Sports." *Fordham Law Review* 53 (November 1984): 157–220.

Leland, John. "Up in the Air." *Newsweek* (1 September 1997): 56–62.

Leonhardt, David. "A Marketing Slugger Steps Up to the Plate." *Business Week* (4 November 1997): 84.

———. "Are Pro Sports Conning Our Cities?" *Business Week* (3 March 1997): 13.

Lesko, Ron. "Twins Sign New Lease; Will Stay Another 2 Years." *Charlotte Observer* (15 August 1998): 4B.

Levinson, Marc. "Fields of Schemes." *Newsweek* (11 December 1995): 60.

Lippman, John. "Murdoch Tries to Turn a Triple Play by Adding Lakers, Kings to His Dodgers." *Wall Street Journal* (20 April 1998): B9.

Lipsitz, George. "Sports Stadia and Urban Development: A Take of Three Cities." *Journal of Sport and Social Issues 8* (Summer/Fall 1984): 10–13.

Litke, Jim. "Baseball Bigger, but Better." *Charlotte Observer* (2 April 1998): 5B.

Lowenfish, Lee. "A Tale of Many Cities: The Westward Expansion of Major League Baseball in the 1950s." *Journal of the West* 17 (July 1978): 74–75.

Mahtesian, Charles. "If You Can't Bribe the Owner, Maybe You Can Buy the Team." *Governing* (March 1996): 42–45.

"Marlins Plan More Salary Slashing." *Charlotte Observer* (7 May 1998): 4B.

McCarthy, Mike. "Fair or Foul." *Wall Street Journal* (12 June 1998): W7.

McCormick, John. "Playing Stadium Games. The Urge to Be a Big-League Town Has Turned Civic Pride Into a Costly—and Vain—Obsession." *Newsweek* (30 June 1997): 55.

McGraw, Dan. "Big League Troubles: Pro Sports Has a Problem. Fans Are Disgusted. What If They Stopped Watching?" *U.S. News & World Report* (13 July 1998): 40–46.

"McGwire's a Top Draw, But So Are Beanie Babies." *Charlotte Observer* (23 August 1998): 2H.

McMillan, Jean. "Patriots' Departure Disappointing to Fans." *Charlotte Observer* (20 November 1998): 10B.

Mecia, Tony. "Arena Committee Completes Tour, Look at Facilities." *Charlotte Observer* (19 November 1998): 1C, 5C.

———. "City to Pay Hornets for Jet to Visit Arenas." *Charlotte Observer* (29 September 1998): 4C

Meggyesy, David. "The National Football League Monopoly." *Society* (May/June 1986): 16–21.

Mehrtens, Cliff. "ABL Refugees Look to WNBA." *Charlotte Observer* (23 December 1998): 1B, 8B.

———. "State of the WNBA." *Charlotte Observer* (10 July 1998): 1B, 3B.

———. "WNBA May Expand Next Year." *Charlotte Observer* (24 August 1997): 3H.

Minker, Melissa. "Expansion." *SportsTravel* (January 1997): 30–34.

Mollenkamp, Carrick, and Jeffrey Ball. "Midsize Cities Scramble to Woo Stadium Sponsors." *Wall Street Journal* (13 May 1998): S1.

Montieth, Mark. "MSA Has No Suites, No Space, and Very Likely No Future." *Indianapolis Star* (18 August 1996): 8.

"Montreal Knows How to Spend." *USA Today* (9 June 1998): 5C.

Moore, Pamela, and Foon Rhee. "Leaders Weigh Twins Strategy." *Charlotte Observer* (19 November 1997): 1A.

Mormino, Gary Ross. "The Playing Fields of St. Louis: Italian Immigrants and Sport." *Journal of Sport History* (Summer 1982): 5–16.

Neale, Walter. "The Peculiar Economics of Professional Sports." *Quarterly Journal of Economics* 78 (February 1964): 1–14.

Newberry, Paul. "Braves Coverage Diversifies." *Charlotte Observer* (22 March 1998): 14H.

Noll, Roger G. "Attendance and Price Setting." In Roger G. Noll, ed., *Government and the Sports Business*. Washington, D.C.: The Brookings Institution, 1974, 115–157.

———. "Baseball Economics in the 1990s—A Report to Major League Baseball Association." In "The Business of Sports—A Case Study: The Economics of Baseball." *Newsweek*, 1995, 1–32.

————. "Professional Basketball: Economics and Business Perspectives." In *The Business of Professional Sports*. Champaign: University of Illinois Press, 1991, 18–47.

————. "The U.S. Team Sports Industry: An Introduction." In Roger G. Noll, ed., *Government and the Sports Business*. Washington, D.C.: The Brookings Institution, 1974, 1–32.

Noll, Roger G., and Andrew Zimbalist. "Build the Stadium—Create the Jobs!" In Roger G. Noll and Andrew Zimbalist, eds., *Sports, Jobs, and Taxes: The Economic Impact of Sports Teams and Stadiums*. Washington, D.C.: The Brookings Institution, 1997, 1–54.

"Norris Poulson Reveals How Los Angeles Got the Brooklyn Dodgers in 1958." In Steven A. Riess, ed., *Major Problems in American Sport History*. Boston and New York: Houghton Mifflin Company, 1997, 408–411.

Observer News Services. "A's on Move." *Charlotte Observer* (24 October 1998): 2B.

————. "Expos Put Deadline on Mid-Summer Dream of New Stadium." *Charlotte Observer* (17 May 1998): 6H.

————. "Indians Seek Chance to Sell Public Shares." *Charlotte Observer* (4 April 1998): 6B.

————. "McCombs Buys Vikings." *Charlotte Observer* (3 July 1998): 5B.

————. "NBC, Turner Say They'll Form League." *Charlotte Observer* (28 May 1998): 8B.

————. "Purdue Coach Steps Down." *Charlotte Observer* (20 March 1998): 10B.

————. "Schott Will Sell to Avoid an Extended Suspension." *Charlotte Observer* (24 October 1998): 2B.

————. "Silas Among Sacramento Candidates." *Charlotte Observer* (22 August 1998): 9B.

————. "Smith, Washington Settle Up." *Charlotte Observer* (27 February 1998): 5B.

————. "USC Tailback Suspended for Opener." *Charlotte Observer* (4 September 1998): 5B.

Okner, Benjamin A. "Subsidies of Stadiums and Arenas." In Roger G. Noll, ed., *Government and the Sports Business*. Washington, D.C.: The Brookings Institution, 1974, 325–348.

————. "Taxation and Sports Enterprises." In Roger G. Noll, ed., *Government and the Sports Business*. Washington, D.C.: The Brookings Institution, 1974, 159–184.

Olson, Rochelle. "Pohlad Pleads for Help to Keep Twins." *Charlotte Observer* (5 October 1997): 4C.

Olson, Stan. "Baseball Has Future in Charlotte." *Charlotte Observer* (29 October 1997): B1.

Orwall, Bruce. "He's Ba-ack! Ovitz Returns as a Mall Developer." *Wall Street Journal* (27 March 1998): B1.

"O's Owner Suggests Scrapping Some Teams." *Charlotte Observer* (25 April 1998): 4B.

Ozanian, Michael K. "Fields of Debt." *Forbes* (15 December 1997): 174–175.

————. "Selective Accounting." *Forbes* (14 December 1998): 124–134.

Ozanian, Michael K., and Brooke Grabarek. "Foul!" *Financial World* (1 September 1994): 18–21.

————. "The Untouchables." *Financial World* (9 May 1995): 42–45.

Ozanian, Michael K., Tushar Atre, Ronald Fink, Jennifer Reingold, John Kinelman, Andre Osterland, and Jeff Skar. "Suite Deals." *Financial World* (9 May 1995): 42–56.

Pedulla, Tom. "Tagliabue: TV Deals a Start." *USA Today* (26 January 1998): 14C.

Pluto, Terry. "Out of Their League." *The Sporting News* (8 January 1996): 22–27.

Pope, Kyle. "Networks' Big Play for NFL May End in Fumble." *Wall Street Journal* (5 February 1998): B10.

Pope, Kyle, and Eben Shapiro. "NBC and Turner Discuss the Possibility of a New Professional Football League." *Wall Street Journal* (30 January 1998): B8.

Pope, Kyle, and Stefan Fatsis. "TV Networks Rush to Splurge on NFL Deals." *Wall Street Journal* (15 December 1997): B1.

Quirk, James. "An Economic Analysis of Team Movements in Professional Sports." *Law and Contemporary Problems* 38 (Winter/Spring 1973): 42–66.

Quirk, James, and Mohamed El Hodiri. "An Economic Model of a Professional Sports League." *Journal of Political Economy* 79 (March/April 1975): 1302–1319.

————. "The Economic Theory of a Professional Sports League." In Roger G. Noll, ed., *Government and the Sports Business*. Washington, D.C.: The Brookings Institution, 1974, 33–80.

Reed, Ted. "A Pro League of Their Own." *Charlotte Observer* (26 May 1997): 8D.

Rhee, Foon. "Ballpark Figures: PSLs Won't Do It." *Charlotte Observer* (19 May 1998): 1A.

————. "Baseball Study Can't Answer All Questions." *Charlotte Observer* (20 May 1998): 1C.

————. "Disputed Tax Builds Taj Mahal." *Charlotte Observer* (15 January 1998): 1A, 18A.

————. "Expos in Charlotte? Team Not on Market Yet." *Charlotte Observer* (17 September 1998): 2B.

————. "In Bottom of the 9th, Twins Get 'Final' Offer." *Charlotte Observer* (17 July 1998): 1C, 4C.

————. "Triad's Big No Puts Areas Group Into the Game." *Charlotte Observer* (7 May 1998): 1A.

————. "Twins Sale on Agenda as Owners Talk Shop." *Charlotte Observer* (11 January 1998): 1A, 18A.

————. "Twins Still on the Fence Over Moving." *Charlotte Observer* (21 July 1998): 1C.

————. "Will Twins Stay, Play in Charlotte?" *Charlotte Observer* (14 November 1997): 12A.

Rice, David. "A Wild Pitch?" *Winston Salem Journal* (14 December 1997): A1.

Rosenberg, Morton. "Proposed Sports Relocation Legislation: Background and Legal Implications." Washington, D.C.: American Law Division. Congressional Research Service. The Library of Congress, 1985.

Ross, Stephen F. "Break Up the Sports Leagues Monopolies." In Paul D. Staudohar and James A. Mangan, eds., *The Business of Professional Sports*. Champaign: University of Illinois Press, 1991, 152–173.

Rozin, Skip. "Growing Pains: the Evolution of Expansion." *Sport* (December 1994): 10.

San Antonio Express News (17 June 1997): 9C.

San Antonio Express News (9 June 1998): 7C.

Sawicki, Stephen. "Spoiled Sports: When Big Cities Steal Each Other's Teams, Everybody Loses." *People Weekly* (22 January 1996): 93–96.

Schacter, Erica. "WNBA Season: Hoops but No Skirts." *Wall Street Journal* (27 August 1997): A10.

Scoville, James G. "Labor Relations in Sports." In Roger G. Noll, ed., *Government and the Sports Business*. Washington, D.C.: The Brookings Institution, 1974, 185–200.

"Selig Presents Wrong Face for Game's Future." *Charlotte Observer* (2 June 1998): 4H.

"Setback for Expos." *Charlotte Observer* (18 September 1998): 4B.

Shea, John. "Selig's Daughter to Keep Brewers on Same Course." *Charlotte Observer* (14 July 1998): 4B.

Sheridan, Chris. "Raptors Trade Stoudamire in 6-Player Deal; Coach Quits." *Charlotte Observer* (14 February 1998): 2B.

———. "WNBA Goes to Detroit, Washington." *Charlotte Observer* (1 October 1997): 2B.

Shorthops. "Baseball Hot on Mexico." *Charlotte Observer* (17 July 1998): 4B.

———. "Marlins Plan More Salary Slashing." *Charlotte Observer* (7 May 1998): 4B.

Soshnick, Scott. "New League to Begin in 1999." *Charlotte Observer* (12 August 1998): 2B.

Spiers, Joseph. "Are Pro Sports Teams Worth It?" *Fortune* (15 January 1996): 29–31.

Sports Today. "LaSorda: Dodgers Sale to Murdoch Good." *Charlotte Observer* (20 March 1998): 2B.

"The Stadium Game." *Economist* (4 May 1996): 26.

Steinbreder, John. "The Owners." *Sports Illustrated* (13 September 1993): 64–87.

Stix, Gary. "Blackballing the Inner City." *Scientific American* 269 (September 1993): 152.

Stoda, Greg. "Sheffield Won't Help Florida Foot the Bill." *Charlotte Observer* (8 May 1998): 4B.

Suris, Oscar, and Rebecca Blumenstein. "Lions and Tigers Help Detroit Roar Back to Life." *Wall Street Journal* (21 August 1996): A2.

Sweet, David. "Catch That Jackhammer Action! Stadium-Building as Cybersport." *Wall Street Journal* (16 July 1998): B1.

———. "Sic Transit Gloria Marlins, or How Baseball Has Gone to the Devils." *Wall Street Journal* (17 March 1998): B1.

———. "Take Me Out to the Ball Game, Take Me Out to the Hair Salon." *Wall Street Journal* (12 December 1997): B1.

———. "To Maximize On-Field Product, Try Hitting Ball Out of Park Often." *Wall Street Journal* (8 May 1997): B1.

Talton, Jon. "Cities May Be Sorry Places If Ballparks Strike Out." *Charlotte Observer* (10 May 1998): 1D.

———. "Stadium Gives Phoenix a 2nd Chance." *Charlotte Observer* (12 July 1998): 1D.

Thurow, Roger. "The Longest Wait: Packer Fans Buy Seats After 32 Years." *Wall Street Journal* (15 September 1997): B1.

———. "On the Field, Baseball Is Integrated; For Fans, It's a Different Story." *Wall Street Journal* (28 August 1998): A1, A6.

———. "Woman's Hoops League Out-Glitzes Rival." *Wall Street Journal* (19 September 1997): B12.

Turner, Richard. "NBC: The Road to Tap City." *Newsweek* (26 January 1998): 42–44.

"Turner Urges Owners to Bar Sales of Dodgers to News Corp.'s Fox." *Wall Street Journal* (13 March 1998): B10.

"Twins Stadium Setback." *Charlotte Observer* (13 March 1998): 11B.

Utter, Jim. "Ackerman Looks at Long Haul." *Charlotte Observer* (10 July 1997): B1.

———. "CISL's Dwindling Members Dwindle to 0." *Charlotte Observer* (28 December 1997): 2G.

Vest, Jason. "Uproot for the Home Team." *U.S. News & World Report* (10 March 1997): 53–55.

Vrooman, John. "A General Theory of Professional Sports Leagues." *Southern Economic Journal* (1 April 1995): 971–990.

Walden, Michael L. "Don't Play Ball." *Carolina Journal* (October/November 1997): 23.

———. "Stadium Follies." *Carolina Journal* (February/March 1997): 23–24.

Walker, Sam. "Craving Cash, Teams Ask Ticket Holders to Pay Twice." *Charlotte Observer* (20 July 1998): B1.

———. "Hair Salons, Hot Tubs and . . . Oh, Yeah, Baseball." *Wall Street Journal* (27 March 1998): W1.

Ward, Janet. "Are Sports Teams Worth the Trouble?" *American City & County* (February 1991): 59–65.

Wareham, Bill. "Minnesota: Give Us a Year." *Charlotte Observer* (20 February 1998): 3B.

Weistart, John. "League Control of Market Opportunities: A Perspective on Competition and Cooperation in the Sports Industry." *Duke Law Journal.* (December 1984): 1013–1070.

Whitmire, Tom. "Bronx or Bust? Yankee Fans in Limbo." *Charlotte Observer* (19April 1998): 1A.

Will, George. "Purists vs. Impurists." *Newsweek* (29 September 1997): 88.

Wilson, Lionel J. "Statement," in U.S. Congress, House Committee on the Judiciary, *Oversight Hearings: Antitrust Policy and Professional Sports* (Washington, D.C.: Government Printing Office, 1984): 416–418.

"WNBA." *Charlotte Observer* (29 July 1998): 5B.

Worsnop, Richard. "The Business of Sports: Are Greedy Owners and Players Hurting Pro Leagues?" *CQ Researcher* (10 February 1995): 123–140.

Wulf, Steve. "How Suite It Isn't." *Time* (10 July 1995): 52.

Zimbalist, Andrew. "Not Suitable for Families." *U.S. News & World Report* (20 July 1997): 9.

Zimmerman, Dennis, and William A. Cox. "The Baseball Strike and Federal Policy: An Economic Analysis." *Congressional Research Service.* The Library of Congress (13 January 1995): 18–21.

BOOKS

Andelman, Bud. *Stadium for Rent: Tampa Bay's Quest for Major League Baseball.* Jefferson, N.C.: McFarland & Company, 1993.

Baade, Robert. *Is There an Economic Rationale for Subsidizing Sports Stadiums?* Chicago: Heartland Institute, 1987.

The Baseball Encyclopedia. 8th ed. New York and London: Macmillan Publishing Company, 1990.

———. 9th ed. New York and Toronto: Macmillan Publishing Company, 1993.

———. 10th ed. London: Macmillan Publishing Company, 1996.

Cagan, Joanna, and Neil deMause. *Field* of *Schemes. How the Great Stadium Swindle Turns Public Money Into Private Profit.* Monroe, Maine: Common Courage Press, 1998.

Chipman, Donald, Randolph Campbell, and Robert Cavert. *The Dallas Cowboys and the NFL.* Norman: University of Oklahoma Press, 1970

Crepeau, Richard C. *Baseball: America's Diamond Mind, 1919–1941.* Orlando: University Press of Florida, 1980.

Danielson, Michael N. *Home Team: Professional Sports and the American Metropolis.* Princeton, N.J.: Princeton University Press, 1997.

Demmert, Henry G. *The Economics of Professional Team Sports.* Lexington, Mass.: D. C. Heath and Company, 1973.

Dickson, Paul. *The Dickson Baseball Dictionary.* New York and Oxford: Facts on File, 1989.

Euchner, Charles C. *Playing the Field: Why Sports Teams Move and Cities Fight to Keep Them.* Baltimore: Johns Hopkins University Press, 1993.

Fizel, John, Elizabeth Gustafson, and Lawrence Hadley, eds. *Baseball Economics: Current Research.* Westport, Conn.: Praeger Publishers, 1996.

Gershman, Michael. *Diamonds: The Evolution of the Ballpark.* Boston and New York: Houghton Mifflin Company, 1993.

Gmelch, George, and J. J. Weiner. *In the Ballpark.* Washington, D.C.: Smithsonian Institution Press, 1998.

Gorn, Elliott, and Warren Goldstein. *A Brief History of American Sports.* New York: Hill & Wang Publishers, 1993.

Guttman, Allen. *From Ritual to Records: The Nature of Modern Sports.* New York: Columbia University Press, 1978.

————. *Sports Spectators.* New York: Columbia University Press, 1986.

Helyar, John. *Lords of the Realm. The Real History of Baseball.* New York: Ballantine Books, 1995.

Hollander, Zander. *The Modern Encyclopedia of Basketball.* New York: Four Winds Press, 1969.

Information Please Almanac. New York and Boston: Houghton Mifflin Company, 1990–1998.

Information Please Sports Almanac. New York and Boston: Houghton Mifflin Company, 1989–1996.

Jennings, Kenneth M. *Balls and Strikes.* Westport, Conn.: Praeger Publishers, 1990.

————. *Swings and Misses.* Westport, Conn.: Praeger Publishers, 1997.

Johnson, Arthur T., and James H. Frey, eds. *Government and Sport: The Public Policy Issues.* Totowa, N.J.: Rowan and Allanheld, 1983.

Koppett, Leonard. *Sports Illusion, Sports Reality: A Reporter's View of Sports, Journalism, and Society.* 2nd ed. Urbana and Chicago: University of Illinois Press, 1994.

Marburger, Daniel R., ed. *Stee-Rike Four.* Westport, Conn.: Praeger Publishers, 1997.

McCarthy, Kevin M. *Baseball in Florida.* Sarasota, Fla.: Pineapple Press, Inc., 1993.

Meggyesy, David. *Out of Their League.* Forestville, Calif.: Ramparts Press, 1970.

Menke, Frank G. *The Encyclopedia of Sports.* 5th ed. Cranbury, N.J.: A. S. Barnes and Company, 1975.

Miller, James Edward. *The Baseball Business: Pursuing Pennants and Profits in Baltimore.* 2nd ed. Chapel Hill: University of North Carolina Press, 1991.

Morgan, Jon. *Glory for Sale: Fans, Dollars and the New NFL.* Baltimore: Bancroft Press, 1997.

Neft, David S., and Richard M. Cohen. *The Sports Encyclopedia: Pro Football.* 5th ed. New York: St. Martin's Press, 1987.

1999 Sports Almanac. Sports Illustrated. Boston and New York: Little, Brown and Company, 1998.

Noll, Roger G., ed., *Government and the Sports Business.* Washington, D.C.: The Brookings Institution, 1974.

Noll, Roger G., and Andrew Zimbalist, eds., *Sports, Jobs and Taxes: The Economic Impact of Sports Teams and Stadiums.* Washington, D.C.: The Brookings Institution, 1997.

Peterson, Robert W. *Pigskin: The Early Years of Pro Football.* New York and London: Oxford University Press, 1996.

Pluto, Terry. *Loose Balls: The Short, Wild Life of the American Basketball Association—As Told by the Players, Coaches, and Movers and Shakers Who Made It Happen.* New York: Simon & Schuster, 1990.

Pope, S. W., *Patriotic Games: Sporting Traditions in the American Imagination, 1876–1926*. New York and London: Oxford University Press, 1997.

Pope, S. W., ed. *The New American Sport History: Recent Approaches and Perspectives*. Urbana and Chicago: University of Illinois Press, 1997.

Porter, David L., ed. *African-American Sports Greats*. Westport, Conn. and London: Greenwood Press, 1995.

Prince, Carl E. *Brooklyn's Dodgers: The Bums, the Borough, and the Best of Baseball, 1947–1957*. New York and London: Oxford University Press, 1996.

Quirk, James, and Rodney D. Fort. *Pay Dirt: The Business of Professional Sports*. Princeton, N.J.: Princeton University Press, 1992.

Rader, Benjamin G. *American Sports: From the Age of Folk Games to the Age of Spectators*. Englewood Cliffs, N.J.: Prentice-Hall, 1983.

———. *Baseball: A History of America's Game*. Urbana and Chicago: University of Illinois Press, 1994.

Richmond, Peter. *Ballpark: Camden Yards and the Building of an American Dream*. Hamden, Conn.: Fireside Press, 1993.

Riess, Steven A. *City Games: The Evolution of American Urban Society and the Rise of Sports*. Urbana and Chicago: University of Illinois Press, 1991.

———. *Major Problems in American Sport History*. Boston and New York: Houghton Mifflin Company, 1997.

———. *Sport in the Industrial Age, 1850–1920*. Wheeling, Ill.: Harlan Davidson, Inc., 1995.

———. *Touching Base: Professional Baseball and American Culture in the Progressive Era*. Westport, Conn.: Greenwood Press, 1980.

Roberts, Randy, and James Olson. *Winning Is the Only Thing: Sports in America Since 1945*. Baltimore and London: Johns Hopkins University Press, 1989.

Rosentraub, Mark S. *Major League Losers: The Real Costs of Sports and Who's Paying for It*. New York: Basic Books, 1997.

Scully, Gerald W. *The Business of Major League Baseball*. Chicago: University of Chicago Press, 1989.

———. *The Market Structure of Sports*. Chapel Hill: University of North Carolina Press, 1995.

Seymour, Harold. *Baseball: The Early Years*. New York: Oxford University Press, 1960.

———. *Baseball: The Golden Age*. 2nd ed. New York: Oxford University Press, 1989.

Shannon, Bill, and George Kaminsky. *The Ballparks*. New York: Hawthorne Books, 1975.

Shropshire, Kenneth L. *The Sports Franchise Game: Cities in Pursuit of Sports Franchises, Events, Stadiums, and Arenas*. Philadelphia: University of Pennsylvania Press, 1995.

Smith, Myron J., Jr. *Baseball: A Comprehensive Bibliography*. Jefferson, N.C. and London: McFarland & Company, 1986.

Sports Encyclopedia. New York: Ottenheimer Publishers, Inc., 1976.

Staudohar, Paul D., and James A. Mangan, eds. *The Business of Professional Sports*. Champaign: University of Illinois Press, 1991.

Sullivan, Neil J. *The Dodgers Move West: The Transfer of the Brooklyn Baseball Franchise to Los Angeles*. New York: Oxford University Press, 1987.

Tarango, Martin. *Basketball Biographies*. Jefferson, N.C. and London: McFarland & Company, 1991.

Thorn, John, and Pete Palmer, eds. *Total Baseball*. 2nd ed. New York: Warner Books, 1991.

Vincent, Ted. *The Rise and Fall of American Sport. Mudville's Revenge.* Omaha: University of Nebraska Press, 1994.

Voight, David Q. *American Baseball: From Gentleman's Sport to the Commissioner System.* Norman: University of Oklahoma Press, 1966.

Weiss, Ann E. *Money Games: The Business of Sports.* Boston: Houghton Mifflin Company, 1993.

The World Almanac and Book of Facts. Mahwah, N.J.: World Almanac Books, 1950–1998.

Zimbalist, Andrew. *Baseball and Billions: A Probing Look Inside the Big Business of Our National Pastime.* New York: Basic Books, 1992.

DISSERTATIONS

Jozsa, Frank P., Jr. "An Economic Analysis of Franchise Relocation and League Expansion in Professional Team Sports, 1950–1975." Ph.D. diss., Georgia State University, 1977.

Kammer, David John. "Take Me Out to the Ballgame: American Cultural Values as Reflected in the Architectural Evolution and Criticism of the Modern Baseball Stadium." Ph.D. diss., University of New Mexico, 1982.

Maltby, Marc. "The Origin and Early Development of Professional Football, 1890–1920." Ph.D. diss., Ohio University, 1987.

MEDIA GUIDES

1998 Anaheim Angels Media Guide.
1996 Arizona Cardinals Media Guide.
Atlanta Hawks Media Guide 1996–1997.
1998 Blue Jays Official Guide.
1996 Carolina Panthers Media Guide.
Charlotte Hornets 1996–1997 Media Guide.
Cincinnati Bengals 1996 Media Guide.
1998 Dallas Cowboys Media Guide.
1996 Indianapolis Colts Media Guide.
1996–1997 Los Angeles Clippers Information Guide.
Los Angeles Lakers 1996–1997 Media Guide.
The Oakland Raiders: The Team of the Decades 1996.
1996–1997 Philadelphia Seventy Sixers Media Guide.

INTERNET SOURCES

"ABL Continues to Fight for Respect." <http://www.cnnsi.com> cited 5 May 1998.

"ABL's Top-25 All-Time Attendance Marks." <http://www.ableague.com> cited 29 August 1998.

"American Basketball League Attendance Report." <http://www.cnnsi.com> cited 27 August 1998.

"Ballpark Financing." <http://www.mariners.org> cited 6 August 1998.

"Baltimore Ravens." <http://www.nfl.com> cited 14 September 1998.

"Banker Joins Milstein's Bid for Browns." <http://www.cnnsi.com> cited 6 July 1998.

"Baseball Owners Approve Sale of Dodgers to Fox Group." <http://www.baseball.yahoo.com> cited 15 March 1998.

"Bengals' New Stadium Receives Approval." <http://www.football.yahoo.com> cited 3 February 1998.

"Big Red Dealmaker. Vikings New Owner Involved in Several Big Projects." <http://www.cnnsi.com> cited 7 July 1998.

"Broncos Stadium Ballot Initiative Approved." <http://www.cnnsi.com> cited 1 September 1998.

"Bullish Expansion Hopes. California Group Proposes $500 Million for NFL Stadium." <http://www.cnnsi.com> cited 8 June 1998.

"Cards' Stadium Drive Gets Big Boost. Developer Pledges $185 Million to Arizona Complex." <http://www.cnnsi.com> cited 3 July 1998.

"Chicago Bulls History." <http://www.nba.com> cited 8 April 1998.

"Clancy Buys Majority Share of Vikings. Novelist, Investor Group Will Dish Out Over $200 Million." <http://www.cnnsi.com> cited 3 February 1998.

"CoreStates No More." <http://www.cnnsi.com> cited 24 July 1998.

"Cubas Waits. Smiley Will Decide This Week on Marlins Purchase." <http://www.cnnsi.com> cited 21 July 1998.

"Despite Crowds, Mariners Lost $4.1 Million in 1997." <http://www.cnnsi.com> cited 11 February 1998.

Ekstrand, C. "Toronto Transformed." <http://www.nba.com> cited 14 February 1998.

"Elway Throws Weight Behind Stadium Tax. Broncos QB Lending a Helping Hand With Positive 30-Second Ad." <http://www.cnnsi.com> cited 31 October 1998.

"Ford Motordome." <http://www.nfl.com> cited 1 September 1998.

"49ers Stadium Deal May be Unraveling." <http://www.cnnsi.com> cited 9 September 1998.

Fraley, G. "Hicks Buying Rangers for $250 Million." <http://www.dallasnews.com> cited 14 January 1998.

"The Franchise of Americans Needing Sports (FANS)." <http://www.consumers.com> cited 10 February 1997.

"Get 'Em Quick. High-End Tickets Selling Fast for New Bengals Stadium." <http:www.cnnsi.com> cited 21 July 1998.

"Going Nowhere Fast. Lawmaker's Guarantee: Twins Won't Move to Carolina." <http://www.cnnsi.com> cited 24 February 1998.

"Hands-On Approach. Politician Wants Controls on Orioles' Ticket Prices." <http://www.cnnsi.com> cited 24 February 1998.

Hayes, N. "Same Old Al Hints at Move." <http://www.hotcoco.com> cited 28 January 1998.

"Headrick Resigns as President of the Vikings." <http://www.cnnsi.com> cited 27 August 1998.

Heath, T. "Pollin: Players Salaries Cause Increase in Ticket Prices." <http://www.washingtonpost.com> cited 3 December 1997.

"A Heritage With a Rich History Baseball: One Hundred Years of Tradition in Montreal." <http://www.montrealexpos.com> cited 6 October 1998.

"Home Sweet Home? Oilers to Play at Vandy." <http://www.sportingnews.com> cited 4 March 1998.

Horgan, Sean. "Mayor, Colts Sign Lease Agreement." <http://www.starnews.com> cited 21 January 1998.

"Hotel Tax Urged to Fund N.C. Ballpark." <http://www.cnnsi.com> cited 10 February 1998.

"Houston Bidding for NFL Franchise." <http://www.cnnsi.com> cited 3 July 1998.

"Huizenga Negotiating to Sell Marlins." <http://www.austin360.com> cited 7 November 1997.

"Huizenga Says He May Keep Marlins Next Season." <http://www.cnnsi.com> cited 21 August 1998.

"Hunt for More Football in K.C.? Chiefs Owner, GM Visiting Arena Bowl, May Get Next Team." <http://www.cnnsi.com> cited 19 November 1998.

"Hunt Looks Into Buying Royals." <http://www.kcstar.com> cited 19 November 1997.

"Hunt Withdraws Bid to Buy Royals. N.Y. Lawyer Appears to Have Inside Track on K.C. Team." <http://www.cnnsi.com> cited 26 August 1998.

"If the ABL and WNBA Can Do It . . . Women's Professional Hockey League to Begin in Fall." <http://www.cnnsi.com> cited 4 February 1998.

"If They Build It—But Where." <http://www.sportingnews.com> cited 22 October 1997.

"If You Can't Beat 'Em, Buy 'Em." <http://www.cnnsi.com> cited 12 February 1998.

"I Have a Handshake Deal. Commodities Trader Says He's Buying Marlins for $150 Million." <http://www.cnnsi.com> cited 11 September 1998.

"Ilitch Might Have to Sell Ballpark Name." <http://www.cnnsi.com> cited 10 March 1998.

"Indianapolis Colts." <http://www.starnews.com> cited 8 April 1998.

Johnston, Kathleen. "Goldsmith Seeks Corporate Funding for Arena." <http://www.starnews.com> cited 3 March 1997.

"Join in. Deposits Secure WNBA Team for Minnesota." <http://www.cnnsi.com> cited 1 September 1998.

"Kauffman Stadium." <http://www.kcroyals.com> cited 19 August 1998.

"The Key Arena." <http://www.ballparks.com> cited 6 October 1998.

"Latest Stadium Plan for Pats Includes Athletes' Tax." <http://www.cnnsi.com> cited 25 February 1998.

"Legislators Seek to Halt Stadium Strong-Arming." <http://www.cnnsi.com> cited 14 January 1998.

Lhotka, W. "Judge Throws Out Suit Against NFL; St. Louis Will Appeal." <http://www.stlnet.com> cited 13 November 1997.

"Loan Closed Tuesday to Finance New Tiger Ballpark." <http://baseball.yahoo.com> cited 26 August 1998.

"Lots of Greenbacks for Redskins. New York Financier Offers $450 Million for Team, Stadium." <http://www.cnnsi.com> cited 29 August 1998.

"Luckout From the Lockout. ABL Hoping for Additional Exposure With the Absence of NBA." <http://www.cnnsi.com> cited 6 November 1998.

Lynem, Julie. "Fans Unfazed by Offseason Rumors. Colts Players Come Away With Exposure and Win Over Bengals." <http://www.starnews.com> cited 11 November 1997.

"Mailman May Not Stick in Salt Lake City. Agent Wants to Make Mountain Out of Malone's Money." <http://www.cnnsi.com> cited 21 August 1998.

"Malone Chides Jazz Owner Miller. The Mailman Says He Is Underpaid and Underappreciated." <http://www.cnnsi.com> cited 17 March 1998.

"Maloof Family Buys Stake in Kings." <http://www.cnnsi.com> cited 15 January 1998.

"Management Shifts Signal Dodgers Sale Will Be OK'd." <http://www.usatoday.com> cited 18 March 1998.

"Mariners Announce Working Agreement With Japanese Team." <http://www.baseball.yahoo.com> cited 18 February 1998.

"Mayor, Colts Sign Lease Agreement." <http://www.starnew.com> cited 14 January 1998.

"Mayor Giuliani Says City Could Woo New Jersey Sports Teams." <http://www.cnnsi.com> cited 28 April 1998.

"McCombs: NFL in San Antonio Unlikely. Vikings Owner Says City's Leaders Don't Want Team Enough." <http://www.cnnsi.com> cited 29 August 1998.

"Mile-High Referendum. Group Seeks Taxpayers' Help for Bronco Stadium." <http://www.cnnsi.com> cited 3 July 1998.

"Millions of Dollars at Stake for Montreal." <http://www.montrealexpos.com> cited 6 October 1998.

"MLB Ownership Committee Gives Smiley Control of Marlins." <http://www.baseball.yahoo.com> cited 18 March 1998.

"A New Ballpark in L.A.? Fox Contemplates Replacing Dodger Stadium." <http://www.cnnsi.com> cited 26 August 1998.

"New Browns Owner Guaranteed a Profit. Cleveland Football Team Could Net $12 Million in 1st Year." <http://www.cnnsi.com> cited 17 March 1998.

"New Rule: You Can Own Two Teams." <http://www.cnnsi.com> cited 19 September 1998.

"New Stadiums to Cost Team Owners More. Pirates, Steelers Consider New Funding Approaches." <http://www.cnnsi.com> cited 10 March 1998.

"New Venue Blues for Niners. Report: Company That Was to Develop Stadium Dissolved." <http://www.cnnsi.com> cited 3 March 1998.

"NFL May Put Cap on Brown's Spending." <http://www.cnnsi.com> cited 21 July 1998.

"NFL, Oakland Urged to Settle L.A. Suit." <http://www.cnnsi.com> cited 19 November 1998.

"NFL Ticket Prices Up 4.7 Percent for '98. Bucs Lead 13 Teams Who Raised Cost of Attending Games." <http://www.cnnsi.com> cited 3 September 1998.

"No Sale? Huizenga Says He May Keep Marlins Next Season." <http://www.cnnsi.com> cited 21 August 1998.

"Nuggets Name D'Antoni Head Coach." <http://www.nba.com> cited 28 September 1998.

"Oilers Get Buyout Approval From Memphis." <http://www.sportingnews.com> cited 4 March 1998.

"On Borrowed Time. Athletics Trigger Year-to-Year Stadium Lease." <http://www.cnnsi.com> cited 27 October 1998.

"Orioles to List at $3.1 Million." <http://www.cnnsi.com> cited 12 January 1999.

"Packers Stock Sale Raises $24 Million." <http://www.cnnsi.com> cited 17 March 1998.

"Padres Get New Home in 2002. San Diego Voters OK New $411 Million Downtown Stadium." <http://www.cnnsi.com> cited 5 November 1998.

"Personal Seating in Pittsburgh. Steelers May Sell Seat Licenses in Stadium." <http://www.cnnsi.com> cited 7 July 1998.

"Plans Progressing on Mets Stadium." <http://www.cnnsi.com> cited 27 October 1998.

Posnanski, Joe. "Hunt Looks Into Buying Royals." <http://www.kcstar.com> cited 19 November 1997.

"Price Check. Amid Dispute Over Athletics' Value, Joe Morgan Emerges as Possible Buyer." <http://www.cnnsi.com> cited 27 October 1998.

"Problems Plaguing the Bills. Lagging Suite Sales Endanger Team's Future in Buffalo." <http://www.cnnsi.com> cited 6 July 1998.

"Raising Arizona. Cards' Season-Ticket Sales Up Above 30,000." <http://www.cnnsi.com> cited 7 July 1998.

"Ravens Kick Off a Stadium of Firsts." <http://www.nfl.com> cited 19 September 1998.

"Realignment Postponed. Leagues Remain the Same Through 2000." <http://www.cnnsi.com> cited 14 January 1999.

"Report: Sumitomo to Bankroll Tigers' Stadium." <http://www.cnnsi.com> cited 17 March 1998.

"Report: Three Brown Bidders Drop Out. NFL to Pick From Remaining Four Groups by September 9." <http://www.cnnsi.com> cited 3 September 1998.

"Rick Adelman Hired as Coach." <http://www.nba.com> cited 28 September 1998.

Rogers, Prentis. "Networks Not Threatened by NBC, Turner." <http://www.cnnsi.com> cited 31 January 1998.

"A Royal Deal. Kansas City Approves Sale of Team to Prentice Group." <http://www.cnnsi.com> cited 19 November 1998.

"Royals Leaning Toward Prentice Bid. Team Says Ownership Group Needs More Local Involvement." <http://www.cnnsi.com> cited 21 August 1998.

"Salaries Keep on Soaring." <http://www.sportingnews.com> cited 3 December 1997.

Sansevere, Bob. "Twins Minus Pohlad Looks Like Good Deal." <http://pioneerplanet. com> cited 13 November 1997.

"Schott on Way Out? Reds Partners Will Match Cash Offer for Share of Team." <http://www.cnnsi.com> cited 19 September 1998.

"Seahawks Get Land for Open-Air Stadium. Proposed Park Would Open in 2002, Seat 72,000." <http://www.cnnsi.com> cited 7 July 1998.

"Slaight Sells Raptors, New Arena to Leafs' Stavro." <http://bball.yahoo.com> cited 17 February 1998.

"Smiley's Group in Position to Buy Marlins." <http.www.sportingnews.com> cited 19 November 1997.

"Sold! Vikings Accept Red McCombs' Bid for Ownership." <http://www.cnnsi.com> cited 6 July 1998.

"Sticker Shock. Best Seats at Astros' New Park Will Be Pricey." <http://www.cnnsi. com> cited 24 July 1998.

"St. Louis Loses Conspiracy Lawsuit Against NFL." <http://www.sportsline.com> cited 3 September 1998.

"Sucker Bet." <http://www.cnnsi.com> cited 3 July 1998.

"Tagliabue Says Sale of Vikings to Tom Clancy May Proceed." <http://football.yahoo. com> yahoo.com> cited 24 March 1998.

"Tagliabue to the Rescue. NFL Says It Will Help Chicago, Arizona Get New Stadiums." <http://www.cnnsi.com> cited 19 November 1998.

"Tagliabue Won't Allow Curbs on Vikings President." <http://www.cnnsi.com> cited 11 February 1998.

"Tampa Bay's New Stadium Get a Name." <http://www.cnnsi.com> cited 7 July 1998.

"A Team of Their Own. Countdown Over for Baseball-Starved Tampa Bay Fans." <http://www.cnnsi.com> cited 31 March 1998.

"Tom Watson Joins Bid to Buy Royals." <http://baseball.yahoo.com> cited 29 August 1998.

"Top Dawgs? Policy Joins Billionaire Lerner in Bid for Browns." <http://www.cnnsi. com> cited 24 July 1998.

"Toronto Raptors History." <http://www.nba.com> cited 8 April 1998.

"TV Azteca and the NBA Extend Broadcast Partnership." <http://www.nba.com> cited 29 August 1998.

"2001: A Stadium Odyssey: Patriots to Leave Massachusetts, Move to Hartford." <http://www.cnnsi.com> cited 19 November 1998.

"Turner Apparently Has Murdoch in His Sights." <http://www.usatoday.com> cited 18 March 1998.

"Utah Jazz History." <http://www.nba.com> cited 5 February 1998.

"Vancouver Grizzlies History." <http://www.nba.com> cited 31 January 1998.

"Vandy Looks Dandy to Bud Adams." <http://www.cnnsi.com> cited 25 February 1998.

"View From the Cheap Seats." <http://imprint.uwaterloo.com> cited 17 June 1997.

"Vikings Accept Red McCombs' Bid for Ownership." <http://www.cnnsi.com> cited 3 July 1998.

"Voters Reject Triad Referendum for Baseball Stadium." <http://www.cnnsi.com> cited 6 May 1998.

"Washington Wizards History." <http://www.nba.com> cited 5 February 1998.

"What Will Switch Do to Brewers?" <http://www.austin360.com> cited 11 November 1997.

Whitlock, Jason. "Keeping Royals' Price Up Is Concern for Baseball." <http://www.kcstar.com> cited 21 July 1998.

"Will Royals Remain in AL?" <http://www.sportingnews.com> cited 19 November 1997.

Wilson, B. "Padres Look to County to Fill Ballpark Funding Gap." <http://www.baseball.yahoo.com> cited 3 July 1998.

Wolf, Bob. "N.L. Brewers Can Go Home Again." <http://www.sportingnews.com> cited 18 March 1998.

Index

About the Authors

FRANK P. JOZSA, JR. is Associate Professor of Economics and Business Administration at Pfeiffer University. His publications have appeared in *Athletic Business*, the *Carolina Journal*, the *Wall Street Journal Review of Books*, and in the *Proceedings: International Conference on Sports Business*.

JOHN J. GUTHRIE, JR. is Associate Professor of History and Economics at Daytona Beach Community College. He is the author or co-author of a number of books including *The Florida Land Boom: Speculation, Money, and the Banks* (Quorum, 1995) and *Keepers of the Spirits: The Judicial Response to Prohibition Enforcement in Florida, 1885–1935* (Greenwood Press, 1998).